Breakthroughs in Practice

*Theorising critical moments
in social work*

Breakthroughs in Practice:

Theorising critical moments in social work

Edited by
Lindsey Napier & Jan Fook

Whiting & Birch Ltd

MM

HV
40
B822
2000

Published by Whiting & Birch Ltd,
PO Box 872, London SE23 3HL, England.
USA: Paul & Co, Publishers' Consortium Inc,
PO Box 442, Concord, MA 01742.

British Library Cataloguing in Publication Data.
A CIP catalogue record is available from
the British Library
ISBN 1 86177 032 4

Printed in England by Intype

Contents

Acknowledgments

We would like to acknowledge the work and patience of our contributors, during the long course which the development of this book required.

Our most grateful appreciation is also extended to Nicole Richards, whose calm efficiency with administrative details was invaluable in the final stages.

1
Reflective practice in social work

Lindsey Napier and Jan Fook

Why this book on reflective practice?

What experiences and ideas led us to produce this book? We start by relating the respective experiences of practice and teaching that fired and sustained our interest in developing reflective practice. In the course of our accounts, both of us note the difficulty in understanding and modelling a reflective process, given the lack of published accounts of reflections on details of practice. Generalised descriptions of fields of practice, which tend to be more didactic, and relate to practice theory in a broad field, do exist (for example, Carter et al, 1995; Hanvey & Philpot, 1994). Material on the theory of reflective practice in social work also exists (for example, Gould & Taylor, 1996). However, almost non-existent is the literature which chronicles the detailed process whereby practitioners learn and develop theory from specific instances of practice. This is our interest, and the interest of the contributors in this book.

Jan...

I began my early career as a social work student in the mid-1970s, when I decided to become a social worker because I wanted to help people. My preferred choice of practice was casework. I quickly learnt that both these aspirations were seen as naive and were most definitely unfashionable. So, armed with the zest of radical critique, I took up my first job as a generic social worker, trying to work out how criticisms of the social structure could help me help families of people with intellectual disabilities, and finding little guidance from my previous studies, or the textbooks. This was my first experience of the disjuncture between theory and practice in social work. However, rather than question either the theory or the practice, I put the problem down to the fact that few practice models existed which could adequately apply broad social criticism to specific direct practices.

This then became my professional mission, which lasted over the next fifteen years. During this time I developed and taught a model for the practice of radical casework (Fook, 1993), a model which I thought brought the theory and practice of radical social work criticism much closer together. In this model, the theory remained prime, the practitioner only needed to be better taught (through illustration) how it could be deductively applied to practice.

Some of the observations I made over the years, however, caused me some concern. I often found, for instance, that students would search elusively for the exact radical practice, which for them must be necessarily different from all traditional practices, which would allow them to enact their radical theory. This would often lead to a worrying inaction, and a devaluing of their own work as 'conservative', because they could not find a piece of action which they regarded as inherently radical, in order to enact their radical goals. In short, some students were experiencing radical approaches to practice as actually disempowering, which in turn led to a rejection of radical perspectives, or a further alienation from practice.

I began thus to question the disempowering way in which theory seemed to be conceptualised by these students. Another phenomenon, which also concerned me, was the way in which social workers seemed to be split into two very distinct groups, the 'radicals' and 'conservatives', the 'community workers' and the 'caseworkers'. These divisions did not seem to me to be representative of the settings and ways in which workers practised, and I began thus to further question the relevance of such theoretical conceptualisations in helping us understand and act in our immediate world.

A particular challenge came when I was involved in the design of a postgraduate course in advanced level practice. I felt intuitively that teaching the traditional content of updated social work practice theory and current issues would be dissatisfying for both the prospective students and myself. There was no way that I as an academic could aspire to know more about the vagaries of practice, the changing and specific contexts, in which our students were working, in order to teach it back to them. Most of what was happening had never been systematically researched and never could be, in order to enable me to regurgitate it in a form, which might be meaningful to current practitioners. Most students had also been recent undergraduates, so would already be familiar with the newer social work theories. Furthermore, a perusal of the literature indicated very little research or thinking about the nature of advanced level practice. What could I teach which would actually help practitioners learn new advanced skills, and more importantly, improve their practice in their immediate situations?

The reflective approach to practice offered some insights about a different way of conceptualising the relationship between theory and practice, as an ongoing process in which theory and practice constantly inform and develop each other. I adapted what was basically Donald Schon's approach (1983) with some insights from postmodern thinking, as a teaching tool (Fook, 1996). Students were asked to present a current piece of practice, which exemplified a dilemma or sticking point for them. Classes became a means of helping them reflect on the practice presented, a kind of peer supervision session, with the focus on assisting the presenter to gain new perspectives, through examining implicit assumptions. Theory was then applied retrospectively, as a way of adding another (rather than the only) type of meaning, and creative thinking was encouraged to develop new strategies for acting in the situation.

What happened was quite remarkable. Many students reported breakthroughs in their practice, in situations, which had stalemated, or presented problems for them, sometimes over years. Some sessions were moving as students came to acknowledge the role of their own emotions and personal needs in the way they had approached or interpreted the situation. Others were quite exciting, as we witnessed the formulation of new practice strategies, and in some cases new models. All sessions were reaffirming, as we revisited the core of values and human concerns which gave meaning to our labours as social justice professionals. In the process of critically reflecting on their practice, students reconceptualised and developed practice theories, and changed practices and situations, in line with strengthened value and theory commitments.

I have since further modified this teaching approach, and now use it in teaching undergraduate students. Many report a much more empowering relationship with theory, and a much greater confidence in their own ability to create practice strategies, to take risks to expose their practice to scrutiny, and so to improve it.

However, a marked downside in taking a reflective approach in educating, has been a difficulty, expressed by some, in understanding the approach, and in appreciating the ways in which it can be used to critically challenge situations. Students with a more 'academic' orientation tend not to enjoy, or do so well in, these classes. The reconceptualisation of the theory/practice relationship is not to their liking, and they do not see how they are learning 'theory' through such an approach. It is difficult for them to shift, indeed to overturn, the traditional values implicit in the traditional knowledge hierarchy, and to value emergent learning from personal experience. Unless it is 'out there' it is not valuable. From my observations, some students who have particular difficulty, are those educated with an explicit 'structural' social work perspective, in which causes of problems are perceived necessarily to be material and empirical, and distanced from the individual (Fook, 1995). They are fearful that if the responsibility of the individual is recognised, this smacks of 'blame the victim' mentality, and therefore must be eschewed. I find in my teaching that this conceptual 'splitting' of the structural and individual, the personal and political, is not a rift that can readily be reconceptualised. Even though students might accept a reintegration of the structural and individual in intellectual terms, I find that basic embedded, almost cultural assumptions about the nature of knowledge, inhibit them from understanding this in a more experiential and holistic way.

I have some sympathy with these dilemmas, but am reminded that it is always useful to question any constructed ways of thinking ... However, in line with a reflective stance, it is appropriate to illustrate with concrete experience, to model the process, rather than to rely on abstract argument (Fook, 1999). Therefore I believe the next important step is to actually provide illustrative material - actual concrete practice experience and personal reflections upon them, which demonstrate the theory building and remaking process which occurs in reflective learning.

Lindsey and I, as you will see in reading her account of her teaching experience to follow, arrived at much the same point in our teaching careers, in pinpointing the need for literature which actually 'does' reflection, not simply just 'talks' about it.

Lindsey...

I lit upon the term reflective practice, through Donald Schon's (1983, 1987) writing, somewhere in the first years of my work as an educator of student social workers. His ideas resonated with my wish for the worlds of practice and theory to better inform each other, just as I considered the worlds of policy and practice should do. His books used to lie around my room, as if by magic I'd find a way through the splits of theory / practice, university / field, and policy/practice.

On becoming an academic after many years of practice, I had been surprised at the reactions of some erstwhile colleagues, who regarded me as having 'crossed sides' and made the choice to be remote from and not concerned about practice. Predictably they ribbed me about escaping into the world of theory and research, and abandoning what in their view really mattered, the daily lived experience of social work. One inference was that theory and practice had little to do with each other. I was fairly immune to such teasing, as for some years previous I had occupied a policy position in health services. There I had come in for regular criticism about being distanced from and therefore lacking understanding of the pressures of the 'front line'.

I rejected such separations. In my work with undergraduate students, I continued my colleagues' well established approach, where competing practice theories were always discussed with reference to their application and expression in practice. I delivered many lectures and held many seminars both for students and practice teachers of our students, drawing on my own practice to illuminate a particular approach or framework. In the absence of published accounts by practitioners, I invited practitioner colleagues to provide 'live' accounts of how they worked with practice theories.

I found this unsatisfactory. It was unsatisfactory because I tended to present theories as discrete and fixed, not as living, changing and partial, creatures of their time. My 'reflection' stopped short of revisioning theoretical ideas; showing how appropriate theories could inform practices was the centre of my attention.

At times this appeared appropriate. Ideas about crisis and crisis intervention appeared to fit neatly the responses of colleagues and myself to rail, air and flood situations, for example, regardless of the individual worker. I say 'appeared', because so much more had been learned from these situations - about timing, about resilience, guilt, and courage, about omnipotence, fear, and humility, about how crisis is defined, by whom, and with whose interests in mind - about the influence of context. When, in the classroom, crisis theory was critiqued and refashioned in the light of structural explanations of crisis, there still seemed an 'emptiness' for students, a gap between the theoretical ideas, their application to particular contexts and the professional experience.

In the course of privileging practice theories I down played the specificity, complexity, unpredictability and immediacy of people and their situations. The moment by moment interactions, which brought me together with the particular politics, places, policies, people, my interaction with their value and theory commitments and the measure of authority they could command were secondary. The people who let me in on their lives, kept me or kicked me out of their lives, sometimes entrusted me with their lives, somehow became secondary. Yet they had been my teachers, different, but just as important as the people who had been involved in my formal theoretical learning.

As well, into this fluid context I tended to present me, the practitioner, as 'fixed', an instrument of the theory. This was not easy: it was like keeping my self in check all the time, keeping myself out of the practice. Yet the 'theories in use' had not been in just anyone's hands. The hands were mine. They had been influenced by my own espoused theory, which led (and leads) me to look first for social sources of inequalities and personal difficulty and to seek out people's strengths and resilience. I knew that I brought to my practice not only 'formal' ideas. I contributed knowledge from experience and the influences of value commitments. I knew that I had not behaved consistently in similar situations. I had behaved more or less determinedly, more or less courageously, more or less imaginatively, more or less clearheadedly, more or less congruently with my 'espoused' theories.

This suited some students. These are the students who want certainty and simplicity - certain ways of explaining, assessing and responding to issues and problems. It is tempting to reduce their underlying anxiety by producing 'grand plans'. In my own field of specialisation - health and illness, I provided that too (George and Napier, 1988). But though theories offered general orientations and guides to action, I found that portraying the practitioner working with them, was more complex. I had been exposed to decades of theories for practice and practice theories. My practice wasn't 'pure' application of theory; it was often contradictory and probably eclectic. I began to think that privileging theory could protect the practitioner from entering the experience of 'others', and from distancing them from the practice.

I am tempted to say that my discovery of postmodernism saved me from reducing context to just that - a set of variables into which one could pour theory. More honestly, it took a disastrous experience of teaching a course on social casework to a diverse group of postgraduate students - some with no formal education in practice theory - to cure me of the belief (or doubt) that introducing theories to practices aside from the practitioner and their context is helpful. For students to review and reassess the underpinnings of their practices required, as if I didn't already know, starting where the practitioner is 'at' - with them in their practice. It is, after all, the person who is the outcome (Jackson and Preston-Shoot, 1996).

While Jan experimented with a reflective approach in her teaching and wrote about reflexivity in research, a colleague and I were delegated to redesign the final two years of our university's four-year Bachelor of Social Work degree. We wanted the curriculum to prepare students to work with change and uncertainty. We also recognised the importance of harnessing the energy, motivation, imagination and fruits of experience that students bring to the classroom. Many are impatient to leave theory behind and to 'get out and practise'. In the curriculum, we have placed the study material - the work of social work - in its messy interpersonal, organisational and political context, and the student worker, at the centre of inquiry. By so doing, we hoped to lessen the tendency to separate theory, context and practice. The study units are called, for instance, 'Social Justice, Social Citizenship and Social Work' and 'Interpersonal Violence and Social Justice'. With an inductive approach, we hoped that students would be able to become aware of and examine their own espoused theories and to consider these alongside the ideas and suggested action pathways of formal theories, the 'guidebooks' of certainty and uncertainty. As well as reaching for the resource of formal theories and discovering how different approaches lead to different understandings, processes and outcomes, we hoped that students could be asked to examine their own prior learning, the theories they bring to bear 'intuitively' on situations. This requires learning to 'reflect', particularly on the values underpinning both.

In practice, this is a tall order. It can be mystifying for some students to consider that there may be no one prescription. It does not make sense to some that they may already be working with theoretical ideas, especially when they claim to have no interest in or no need for theory. It can be daunting for some students to consider that 'owning' their ideas is important because there are consequences for clients and policies. It can also be exciting for students to think that they can contribute to theory building, that through examining how they work with theory, new ideas and ways to practise may emerge. It is arguable, of course, whether and how it can be helpful to read about how practising social workers work with the process of action and reflection. But it has been a source of frustration for me as a teacher that, so far as I am aware, there are no accounts which model knowledge building through such a process.

As we discuss below, though there is a substantial amount of discussion, both circumspect and enthusiastic, about developing reflective approaches in education and practice, there is little published demonstration of reflective processes on which to base judgment about the extent and nature of its helpfulness in developing practice theories and theory for practice. To place the reflective accounts of this book in context, let us begin by providing an overview of the various ways in which reflection has been discussed in social work.

The reflective approach

In broad terms the reflective approach is based on a questioning of traditional assumptions about the nature of knowledge generation, theory and practice. Traditional approaches assume that theory should inform practice in a deductive, 'top down' manner. In a traditional view, knowledge is believed to be generated from an empirical 'objective' standpoint, from 'outside' the practitioner, or person experiencing the situation. Theory is thus developed through generalising knowledge, which has been systematically ('scientifically') researched. It is only therefore generalised theory, created in this way, which can be validly applied to specific situations.

A reflective stance questions the traditional approach in that it can lead to a perceived insurmountable gap between 'theory' and 'practice', between the abstractified and generalised theory taught in formal settings, and what practitioners actually do in specific situations. As a tool for understanding and improving practice, traditional conceptions therefore have limited usefulness.

Instead, a reflective approach posits that contrary to traditional conceptions, 'theory' is implicit in the way people act, and may or may not be congruent with the more formalised theory they believe themselves to be acting upon. In a reflective approach theory is induced from practice, in more of a 'bottom - up' manner. The best way to access this 'theory 'is thus through processes of reflection on specific actions, and a linking of these with unacknowledged assumptions and features of the specific context. This is particularly important, since practice often takes place in 'messy' situations, which are uncontrollable, unpredictable and changing. Through use of intuition and artistry, the practising professional learns to act in ways which are relevant to the specific situation or context. Through this type of process the practitioner is able to build up more generalised theories, by an ongoing interaction of learning from experience and reformulation of practice principles.

In a reflective approach, the specific context, and the holistic experience of it, become important, so that practice can be developed in ways which maximise responsiveness. Interpretive approaches also become important, since there is a recognition that unacknowledged assumptions may be influencing actions. The reflective stance is non-positivist and experiential, in its assumption that knowledge is generated from the experiences and interpretations of practitioners.

Donald Schon (1983 and 1987) is credited with the early popularisation of the reflective approach for teaching practising professionals, but there has been a subsequent burgeoning of interest in the educational field (for example, Brookfield, 1995). However, until recently, there has been little literature which documents the use of the reflective approach in social work. It is this recent literature which we now discuss.

The reflective approach in social work

One set of arguments in favour of developing reflective practice emerges from analysis of the changing political and economic context of professional practice. As responsibility for care and service provision is steadily privatised and a language of consumer choice in a welfare marketplace replaces a language of need, the task of explicitly describing what social workers do and the knowledge they actually use in practice is imperative. It is important to know whether social workers are positioned to deploy professional knowledge and how they continue to exercise discretion. Do they, for instance, use knowledge to resist the values of 'user pays' and to influence who receives or is refused resources? If so, how? If social workers are more than technicians, brokers and mediators between efficiency conscious managers and more or less competent 'consumers', it may be important to know whether there is a place for knowledge about, for example, how to establish trust or when to turn 'problems' into 'issues'.

Jones and Jordan (1996) have argued that there remain continuities in practice, that professional authority and autonomy remain, but that to learn how knowledge is built and theory and practice are integrated require 'critical' and 'flexible' reflection on live practice experience. For them, reflection means focusing on 'the interactional competence' of the worker, where 'values, empathy and support for the service user as a person' are at the heart of role performance.

'Reflection' in social work has a longer history, of course. Freire (1970) regarded 'critical reflection' as central to engagement in a liberation process. What he termed 'conscientisation' is in his thinking inseparable from 'transformative action'. Here it refers to a process where people gain knowledge and find a springboard to action through active reflection on the oppressive conditions of their lives. The practitioner is primarily an educator, enrolled not to deposit expert knowledge but to provide opportunities for shared critical reflection; knowledge building and action become collaborative tasks.

Within feminist traditions (for example, Fawcett et al, 2000), it is accepted that crucial truths are generated from women's own accounts of their experiences, accounts which are often silenced or disregarded. Women are as expert as workers in discovering 'the truth'. At the heart of feminist practice is the practitioner's involvement with women in reflection - the practice of consciousness raising, - a mutual engagement in reaching understanding, generating knowledge and changing life conditions. Theories for action are the product of joint endeavours.

Postmodern and poststructural thinking challenge the premises of modernist social work and the traditional oppositions: theory - practice; individual - structural; school - field; direct - indirect; micro - macro (see Healy & Fook 1994; Leonard 1997, for instance). Our own overall experience is that these theoretical developments strengthen social work's appreciation of the complexity and diversity of people's lives. Not only can they impel and support social work's commitment to citizen and client participation in searching out multiple accounts and perspectives. They require social workers to reframe interactions as joint enquiries, joint endeavours.

Within social constructionism, knowledge generation is regarded as a conscious creation of workers' and clients' interactions. Here, reflection is invoked to describe a process of discovering and giving voice to the multiple meanings possible to confer on experience. In therapeutic work with individuals and families, these are offered not as expert and overriding truths but as different ways of deconstructing and retelling a person's or family's narrative. The reflective practitioner is 'infinitely curious' (Laird, 1995), a 'respectful stranger' (Anderson and Goolishian, 1992; Laird, 1989, 1994), The goals are to create a context where multiple ways of knowing are acknowledged; to act as a catalyst for family members to narrate and recreate understanding of situations and lives; and to offer feedback and possible alternative meanings to experience. Rather than imposing one truth, they must attend to the range of meanings, meaning systems and their social context (Saleeby, 1994) and be particularly curious about the voices and discourses which are silent or suppressed.

Both these political and theoretical developments have influenced the conceptualisation of social work education, both in regard to structure and process. A reflective approach implies the importance of experiential learning (Moffatt, 1996). Enquiry and action learning programs (Burgess, 1992, Taylor, 1996 and 1999) and issue based learning programs (Davis, George and Napier, 1996) explicitly engage with self directedness. When the teacher takes a reflective stance with students, it is assumed that knowledge will flow from the interaction with students, however resistant students are to embracing uncertainty and to considering knowledge as provisional (Papell and Skolnick, 1992; Parker, 1997). Students are asked to position themselves as active contributors to knowledge building. Multiple sources of knowledge are valued, including students' subjective knowledge (Boud et al, 1993, Eraut, 1994; Fook et al, 2000).

Starting points for learning are concrete situations, where students must confront the unexpected, the unusual and the complex, situations which defy quick technical fixes. Problem posing, not problem solving becomes the focus (Moreau, 1989) and inductive learning processes are highlighted. Students demonstrate what they bring to situations in terms of subjective knowledge (previous experience, values, attitudes, intuitive capacities) as well as a relative capacity for engaging with and being guided by formal theoretical ideas and techniques of practice. Practice is conceptualised as research, and the moments of 'not knowing' prized for what they can generate - recall of how such moments were resolved, what knowledge helped or could have helped, what the student contributed of 'themself', and where new knowledge might be needed.

Well known ways of highlighting 'difference' in understanding and performance are highlighted - observation, historical and international perspectives (Cox and Hirst, 1996), examining how knowledge has been arrived at and a particular perspective assumed, why particular accounts of people and their situations have been privileged and whose versions of the facts have been ignored or distorted.

The use of critical incident analysis has been developed in education, practice and research to focus reflection (Fook, 1996, Rossiter, 1994). By selecting an incident, perhaps one where the worker feels there is something important to be learned about their way of working, something routine or which stopped them in their tracks, a process of continuous unpacking can take place. It is posited that by extricating and naming specific responses in specific situations, both routine ways of understanding and acting and 'out of character' ways can be identified.

The theory and practice of critical reflection has been developed to a beginning point in social work; but there are further questions raised by our experience as reflective educators and learners in social work. Let us summarise our understanding of the elements of a reflective approach to date. The reflective approach seems to stand for the following:

- Emancipatory practice : reflection links awareness to liberation;
- Artistry - intuitive, creative action: reflection promotes a more effective 'use of self', where the whole of knowledge is valued and uncritically embraced.
- Coherence: reflection enables a 'clearing of the ground', a discovery of the differences between what one thinks informs one's practice and what it actually constitutes, in terms of value commitments, ruling ideas, and attitudes.
- Inquiry about power: critical reflection focuses on whose account of truth is privileged, on looking for silences and on demanding multiple perspectives;
- A new theory of knowledge building: reflection is a theory about transforming the theory / practice relation.

Reflection and social work

How will good reflective practice in social work be recognised? The behaviours which flow from intuition and past experience may be at odds with behaviours demonstrating empathy and fairness. Is there a danger that reflection becomes yet another avoidance of some 'absolutes', that 'anything goes', that it is not informed by social work values? What about theories of explanation? Does it matter which ways of understanding are employed? Is coherence to be valued at the expense of understandings which privilege particular explanations?

Practice has to take account of context, the imperatives of agencies - legal, political and economic - but must not the practices also be judged against the binding values of the profession social work and the meanings given to justice - fairness, inclusion and participation, for instance?

A critical reflective approach

These doubts and further questions that have arisen about the reflective approach from our own experience are to some extent echoed in formal criticism. For instance, the reflective approach, in particular the work of Schon, has been criticised for its lack of political awareness. We are also reminded that it has easily become an all - embracing concept, overused and too easily misunderstood (Brookfield, 1995). Reflection, as a process, can be used for all manner of purposes, to perform all manner of functions. It is still necessary to ask the further questions of reflection : for whom, and for what? Whose interests does it serve, and for what purposes?

Our tendency as we started to talk with contributors was to distinguish reflection and critical reflection. With a critical reflective stance, we wanted reflection to be coupled with a political analysis: we espouse ideas about an emancipatory practice. This type of approach draws on the work of critical social science (for example, Carr and Kemmis, 1986; Fook, 2000), and specifically uses reflective processes to analyse and uncover the ways in which unacknowledged assumptions and discourses construct power relations. In a critical reflective approach, the types of reflective questions asked will direct the practitioner towards the political, and potentially emancipatory, aspect of the situation which may be changed.

This doubtless influenced our choice of contributors; however our primary interest was not in choosing contributors with whose espoused approach or actions we might necessarily agree. Indeed, when reflecting on all the accounts (including our own), it is easy to see many different ways the situations could have been interpreted or acted upon, differently. Our purpose was not to present model interpretations or practices, but rather to discover the divergent learning, which the process of deliberate reflection could generate.

The contribution of this book

It is relatively easy to talk about the theory of reflection and critical reflection, and as we have shown, there is a burgeoning literature about the approach. However, our experience has shown us that it is often difficult to grasp its relevance and usefulness, and to come to a full appreciation of it , without experiencing it.

What follows therefore is a collection of accounts of social workers' practice experiences, their reflections on them, and the practice theory building which has arisen out of these reflections. It represents an attempt to illustrate the reflective approach in action through the practice experience of a number of social workers, drawn from a variety of backgrounds and practice settings. It represents an attempt to illustrate the reflective approach in action through the practice experience of a number of social workers, drawn from a variety of countries, backgrounds, experience and practice settings. The contributors are of different ages and have varying years of experience as social workers. The events, which they describe, occurred at different times and in different places, some recent, some long gone.

We acknowledge that such diversity might make it more difficult to develop a central and clear understanding of reflection. Yet on the other hand comparisons might help build a more complex appreciation of its potential uses. We hope that as you read, you will pause and consider how you might have acted in the situations described. The contributors' processes of thinking, feeling and acting should prompt you, the reader, to consider your own responses to them and to the work. How might you have used your authority, your voice? What might be its sources? Which ideas and values do you imagine might have informed your actions in any of these situations? What might have put barriers in your way? We hope that in this varied collection, many of you will be able to discover an experience or reflection that will trigger your own learning about your own experience.

References

Anderson, T. & Goolishian, H. (1992) 'The client is the expert: A not-knowing approach to therapy'. in McNamee S, & Gergen, K. J., *Therapy as Social Construction*, Sage, Newbury Park

Boud, D., Keogh, R. & Walker, D. (1993) *Using Experience for Learning*, Open University Press, Buckingham

Brookfield, S.D. (1995) *Becoming a Critically Reflective Teacher*, Jossey Bass, San Francisco

Burgess, H. (1992) *Problem-Led Learning for Social Work*, Whiting and Birch, London

Carr, W. & Kemmis, S. (1986) *Becoming Critical*, Deakin University Press, Geelong

Carter, P., Jeffs, T. & Smith, M. (1995) *Social Working*, Macmillan, London

Cox, P. & Hirst, G. (1996) 'Putting Young Heads Onto Older Shoulders: Social work education for work with children, young women and young men' in Preston-Shoot, M. & Jackson, S. (eds.) *Educating Social Workers in a Changing Policy Context*, Whiting and Birch, London

Davis, A., George, J. & Napier, L. (1996) 'Hidden partners? Inviting partnership in the social work curriculum', in McDonald, D. & Cleave, L. (eds.) *Partnerships that work?* Proceedings of the Asia - Pacific Regional Social Services Conference Christchurch, New Zealand, 1995, ICSW - AP/IFSW - AP/APASWE , 93- 97

Eraut, M. (1994) *Developing Professional Knowledge and Competence*, Falmer Press, London

Fawcett, B., Featherstone, B., Fook, J. & Rossiter, A. (eds.) (2000) *Practice and Research in Social Work: Postmodern feminist perspectives*, Routledge, London

Fook, J. (1993) *Radical Casework. A Theory of Practice*, Allen and Unwin, Sydney

Fook, J. (1995) 'Beyond Structuralism?' paper presented at the 'Narratives of Change' conference, Monash University, Nov. 28, 2-10

Fook, J. (ed) (1996) *The Reflective Researcher: Social workers' theories of practice research,* Allen and Unwin, Sydney

Fook, J. (1999) 'Critical reflectivity in education and practice', in Pease, B. & Fook, J. (eds.) *Transforming Social Work Practice: Postmodern critical perspectives,* Routledge, London, 195-208

Fook, J. (2000) 'Critical Perspectives on Social Work Practice' in O'Connor, I., Smyth, P. & Warburton, J. (eds.) *Contemporary Perspectives on Social Work and the Human Services,* Longman, Australia, 128-138

Fook, J., Ryan, M. & Hawkins, L. (2000) *Professional Expertise: Practice, theory and education for working in uncertainty,* Whiting & Birch, London

Freire, P. (1970) *Pedagogy of the Oppressed,* Herder and Herder, New York

George, J. & Napier, L. (1988) 'Social work and health care', in Vinson, T. (ed) *Advances in Social Work Education* 2, University of New South Wales Press, Sydney

Gould, N. & Taylor, I. (eds.) (1996) *Reflective Learning for Social Work,* Arena, Aldershot

Hanvey, C. and Philpot, T. (eds) (1994) *Practising Social Work,* Routledge, London

Healy, B. & Fook, J. (1994) 'Reinventing social work', in *Advances in Social Work and Welfare Education,* National Conference of the Australian Association for Social Work and Welfare Education, University of Western Australia, Perth, 42-55

Jackson, S. and Preston- Shoot, M. (eds.) *Educating Social Workers in a Changing Policy Context,* Whiting and Birch, London

Jones, M. & Jordan, B. (1996) 'Knowledge and practice in social work', in Preston-Shoot, M. & Jackson, S. (eds.) *Educating Social Workers in a Changing Policy Context,* Whiting and Birch, London

Laird, J. (1989) 'Women and stories: Restorying women's self-constructions' in McGoldrick, M., Anderson, C. and Walsh, F. (eds.) *Women in Families: A framework for family* therapy, W.W. Norton, New York.

Laird, J. (1994) ' "Thick description" revisited: Family therapist as anthropologist - constructivist' in Sherman, E. & Reid, W. (eds.) *Qualitative Research in Social Work,* Columbia University Press, New York

Laird, J. (1995) 'Family centred practice in the postmodern era', *Families in Society,* March, 150-162

Leonard, P. (1997) *Postmodern Welfare: Reconstructing an emancipatory project,* Sage: London

Moffatt, K. (1996) 'Teaching social work as a reflective process', in Gould, N. & Taylor, I. (eds.) *Reflective Learning for Social Work,* Arena, Aldershot

Moreau, M. (1989) *Empowerment through a Structural Approach to Social Work,* Carleton University School of Social Work, Ottawa

Papell, C. P. & Skolnik, L. (1992) 'The reflective practitioner: A contemporary paradigm's relevance for social work education', *Journal of Social Work Education,* 28, 1, 18 - 26

Parker, S. (1997) *Reflective Teaching in the Postmodern World,* Open University Press, Buckingham

Pozatek, E. (1994) 'The problem of certainty: Clinical social work in the postmodern era', *Social Work*, 39, 4, 396 - 403

Rossiter, A. (1994) 'Teaching social work skills from a critical perspective' in Hesser, K.-E. H. (ed) *Social Work Education: State of the Art*, Official Congress Publication, 27th. Congress of the International Association of Schools of Social Work, Amsterdam, July, 91 - 96

Saleeby, D. (1994) 'Culture, theory, and narrative: The intersection of meanings in practice', *Social Work*, 39, 4, July 351 - 359.

Schon, D. (1983) *The Reflective Practitioner*, Basic Books, New York

Schon, D. (1987) *Educating the Reflective Practitioner*, Jossey - Bass, San Fransisco

Taylor, I. (1996) 'Enquiry and action learning; Empowerment in social work education', in Preston-Shoot, M. & Jackson, S. (eds.) *Educating Social Workers in a Changing Policy Context*, Whiting and Birch, London

Taylor, I. (1997) *Developing Learning in Professional Education: Partnerships for practice*, Open University Press, Buckingham

2
They took my baby

Sheila Sim

I read 'Sandra Albert's' medical file again today. A flood of conflicting emotions swept to the surface: shame, anger, sadness. I saw the double-binds, the swings from optimism to pessimism to despair. 'It's a mess!' I thought.

What happened? Why, with my twenty three years of social work experience, did I not/could I not take better control of all the elements in this volatile situation and create a different outcome? or - at the least - create a better path to the same outcome? The questions simply lead to further questions: did I expect myself to 'create' solutions in isolation? 'Take control' of what - what were and are the limits of my authority?

I've chosen to write about this case precisely because it is a failure and a mess. I'm feeling somewhat apprehensive about what my account will reveal about my social work practice. I don't get the same comfortable feeling that I'd have if I were writing about my work in the area of reproductive loss, for example. But I have to confront 'what really happened', since only an examination of this story will illustrate whether anything different will emerge to transform my future practice.

Tommy Lee is born

Let me introduce you to Sandra as I met her on a humid Sunday afternoon six years ago.

I was 'on call' that weekend for social work emergencies in the specialist women's hospital where I work. The insistent tone of the pager broke into my slow Sunday breakfast. 'Sandra', a 34 year old multigravida, had been admitted to Labour Ward by ambulance and had given birth to a baby boy at 9.30 that morning. Her six previous children were in care. Could I come and see her?

Sandra was sitting up in bed on the post-natal ward - in a shared, four-bedded room. She was a slight woman, sitting half way down the bed with

16

shoulders hunched. Her hair was drawn back in a loose ponytail with an elastic tie. Her face looked worn and worried, as if she half expected someone to come and turf her out of the bed at any minute. She was wearing two hospital gowns - one back, one front - standard improvisation for women admitted without a nightie.

I introduced myself. She looked pleased to see me. I said I'd been asked to come in and meet her because of the speed of the baby's arrival and the fact that her other children were in care... just to see if we could help set her up for life with this baby in the best possible way. I made my voice and my behaviour as soft and non-threatening as I could. I acknowledged that she'd only just given birth! and that today was just so we could meet each other.

Her expression, tight as I voiced the word 'care' - her right hand crept to touch the side of the baby's crib - relaxed when I asked about the baby. She showed him off, sleeping in a bundle beneath the bunny rug: a big boy, 4.25 kilos, shock of brown hair and a solid sort of air.

'I didn't know I was in labour! They had to press the emergency button! I was visiting these friends in Bondi and I was just on the train when the pains started'. The story of her labour poured out. The baby was born within twenty-five minutes of her arrival at our hospital. She had named him 'Tommy-Lee'. She was going to move down the South Coast to stay after they left hospital. Her voice dropped. 'Sean, that's my partner, he doesn't know I've had kids before. He thinks this is my first' - and dead on cue Sean arrived from the kiosk where he'd been buying her a Coke, a lanky man in his twenties. He too expressed his amazement at the speed of the baby's arrival. This was all new to him. We stood round the crib admiring Tommy-Lee. I promised to dig out a nightie and some toiletries, and after I'd given her these, I left.

I notice from the medical record that I rang the Department of Community Services (DoCS), to liaise and to clarify why Sandra's previous children had all been removed. The after-hours worker could give me no information except that Sandra's local office in the western suburbs was actively involved. We weren't conveying any concerns to them: after all, this was only five hours after Tommy-Lee's birth! 'Give her a chance', was our unspoken agreement. Tommy-Lee was a lovely chubby baby and his apgar scores, which measure reflexes at one and five minutes, were high. Sandra had obviously nurtured him well in her womb.

On the following day, Monday, both mother and baby were doing fine, and nursing entries in Sandra's notes are brief: 'fundus firm', 'seen by social worker'. I was trying to understand Sandra's story, what had gone wrong between her and the other children. I still don't know exactly how many children Sandra had given birth to. You could call her a 'poor historian' - details, dates, names came tumbling forth out of sequence. You could call me a 'poor history taker' since I was so concerned to hear her life story from her own perspective that I didn't interrupt unless I was hopelessly lost.

She'd grown up in South Australia, the youngest of three children. She'd never got on with her parents and it was her aunty in Ceduna whom she saw as 'mum'. She'd left school early, could only just read and write. She said she 'winged it' when she had forms to fill in, asked for help or pretended she'd left her glasses behind. She drifted across to NSW, and had her first child when she was eighteen. She seemed to be able to manage until he was two years old. She got fed up, went out for the night, and left him on his own. This pattern - managing so far, but not far enough - seemed to be repeated with all the children. She'd left Catriona for three days once with a babysitter. She'd 'forgotten' to collect Angie from Kindy and turned up the next day puzzled by the hullabaloo this had caused. One baby died of cot death at three months of age. She'd had a stillborn baby boy in the pregnancy just before Tommy-Lee. Another boy had died in a house fire, aged two and half. Tommy-Lee's father, Andrew, had died in a car accident when she was five months' pregnant ... the litany of loss was overwhelming. I'm amazed that on that second day of her baby's life both Sandra and I were so hopeful. She didn't want to lose him, and together we talked about how she would get support when she got home. I told her that I'd rung her local DoCS office and she told me all about the operation that Harry, her district officer, was about to have. Together we rang Tresillian, to see if she could book in for continued support, and a pregnancy help centre to put in a request for nappies. We had a cup of tea and sifted through the Social Work Department baby clothes pile, stored in an unused bathtub!

As the week continued, these cosy plans unravelled. What went wrong? Did Tommy-Lee 'wake up', realise he'd been born, and impose his demands in a more urgent way? Did Sandra experience that third-day hormonal mayhem? Did we simply see more of the impact of her mild intellectual disability, her rather scattered thought processes?

I was away from the hospital on Tuesday. By the evening Sandra was in tears, increasingly agitated by the baby's never-ending need for a breastfeed. Twice she stomped off the ward, fed up, but always returned after she'd had a cigarette in the cool air downstairs. She had after-birth pains, her haemorrhoids were hurting her, she was beginning to have a sore throat. 'Look after ME' she was telling us.

She and the baby had a restless night. He was unsettled and at 1am was moved to the nurses' station. Sandra had a temazepam to help her sleep. Needless to say, in the morning she was tearful, fragmented, kept putting Tommy-Lee to the breast and then taking him off 'to burp him' every five minutes. He didn't appreciate this inconsistency and became increasingly grizzly. 'I can't fucking win!' Sandra shouted.

She couldn't tell me what it was that was making her so upset that day. It wasn't hard to make a long list of contributing factors. I tried to acknowledge all the fears that must be going through her mind, all the loss and anxiety - and to keep reminding her of what she had achieved for

Tommy-Lee. The midwife looking after her that shift was a sturdy woman who exuded confidence, didn't condescend, and kept her focus on the task of the moment. Together we tried to create a holding environment where Sandra could get it all together with her baby. It was still only day four, after all.

Just before I left the hospital for a meeting elsewhere, DoCS rang in response to my earlier calls. They were agreeable to Sandra being discharged with the baby when both were pronounced ready to leave.

I returned to work the next morning to find the midwives and Sandra stunned. DoCS had faxed through a care order late on the previous day! The care order stated that she'd had *eight* children removed due to her neglect as a result of her intellectual disability. Meanwhile - of course - Tommy-Lee had developed jaundice (brewing away the previous morning, I'd guess) and was now in the nursery having phototherapy, the care order stuck to his cot. Sandra had a sore throat and could hardly speak. What was there to say? She'd lost his birth registration form, but then, was he really her baby to register? In her demeanour, she seemed actually calmer than before. While her struggle to establish herself as Tommy-Lee's parent was still going on, she too was struggling with confused dreams and regrets. Now that in a sense, he was no longer hers, she seemed more relaxed. She'd embarked on a familiar path, after all.

It was the midwife and I who waxed indignant. No-one, least of all Sandra, had been contacted about this care order. The fax had just appeared and had to be obeyed. Together Sandra and I rang DoCS from the Nurse Unit Manager's office. Her caseworker was having an operation - well, she'd told me that herself! - and wouldn't be at work until the next day. We were reassured that he would call us then.

Overnight, Sandra asked the mum in the next bed if she could 'have a cuddle of her baby' but pushed the baby back towards her neighbour when she heard footsteps in the corridor. I hope they were wheeling Tommy-Lee back to his cot by Sandra's bedside. He was there for her to cuddle all the next day. She worried about the look of his stools, and developed a lump over her right nipple, which the midwives helped her to ease with a cold pack. She was anxious too that 'Sheila had forgotten her'. I saw her twice that day, and when we didn't receive the promised call from her caseworker Harry, we commandeered the Nurse Unit Manager's office again and arranged for him to meet us all at the hospital after the weekend.

The baby's care order expired on that Sunday. Sandra meekly agreed to Harry's request to stay in hospital until our joint meeting. The Nurse Unit Manager kindly agreed that we would let them both stay! It was a calm weekend: the notes record 'in good spirits', 'independent with all baby cares'.

Next morning Sandra and I met early. Her post-natal check had been completed; her 'baby bundle' was waiting for collection. Tresillian were offering a pre-admission interview. Her Early Childhood Health nurse was primed to call on her at home. That seemed to add up to a considered plan for her discharge, which we could discuss with the DoCS workers when they arrived.

Sandra worried about Harry. How would he know where to come? He'd just had an operation, and she didn't want him to be wandering the grounds, lost. She went down in the lift to see if she could spot him. I sat contentedly by Tommy-Lee's cot. It was a rare moment of peace.

She burst back into the room. It wasn't Harry! They'd come to take the baby away! To take him off her!

She'd been riding back up to the ward in the lift. She hadn't seen Harry anywhere. Two men got in on the ground floor, one with a baby carry-bag. She chatted away to them about waiting for Harry. 'Are you Sandra Albert?' asked one. She said yes, she was. 'We've come to remove your baby', he said. The lift stopped at the second floor and she fled to the ward. She was distraught.

I couldn't believe it. I sat her down on the bed, put my arm around her and said I'd find out what was happening. Outside at the nurses' station were two district officers. One did have a carry bag - and a renewal of the care order.

I said as firmly as I could - I was shaking - that we had been expecting Harry, who knew Sandra's history, and that we had agreed to have a joint discussion about plans for the baby's care. The district officers had the grace to look sheepish. By then the ward was in an uproar. The midwives and the other mothers were glaring. Tommy-Lee had stirred and was demanding a breast feed. We didn't trust these officers not to snatch him from the breast and so spirited Sandra into the Nurse Unit Manager's office to give him his feed and have time with him in private.

I rang the DoCS office to protest about the unprofessional way in which they'd conveyed this latest development to Sandra. In the lift! While she was helpfully giving them directions! Without any prior discussion! I was thinking 'high-handed', 'brutal', 'totalitarian'. My spoken language was more conciliatory. I outlined our arrangements for support; I tried not to sound like a rosy-eyed maternity social worker. It was no good. Tommy-Lee had to go into foster-care, at least until court on Friday.

Our only act of defiance was to delay Tommy-Lee's departure until he had had a gargantuan feed and Sandra had given the awkward district officers a run-down on his needs and quirks. Their stock fell further in our eyes when we realised they had come armed only with the carry bag - no bunny rug, no spare nappies, no milk supply. We bundled him up in all we could find and made them promise that Sandra's own district officer would visit her at home the next day. They gave her some written information about care orders and the phone numbers of Legal Aid. Then they left, carrying Tommy-Lee.

One of the midwives brought us a cup of tea. I think we were both speechless. Sandra began to cry; I began a rousing speech about 'just because you had difficulties with your other children doesn't mean you can't look after him...' and let the words fall into the space between us. I didn't actually know whether she *could* look after Tommy-Lee at home. I'd seen her tune in to his needs and walk away from them, often two or three times in the one day. I still didn't really understand what had gone wrong before.

The afternoon must have trailed on. The lactation consultant helped her express her breast milk and gave her a supply of bottles. We rang the legal aid number and got her an appointment. I made sure she had the DoCS office phone number, the time Harry would visit, and enough money to last the week, a cab-charge to get back home. She must have gone home. In her medical notes there isn't a nursing entry after the 7a.m. 'All's well'. Instead there's a stamp with the date, the hour and the word 'discharged'. The baby is absent from this entry, just as he was for Sandra as she made her way out onto the street.

For months afterwards the Nurse Unit Manager's office bore the image of Sandra sitting on a vinyl chair, hugging Tommy-Lee and crying wet tears onto his spiky hair. 'Did you see that film 'Ladybird, Ladybird'?' the midwives asked each other.

We were expecting to see Tommy-Lee on Friday, at the Children's Court. It was a hot, dry day, the temperature soaring. I got lost in those outer suburbs, couldn't find the entrance drive, and walked, I thought for miles, across a sort of paddock. The earth was red and dusty. I could have been in Alice Springs. Inside the court house fierce air-conditioning negated the outside day. Volunteer ladies dispensed tea. All the seats were taken by shifting family groups, some sullen, some argumentative. Sandra and her solicitor Michael were waiting outside, I discovered, under a flame tree, having a cigarette. She looked anxious, scrubbed up for the occasion. Harry emerged from the courtroom - no baby: too hot. Sandra's shoulders sagged.

In court, as we expected, the matter was adjourned. I explained to the magistrate our plans for support, our interview date at Tresillian. Sandra was outnumbered by helping professionals in the courtroom, social work, legal, and clerical, by eight to one.

Outside, the waiting families were more restive. We sat in the cool and drank a cup of tea while we planned the next step. I was impressed by Harry, who was large, reassuring and straightforward. He'd brought Sandra news of Tommy-Lee and details of an access visit - only in the office, not at home, but at least a visit. She handed over her gift of expressed breast-milk; she and I confirmed the day and time of her interview at Tresillian and organised where I'd meet her to take her there. We made an appointment with the Citizen Advocacy Scheme so she'd have an advocate, an ally.

At least Tresillian was familiar territory to me. It seemed only marginally less terrifying than the court house to Sandra, and much crisper and neater than our down-at-heel chaotic postnatal ward with its continual baby noises. However, a date was fixed for her admission with the baby. She would stay there for a week, and they would provide an assessment for the court.

The second time at court I realised the entrance was exactly where one would expect it to be. This time Harry had given Sandra a lift and brought Tommy-Lee. Their time at Tresillian had been fragmented. She'd hung in for three days, and then disappeared. They were recommending a psychiatric report.... 'Anyone would be psychiatric after that carry-on!' commented the midwives when I brought them this news.

The third time at court, I was overseas. Sandra had not kept her appointment with the psychiatrist. She'd forged a bond with Tommy-Lee's foster mother Jan. Jan let her come and go, feed him and walk away, pop into their lives again and disappear. I thought that Jan coaxed the best from her and that the rest of us had let her down.

Every now and then, Jan and Sandra would ring me to give me news of Tommy-Lee, blooming by all accounts. When he was ten months old, Sandra signed a consent for him to be placed for adoption. I never heard from Sandra again.

Reflection

Two things strike me as I read over that account:

The first is the contradiction between the overwhelming sense of futility and powerlessness, and the actual presence and stamp of power at every level of the story. More of this later.

Stories

The second is the language I've used. It reads like a short story! or almost. I mean the way I've chosen to begin with the beep of the pager, to race along to the denouement of Tommy-Lee's removal, and to end with that stark sentence about never hearing from Sandra again. The language is concrete, graphic and almost devoid of any social work or psychological terminology: I can find 'multigravida', 'intellectual disability', 'holding environment' and 'care order', a small presence of four semi-technical terms out of a total of I don't know how many words.

The characters are presented almost as if they are in a Greek drama: the cruel and powerful DoCS occupies the same role as King Creon, the autocratic and unmoving uncle of Antigone who wanted only to mourn her dead brother; the DoCS officers are the standard messenger-figures, bumbling, ineffectual, just there to carry out orders as servants of the king. The midwives are a sort of Greek chorus; and Sandra is the tragic heroine, her inner fatal flaw her own inability to be a mother to Tommy-Lee. I'm not sure what role I play in all of this - the old nurse, trying to be wise but constantly wringing her hands? Ismene - the sister of Antigone - who counsels obedience to the commands of Creon?: 'I cannot go against the State. I am not strong enough' (Soph. *Antigone*, Act I). This comparison won't sustain any more vigorous analysis: it's enough to point out the resonance that occurred for me while I was reading.

I was, and am, an avid reader: of books, train timetables, the labels on bottles! 'Sheila's always happy when she's got her nose stuck in a book' was the family observation. Reading the story, entering into the life on the page, opened up perspectives and ways of looking at the world that I obviously craved, or I wouldn't have haunted the public library. A story offered me a way to make sense of life. A good story was like the ah-ha! of gestalt therapy, a potent medium for altered consciousness.

I remember how delighted I was to find some novels included in the 'essential reading list' sent to first year students before we began our social work degree course: and not just the expected *Anna Karenina* and its unhappy family, but *Catcher in the Rye*, *To Kill a Mockingbird* and a wonderful account of life as a child care officer, *The Shorn Lamb*, whose author I've forgotten, a sort of James Herriott of child welfare. I was relieved that works of fiction, so important to me till then, could still have a place, or be seen as somehow relevant to the mysterious practice called social work which I was about to learn.

Before my social work degree, I had limited experience of 'work with people': nights in a shelter for homeless men and women, and a year living with a gentle group of long-term psychiatric patients. Listening to their experiences, I could hear the story contained inside it. 'If only other people knew what it was like!' (they'd understand and accept the mentally ill, the alcoholic....) was my tacit assumption. I think that's why I began writing 'stories' about women escaping violent husbands, a disabled woman whose window looks onto an amusement arcade... As a new graduate in Glasgow, I taped conversations with Donald and Archie, talking out loud about their years of unemployment, and together we transcribed their words and sent them off to a radical magazine. Perhaps that's why I read aloud to medical and nursing students if I'm giving a lecture: *Head above Water*, Buchi Emecheta's life as a black single mother in London; *Swimmer in the Secret Sea*, a father's tale of his stillborn baby; and *The Day I Held Up the 7-Eleven*, a hilarious one-pager on the turmoil of the first trimester of pregnancy. The theoretical frameworks, which I'm trying to convey - the bereavement theory, the psychodynamics of parenthood - spring to life in these stories.

I can't just teach them the abstract terminology ('role identity', 'attachment', 'loss'); they have to 'understand what it's like' in an actual, living sense, to experience loss or attachment.

By telling what happened to Sandra and Tommy-Lee as if it were a story, I'm hoping I will understand her experience from the inside.

However, working life isn't fiction!

A story no matter how postmodern has a beginning, a middle and an end. Perhaps we are left on the last page wondering how the characters get on after the story's over, perhaps we are left with alternative endings, or the account is told from many different perspectives. No matter: the characters actually do not have life unless it's on the page. The last page is the last word!

A 'case', the story of an interaction between a client and a social worker, has less clear boundaries. After all, the lives of Sandra and Tommy-Lee didn't end when I wrote my last sentence. I, the DoCS officers, the midwives and the magistrate presumably all went on with the practice of our professions well after the point where I chose to end my account. I write 'chose' advisedly, since that particular ending was where the story ended for me. Sandra, the baby and the adoptions branch of DoCS continued on with their interaction and for all I know still do.

I was also the one who decided where to begin and who put the events of day nine of Tommy-Lee's life at the centre of the piece. These beginnings, middles, and endings shift depending on who it is who's telling this story. For Sandra, perhaps the beginning was her decision to come into town, or the death of Andrew, or a point far back in her own life. For Harry, the beginning was the day he came back to work from sick leave, although he'd had multiple other beginnings with Sandra and her other children. For Tommy-Lee, the beginning was his conception (although he was safe in there) or his speedy arrival.

So the shape of the story depends on who is telling it, the author; but the fact remains that the story continues off the page, can't be confined to the ten or twelve days of work presented here. A construction, which I place upon it by selecting this period of time, is of necessity artificial. In real live social work it's harder to see any pattern or parameters at all in the dense material we're surrounded by.

I begin to wonder what I can learn from my comparison of Sandra's story with Greek tragedy. From my distant studies of classical Greek I recall descriptions of the amphitheatre at Epidauros, the actors, figures in robes, wearing tall masks with set expressions and high heeled wooden shoes so that they could be seen and heard from a distance: immobile, rigid, and rather static figures. The plot was also a constant: the circumstances of the story might change but the essential drama, the action, was always the struggle of the protagonist against powerful forces including his/her own essential nature. My analogy with Greek tragedy serves to underline the set, conventional nature of the roles we all played.

It's as if we are enacting a drama to which we all know the conclusion. Sandra and the baby are bound for tragedy and we all played it out to the inevitable end. Sandra seemed to reach this awareness before the rest of us: when she 'gave up' on day four in response to the first care order, lost Tommy-Lee's birth registration form and lost her voice. After all (as I wrote) she was all too familiar with the way in which these texts developed.

What purpose is served by bestowing on the actors in Sandra's story, the stiff gestures, masked faces and circumscribed roles of Greek drama? Am I hoping to exonerate myself from any responsibility for the final outcome? After all, I was only playing a minor role... it's only a walk-on part, really. Am I unwittingly reinforcing the motif of women's powerlessness in the face of the laws of the patriarchy? I'm not sure that a scrutiny of the actual events will sustain such a theme in any case... so I decide to get closer to the power and powerlessness and see for myself.

Who's got the power?

The power - if we can treat it for a moment as if it were an entity, in contradiction of postmodern discourse - seems to rest in the hands of the men in this situation: but not all the men. Sean, for example, faded away at the first hint of trouble and was never seen again; Sandra's partners were almost invisible as she relayed the history of her many pregnancies.

No: it's the men from DoCS who, at first glance, appear to be possessed of wide-ranging, inflexible, and unarguable powers. It's they who create in us a misleading sense of security in the first days of Tommy-Lee's life, by conveying that they will happily accept whatever discharge plans I arrange. It's they who fax through the care order, which sets us all reeling. It's they who arrive armed with a baby carry-bag in full view, who announce the reason for their arrival in the lift, and who walk out of the hospital with the baby. It's they who invoke the power of the courts, the Children (Care & Protection) Act, 1987, Section 62A, the imperatives of a child protection agenda.

And the women? At first sight, the women seem helpless and slow to organise. Sandra can't even organise her labour so that she has time to get to the hospital she's booked into, and time to settle in there before the baby emerges. She seems buffeted this way and that by events, by her own feelings and the baby's demands. In the face of the power of the Children Act I, her social worker, seem almost as powerless to slow down or alter the course of events, much less to influence the final outcome. The midwives check Sandra's perineum and look after the baby when Sandra storms off the ward, but when the DoCS officers arrive they look for me. Tommy-Lee knows only how to lie in his cot, eat, sleep and breathe. Together we seem immobilised by a counsel of despair, a deep sense of futility about the point of any action on our part.

Somewhere in here we have to take cognisance of the fact that these events took place in the first few days and weeks after Sandra had given birth: chaos, muddle and confusion are endemic. The baby is just finding himself in the world, learning the meaning of overwhelming bodily sensations and outside sensory data like smell and sound. Even that way of describing his first days is too simplified: in this immediate postnatal period he makes no such distinction as inside and outside, self and not-self. Similarly, the mother is just finding her baby. There's an inevitable period of transition as she replaces the internal baby with the actual baby who's been born. This real baby can be cute, chubby, 'good' i.e. eat and sleep in sequence; but even a 'good' baby produces sighs, snorts and gurgles, which his mother has to learn to interpret. Even a 'good' baby has to be fed, burped, changed, bathed, held, soothed, puzzled out, and not just once but several times a day, day after day. This transition can hardly be accomplished overnight, and so time and again on the postnatal ward I detect a sort of suspension of judgement, a tacit agreement: 'let's give her a chance'. We know the muddle will eventually settle into some kind of shifting but recognisable routine. In the meantime, we work along with the muddle (see Cornwell, 1983, p.28). Doctor Spock and others of his era might have forced their will on the baby; we wait to see what kind of rhythms the baby creates. The word 'wait' perhaps implies passivity, but it's a highly active, observant and experienced kind of waiting.

What did I do?

So already I've begun to admit that the midwives and I were engaged in the act of assessing Sandra and her baby in their first days. I made a list of all the other 'I' actions to see if I could prove/disprove the notion of myself as powerless in this situation. They came two-thirds of the way down the page!

In the first place, I accepted the referral. I went into the hospital to meet Sandra, to assess the situation and to respond to some anxiety, albeit nebulous, on the part of the nursing staff. 'Not much antenatal care, emergency admission, western suburbs, all her many previous children have been removed from her care'. My intention, I know, was to step in between the stereotypical picture that they implied and the real Sandra, not to jump to conclusions but to make an assessment of her needs and wishes. The fact remains that I didn't simply reply 'I'll see her on Monday'. I concurred with the misgivings of the midwives and agreed to come in out of hours, thus elevating the status of this 'case' from the word go.

I rang DoCS on day one. Something in my assessment of her at the first meeting - the vague story, the sense of chaos, the inconsistency - impelled me to acknowledge at once with Sandra the removal of her other children and to 'liaise' with DoCS and let them know this baby had been born. What was I doing? Fulfilling my statutory duty as a Health Department employee? Covering all the bases in case the removal of the other children had occurred after horrendous abuse? Whatever my rationale, I can't escape the responsibility for having alerted DoCS to Tommy-Lee's existence and thus for waking up the sleeping giant.

I rang them again on day two, getting through to Sandra's local office to see if I could clarify what supports they were providing and to let them know what we would be arranging. I spoke to the duty officer, who of course didn't know Sandra. I wanted him to take note of the fact that so far, all was well. I wanted him to know that it wasn't always thus: there were women who thought they'd given birth to a stone, or who left the baby wobbling on the edge of the bed while they went off and had a cigarette. Their Sandra, for all her intellectual disability, was mothering her baby well and I wanted him to acknowledge her expertise. I rang DoCS I continued the process of defining this as a 'case' and a 'child protection case' at that.

My other actions can more clearly be considered part of my advocacy role:

- I organised practicalities, like a nightie, clothes for the baby, discharge plans.
- I rang DoCS on the day after the care order had been placed, and again on day six when Harry had not been in touch with Sandra by mid-afternoon.
- I confronted the DoCS officers in their errand of removing the baby and made my protest known to the office manager. I engineered the baby's departure in a damage-control sort of way.
- I went to court with Sandra twice. I went with her to Tresillian.

In court I asked if I could speak and presented the information I had about Sandra's early care of Tommy-Lee as clearly and convincingly as I could. As I spoke I remembered the day I'd accompanied Jean MacNamara to the small claims court in Glasgow after she'd been caught reconnecting her disconnected electricity supply. I'd made an impassioned speech about her need to feed and keep warm her two children, her helplessness against her man's habit of drinking away the 'light money' that she'd stashed away. The magistrate had told me in withering terms to mind my own business. Such pleading had no place in his court. I don't know if my pleading for Sandra had any place, but I didn't sit silently.

In the end, however, I let myself fade away. I accepted an implied time limit for my advocacy. As the baby grew older the impressions and conclusions drawn from Sandra's mothering of him in days one to nine, grew increasingly less relevant in the face of the mounting evidence of her erratic behaviour since then. I did what everyone else had done: her children, her previous partners, Sean, her last DoCS officer Sally, all disappeared from her life. I could rationalise my action by reminding myself that I worked in an acute hospital setting, that we couldn't provide long-term postnatal follow up of any value to someone who lived fifty kilometres away, that I was allowed to take four weeks' leave even if it did coincide with a court date. I conveyed to Sandra the message that she knew only too well, that people just abandoned her and gave up on her.

I have to acknowledge, then, that I was a key and influential player in the sequence of events I've described, rather than helpless sister Ismene, standing in the wings. I accepted my powerful role as a delegate of 'the welfare'. I acted as an agent of state control, an aspect of the social work role I was already struggling with as a social work student on my second placement in Holloway Prison or in the slum clearance housing scheme of Glasgow......

...People appear who make it their business to involve themselves in other people's lives, health, nutrition, housing; then... there emerge certain personages, institutions, forms of knowledge: public hygiene inspectors, social workers...
(Foucault, in Gordon, 1980, p.62)

Marginalised voices

This uncomfortable tension between my attraction to social work and its social control functions, led me to explore and embrace marxism and feminism in the heady days of the seventies. But it wasn't until I found myself immersed and frequently lost in the writing of Michel Foucault that I reached a more liberating perspective on the discourses of power within society.

And the dominant discourse within the child protection field gives centre stage to the loudest voice, the one proclaiming the rights of a child to a safe, nurturing environment. Sandra's voice was almost completely inaudible: she could tell me what had happened to her, but not always what she wanted. She yelled that she couldn't win, and then lost her voice because there was no point in speaking. She knew she was marginalised, living on the edges of normal urban life, dogged by poverty, gender, semi-literacy and disability. She instigated subtle acts of resistance, like cuddling another mother's baby or staying the night with Jan, the foster-mother. I've even described her last breastfeed of Tommy-Lee as an 'act of defiance'.

Mostly, though, she fell into the disparaging, self-defeating, withdrawn behaviour that was condemned by society as a kind of irresponsibility - but which paradoxically 'protected the one narrow space of autonomy left...: (the) freedom not to care' (Marris, 1996, p.107). Sandra, faced with such great inequality of control, actually undermined her own hopes of being a mother for Tommy-Lee, and lived out our expectations.

Creating a definition may even be an 'actiological factor' in creating the situation one has defined... Social situations are the field for the self-fulfilling prophecy (Laing, 1969, p.17)

I'm presuming that my own intentions were not to aid in her further marginalisation, but to empower her, to help her negotiate the possibly hostile terrain of the health and welfare systems. I didn't set out to be such a dragon as was revealed by that examination of 'what I actually did'. I can see where my voice, too, was marginalised, and where my specialist knowledge went unheard. Some of this knowledge was a result of my exposure to the particular medical setting in which I work: the energising effect of the endorphins in the immediate post-birth period, making Sandra chatty and optimistic; the likelihood of a speedy labour in someone with Sandra's obstetric history; the increased risk of post-partum haemorrhage and hence the unspoken imperative to keep her in hospital and talk her out of early discharge.

My social work knowledge must by now be deeply embedded (or do I mean embodied!) in my practice. How often as a beginning practitioner I'd hear the advice, 'start where the client is'. Now it's so completely internalised that I can hear myself saying it to myself if I'm tempted to branch off on an irrelevant track. I hope I bring to any encounter the classic casework qualities of empathy, respect and acceptance. I set out to welcome my client with the kindness, courtesy and respect required 'when strangers meet' (Bruch, 1974, p.5). I wanted not to jump to conclusions about Sandra, not to accept at face value the intrinsically dismissive summary of 'Sandra' that I'd been given by the nursing staff, but to remain open and non-judgmental. Intertwined with these social casework concepts, was my awareness of social justice issues: the right of an intellectually disabled woman to parent her own child, the rights of a biological mother to decide for her children, the rights of the child to a safe and healthy environment.

Already I can see the contradictions lodged within those beliefs. Could I remain open and non-judgmental when Sandra described 'forgetting' to collect Angie from kindergarten until the following day? Could I reconcile the right of Tommy-Lee to a good enough childhood, with the right of Sandra to be her own baby's parent? No wonder many social workers experience a sinking feeling when child protection issues surface: how can we find an honest way through the tensions that are inherent between our humanist values and the unarguable authority of the child protection legislation?

Perhaps because the rights of mother and child were conflicting and irreconcilable, the DoCS workers and I fell into an oppositional stance. There was 'no right answer', and rarely is, for the complex and painful lives of parents and children when things go wrong. In the face of such uncertainty, as a response to almost unbearable tensions, we each reverted to a defensive position. They became the unswerving defenders of the rights of Tommy-Lee, and I have almost demonised them in my account. I became an advocate for motherhood, and so they left such motherly things as breast milk and Tresillian up to me. Inadvertently, we indulged in the sort of splitting that characterises 'child protection' in our society. The protection of children is seen not as the responsibility of all - when did you last see someone help a struggling woman, stroller and toddler onto a bus? - but is hived off to a specialist agency which takes care of our moral and legal responsibilities towards children. That way, we can stay well defended against the unique pain of each unhappy family, except when their story hits the headlines; we can continue to ignore the structural and cultural causes of child abuse and we can dodge altogether even wider issues such as the influence of the global economy in the reduction of public services.

The child protection system, safely located off at the edges of public awareness, is also in itself deeply oppositional: our intention is that the rights and needs of families are attended to, but the hub of such activity is the magistrate's court with its echoes of prosecution and defence, guilt and innocence, the legal paradigm an imperfect fit for the complexities of each family.

....when there are conflicting paradigms of professional practice... there is no clearly established context for the use of technique. There is contention over multiple ways of framing the practice role. (Schon, 1983, p. 41)

Context rules OK?

I haven't explicitly stated, though it's inescapable, that (social work) practice is deeply contextual. For me, a social worker in a women's hospital setting, nothing illustrates this more clearly than the changing practices in adoption in Australian society.

In the years since Sandra was a patient, our hospital has relocated. At the time of our move, I packed up four decades of social work files. The earliest records are large brown index cards with the client's name and details entered in the most beautiful copperplate handwriting: 'nice lass', 'BFA' (baby for adoption) are the brief and frequent comments. The social work department case-sheet lists 'keeping/not keeping' as an item for the worker to complete until the 1970s. The earliest almoner and her successors said their work was almost exclusively with unmarried or separated pregnant women, who had no access to benefits, child support, daycare or housing. The women and the workers were steeped in the sociopolitical context and beliefs of their time. There was little opportunity for resistance. In the face of such limited options, the workers tried to humanise the time of birth and hospitalisation, donating a sofa to the pre-maternity wing, facilitating tense interviews between the young women and their families, keeping an eye out for the Visiting Medical Officers who refused women abortions and encouraged them in adoption. There could hardly be a greater contrast than with our accepted practice of open adoption today, when there's time for the woman to be with her baby, to articulate the sort of adopting parents she would wish, to meet them and have ongoing news as her baby grows up.

Now, the sight of all these files might make me glad that our current practice is more enlightened - oops, that we've moved with the times! I can't help wondering what other practices of today will be looked at askance in twenty years' time. The context is all powerful. There's no jumping out of the dominant discourse even while you are thinking and writing about it. It blocks the other knowledges, those naive and subjugated knowledges of Foucault (Foucault, in Gordon, 1980, p.81). No wonder I felt blocked and disempowered while working with Sandra. No wonder I feel more comfortable with bereaved parents after pregnancy loss, since the context allows the expression of mourning and the enactment of ritual, indeed it almost demands it.

Any way out?

Is there any way out of this dilemma? Will all my child protection work in my present work setting be doomed to embody this adversarial, fragmented practice? Will I keep meeting future Sandras and end up feeling that we've all lost?

I wonder what would change if I uncovered the subjugated knowledges and made them speak up.

Example 1

We, the professionals in the obstetric unit, the midwives, social worker and registrar, know about giving birth, although some of us have done it and others haven't. I've alluded to some of this specialist technical knowledge above. Our constructs of pregnancy are at odds with the prevailing belief that 'you just get pregnant and then in nine months time you have a healthy baby'. We know that even 'getting pregnant' is fraught: a pregnancy occurs when you don't expect it, and may not happen when you desperately desire it. 'Nine months time' omits the stories of the parents and their babies who are born too early, or who die in utero. 'Healthy baby' assumes your baby is free from disability, birth trauma or congenital abnormality.

After birthing comes attachment, also known as bonding. 'You just look at your baby and fall in love (happily ever after)' runs the rubric. We the workers, know that the process is just that, a process. You may or may not fall in love with that red, wrinkled, ancient-looking face. You may feel such strong and tender feelings for this new human being, or you may wonder what on earth this baby has to do with you. It takes time to acknowledge that the baby in the cot beside you is the baby you have been carrying in your womb. In the first few days the baby seems in the same dreamy, disconnected state: riding along on the nourishment sustained in the womb he spends twenty two hours of the twenty four, peacefully asleep, although sometimes he may jerk and startle as if he's dreaming of a fall. As he wakes up and begins to feel hungry he may cry, perhaps even all day and no matter what comfort or care you provide. In the meantime you discover, perhaps to your dismay, that you don't magically know what he wants whenever he wants it, that you can't read his mind. It's only gradually that mother and baby become attuned. Sometimes, but only sometimes, the woman and her baby fall on each other as if they've never been strangers. Mostly, that squalling, needy baby is someone you have to get used to.

Synchronous with these psychic shifts are the physical sequelae of birth: the exhaustion; bleeding; pain going to the toilet; constipation; sleeplessness; sore breasts, cracked nipples, milk that squirts itself onto your clean nightdress, milk that dribbles out even when the baby's jaw is firmly clamped around the areola. Walking like an ancient grandmother to the shared bathroom, on the postnatal ward you discover that a horde of visitors have arrived for you. Turning with gratitude to the cup of tea on your tray now that the baby is sleeping at last, you discover that the tray's been whisked away.

What would happen if we, the obstetric professionals, demanded that attention must be paid to the imperatives of this immediate postnatal period? Insisted that no baby can be removed, even under the terms of the Children Act, until this sensitive period is over? After all, the Adoption of Children Act 1965 currently allows a woman to sign consent for adoption five days after giving birth and yet current practice has pushed the actual time of signing consent to something more like three weeks at the least.

Example 2

I, the social worker, hold certain intrinsic values and knowledges, which are apparent to my midwife colleagues. I know all about resources, negotiating and feelings; anything to do with these prompts the response, 'Call the social worker!' My knowledge, and my brief, extends beyond the medical model of the 'primigravida in room 3', to the person-in-environment, her history, dreams and social circumstances. My knowledge is founded on the humanist values that are the core of social work: a belief in the worth of the individual; a commitment to social justice; an opposition to oppression and discrimination on grounds of race, gender, class or disability.

These values must have been the reason I became a social worker rather than a computer programmer. They were reinforced by my early contact with real social workers. I'm thinking of Bill Jordan, tutor at Exeter University, who worked part-time as a probation officer, played football with his clients, helped start the Newton Abbott Claimants Union, and managed to write as well. There were colleagues at the Glasgow Family Service Unit, conversations over lunch about politics and Christianity, and since our 'office' was a four bedroom council house in a tenement, none of us were in danger of developing delusions of grandeur about our status as professionals.

There was even my supervisor in my second job, whom I could always find in the pub across the road if he wasn't at his desk, but who radiated respect and a readiness to listen as he ushered his worn, harassed clients into his office. These core values are still espoused and recognised by social workers from every practice setting. They are undoubtedly under threat from the tenets of economic rationalism and empiricism (see Ife, 1997). However, a roomful of social workers still generates impassioned and animated discussion about them and how they translate into practice. We recognise each other's language and values. We include those values implicitly even when we're working with new managerialist concepts such as 'casemix' and 'benchmarking'.

What would happen if I, the social worker, demanded that these values must be respected? If I made overt the breaches of social justice inherent in our child protection practice? If I actively enlisted the citizen advocate, the Ombudsman, the Human Rights Commission? Would I be scorned out of court, as I was with Jean MacNamara? Would it matter?

Voices again

I feel as if I'm being led back to the most elemental aspect of the practice role, to the very heart of social work practice.

In the swampy lowland, messy, confusing problems defy technical solution. (Schon, 1987, p.3) to return to a much-used quote.

If there is 'no right answer' to be achieved by following the protocols and checklists of technical rationality because 'the case is not in the book' (Schon 1987 p.5), then I am thrown back into my not knowing, a state of complete uncertainty.

When concern holds back from any kind of producing, manipulating, and the like, it puts itself into what is now the sole remaining mode of Being-in (Dasein), the mode of just tarrying-alongside...... 'dwelling' autonomously alongside entities-within-the-world. (Heidegger, 1927/62, Sec.62)

It's as if Sandra is standing in a field, which is itself layered and overlapped by other fields. She is surrounded by the elements and key concepts of the theory that's described by each field (Marxist, systems, bereavement...). The elements are like the flowers, shrubs, trees and stones that we'd find if we really were in a paddock! I am simply 'tarrying' nearby, looking round at this landscape, which is not new to me. But I don't know her truth. I don't yet (and perhaps never truly?) know which elements she'll be drawn to, which tree she might lean against. I don't know which concepts speak to her own lived experience. I'm doing my best not to jump to conclusions or to grab hold of an answer, just so I feel more comfortable.

I'm assuming that she has the ability to tell her own story about what life is like for her. Heidegger says that every one of us is a 'self-interpreting being'.

Almost simultaneously I'm observing and intuiting which concepts and paradigms do belong in her story. No, I'll put that the other way round: to hear what her story contains according to her own interpretation: loss, attachment, marginalisation. What was the meaning for her, of her auntie in Ceduna, her substitute mother? Or the meaning of her slowness to learn, mouthing along with the other kids and hoping no-one would notice she couldn't read the words in front of her? Or the meaning of the loss of each child : after all, they were all different children, not one conglomerate: four boys, now five, and four girls, some lost to her in their babyhood and others like Angie, whom she saw in stiff access visits every few months. Sandra has her own truths. The medical or midwifery angle on Sandra's history illuminates for us one kind of truth. The social work competencies can identify the clear indicators of 'loss' or 'marginalisation'. But the art of social work practice is to bring out and speak the truths contained in her story, and to do this in her service. When she hears this, she'll find her voice again.

Scottish accent

I could end there.

I've begun to think that my telling Sandra's story, and in everyday language, is an act of reclaiming of marginalised voices: mine, the baby's, and possibly hers, although I write that with great hesitation. The language could also be considered as an 'act of resistance' in Foucauldian terms, against the technical rationality of protocol-driven, pedestrian social work practice. After all,

> *the reality of the human life is not like the reality of liquids and solids in physics; it is closer to the reality of metaphor and story....... the human universe is made of stories, not atoms.* (Moss, 1989, p.201)

My work voice, the way I work, is what is being reclaimed here.

My actual voice is quite soft. I have an East Coast of Scotland accent. When I pick up the phone and answer 'Hallo' it's unmistakably me on the line! The sound of my voice when I'm at work tells me how present and available I am to the client who's sitting there: the tone, the timbre, the degree of softness, the hesitation, and sometimes a crisper sound of authority. My accent seems to change, I almost find myself talking more broadly and pithily when people are wary or frightened. Silence doesn't seem to worry me: I hope it doesn't worry my clients! I can tell by a dry, slightly off-key quality, when I'm 'off-key' and speaking mechanically. The older I get, the more often words fly out of my mouth without my conscious intention; I think 'Where did that come from?' or 'I hope I haven't gone too far!' Luckily my clients mostly look relieved to hear me say what they're hoping I'll help them think.

My good days bring encounters with clients that are full of surprises, for them and for me. Last Friday morning I met two new clients in a row and found myself reflecting how lucky I am, to spend my days meeting remarkable people confronting incredible questions: life choices, questions of identity, attribution of meaning. It's hardly surprising that the 'self' in the social worker is touched by this exposure constantly, and is being re-made. It's not just the technical skills and knowledges that are being tested and re-evaluated. The artistry of the social worker undergoes the same kind of process, a sort of daily master-class. I know that I'm at my most authentic as a social worker, and am most authoritative, when I'm speaking in my own voice: the best social work happens when knowledges, values and artistry come together in praxis.

I return to what I wondered initially, 'what happened?' in my work with Sandra, what went wrong? It's intrigued me that I've unearthed so many anecdotes and examples from the start of my life in social work. Is that a reflection of the fact that I graduated in 1971, in a decade when it was acceptable to espouse humanist values, a time when I probably experienced the least conflict between my self and my work role (even as I was struggling to understand both)? My work role and my humanism were unavoidably at odds as I worked with Sandra. I forgot to speak in my Scottish accent, and so there were no surprises, no unexpected outcomes, only the old story: 'they took my baby'.

After words

I can't walk away from Sandra without reflecting on why I chose to write about her. I didn't choose her because it's a 'good story'...there's something about her which captured me and has made me remember her, out of the hundreds of women I could have written about. I carry in my mind the image of her, standing with Michael under the flame tree at the Children's Court: a slight figure in a thin sleeveless dress, Target sneakers on her feet, brown hair shiny and sternly pulled back, in her expression both apprehension and hope. It's as if the events of Sandra's life hold for me a connection to one of the fundamental themes of my own life, separation and loss. And there must be something about the loss of children, children lost to their mothers, mothers absent from their children, that's kept me working with children, families and babies since graduation. Am I a slow learner? or is it that there's a lifetime's learning in this one theme?

When I arrived for my first day at work as a social worker with families, I can't have known that I would never have children myself. That came later. I have to look earlier in my life history for some thread that links me, Sandra and the theme of separation, and has led me to spend so much of my life working with these sorts of issues. When my sister Morag was born, did I mind staying with my grandmother while my mother spent the customary ten days in hospital? I was eighteen months old at the time. Did I know, in any sense of the word, about the miscarriages that were interwoven with my mother's full-term pregnancies? Were my parents ready for me when I was born? (my father wanted a boy!). With what part of my self do I know about my twin, who miscarried at an unknown number of months and left me to wait in the womb alone? Is he where it all began, my earliest separation?

My earliest conscious memory is of lying on a tartan rug in my grandmother's garden. I think it's the lovely summer of 1947, now a legend in the annals of British weather! The air is laden with the scent of stock and droning bees. I can't sense any nearby adult - perhaps I'd been left placed carefully in the middle of the rug to kick my legs. My overwhelming sensation is of being one with the rug, the grass, the sky, the bees, overlapping and contiguous with every other living element. Not a hint of separation, only connectedness.

The other memory that nudges at me is a day when I was six or seven. An Indian man had been going the rounds of the houses in our street, selling brushes and gadgets from a suitcase. I can't remember if my mother bought anything - she may well have. I can recall my sense of shock that a man should have to travel so far from his family and sell to harassed Edinburgh housewives, just to make a living. He probably came from Bradford, not Islamabad! It still seemed to me an inhuman and senseless way for him to make ends meet and for the housewives to buy their household goods. I can remember my sense of indignation and sadness that the world was organised in such a way. I ran after him and gave him my pocket money. It was all of sixpence.

The 'who I am' at work, the 'I' who is re-made in every encounter with a client, is surely deeply rooted in both the personal and the political, the spiritual and the secular dimensions. I think I chose the story of Sandra and Tommy-Lee precisely because it reconnected me to my indignation about the way our world is organised and to my knowledge of how it once was and may yet be: whole, complete and harmonious. Sometimes!

References

Bruch, H. (1974) *Learning Psychotherapy*, Harvard University Press, Cambridge MA

Cornwell, J. (1983) 'Crisis and survival in infancy', *J.Ch. Psychotherapy*, 9, 25-31

Emecheta, B. (1986) *Head above Water*, Fontana, London

Foucault, M. (1980) in Gordon, C (ed) *Power/Knowledge*, Harvester Press, London

Heidegger, M. (1927) *Being & Time* (trans. Macquarrie, J. & Robinson, E.)(1962) SCM Press, London

Ife, J. (1997) *Rethinking Social Work: Towards Critical Practice*, Longman, Melbourne

Kotzwinkle, W. (1975) *Swimmer in the Secret Sea*, Flair Books, NY

Laing, R.D. (1969) *Intervention in Social Situations*, Association of Family Caseworkers, London

Marris, P. (1996) *The Politics of Uncertainty*, Routledge, London

Moss, D. (1989) 'Psychotherapy and human experience' in Halling, S. & Valle, R. (eds.) *Existential-phenomenological perspectives in psychology*, Plenum Press, New York

Sagan, M. (1989) 'Armed robbery: The day I held up the 7-Eleven', in *Cradle and All*, Chester, L (ed) Faber & Faber, Boston

Schon, D. (1983) *The Reflective Practitioner*, Basic Books, New York

Schon, D. (1987) *Educating the Reflective Practitioner*, Jossey-Bass, San Francisco

Sophocles (1947) 'Antigone', in *The Theban Plays*, (trans. E.F. Watling) Penguin, Harmondsworth

3
Changing the system through casework: A critical incident analysis

Silvia Alberti

Introduction

I was introduced to critical incident analysis using a reflective approach while undertaking postgraduate studies a few years ago. When I first utilised reflective practice as a learning instrument, I was surprised at its power. I was able to freely examine myself and my practice in a way which encouraged me to be true to my experience while challenging myself to look beyond it. Although my work context has changed over time, reflecting on and examining my practice in formal and informal ways has remained an important learning mechanism for me. In the chapter which follows, I will detail the context of my work and describe the critical incident which I chose to focus on. My reflections on the incident and the group discussion which followed are outlined, as are the theoretical concepts I used to assist me to move forward in a more positive manner. I conclude with thoughts on the reflective process and how it has the capacity to inspire professional development.

Context

At the time of the critical incident, I was working as a Senior Clinician in a community-based alcohol and drug centre. A significant part of my role included working in a maximum security prison in Victoria. The prison was very old, and imbued with a culture and structure reminiscent of the last century. Within this context, it was my task to deliver a range of psychosocial interventions to prisoners who were identified by themselves or management as having substance use issues. The critical incident I chose to analyse relates to the dysfunctional way a prisoner was managed.

The critical incident

Some months into my work at the prison, senior management requested a 'priority' assessment of a prisoner considered a 'special case'. They reported that this person had been charged with, and was currently being punished for, a drug related offence within the prison.

The prisoner was around 55 years old and was from a non-English speaking background. He understood very little English and had only been in prison a short time. Given the minor nature of his offence, and his good conduct in prison, he had been moved to a minimum security prison in the country several months before. While there, as part of the prison's usual drug screening regime, he was drug tested and returned a positive result. As a result of this, he was immediately transferred back to a maximum security prison.

A number of sanctions were applied including a cessation of visits with his elderly mother and sons and permanent placement in maximum security until his drug status was converted.

He was very confused and distressed about the entire situation, maintaining that he had not used drugs 'ever in his life'. The message I received from prison officials (via other sources) was that I was to do 'whatever' in order to allow this prisoner to be moved back to the country prison so that his visits could be reinstated immediately. The interest invested in this prisoner's situation by officials was unusually high. Never before had I received so many requests to assist a prisoner. I was therefore curious about this prisoner and the circumstances around his drug use.

At assessment, it was immediately apparent that there had been a mistake made and that this prisoner had been wrongly charged. It was clear to me that he had very little knowledge of drug use and no contact with it in a prison context. In addition to this, all other indicators suggested that this man had never had an issue with problematic substance use.

When I reported the outcome of my assessment I was told that there had been 'an unfortunate mistake in the system'. When I suggested that the system correct it, I was promptly told that wasn't possible. Therefore, although it was accepted that he was innocent of any wrong doing, the officials maintained that the only 'fair thing to do' was to 'put him through a drug intervention', despite the fact that he had no drug using history and no issues related to drug use. To deny him this service would mean his right to contact with his family would not be reinstated and that he would have to remain in the maximum security prison. Given that he was now registered as an 'Identified Drug User' (known as an IDU status) he also lost many other 'privileges'.

I chose this incident because I found myself angered and astonished by the unfairness of the situation. I was particularly moved by the circumstances of this man's life and the repercussions for him and his family. At the same time, I felt that I wanted to do something which would stop this sort of incident from occurring again, but was at a loss as to how to achieve this.

The underlining themes

I presented an account of the incident to a group of peers. At the time of my presentation I felt angry about the misuse of power which resulted in much pain for this man and his family. I also felt annoyed and frustrated at my inability to convince these officials to 'do the right thing' and accept responsibility for their error. On reflection, my presentation of the incident carried an air of cynicism, which I think contributed to my inability to generate positive alternatives in the situation.

When I think about my thoughts, feelings and assumptions, several themes emerge. Firstly, I realised that I had become absorbed by the system. I have, in some ways, become so used to it that I now simply 'write things off' as 'part of the way the prison is'. This belief contributed to my resolution at the time that the situation was 'hopeless'. In this way I mirrored the feelings of the prisoners, other treatment staff and some of the officers.

Secondly, I had started to relate to my work environment as 'so big' that it was untouchable and unchangeable. My perception of the system as 'so big' acted to disempower me and to immobilise any creative ideas. It led to the belief that any intervention aimed at effecting change would have to be powerful and very big. This further added to my resolve that nothing could be done to truly change this system.

It became obvious on reflection that the 'client group' extended beyond the prisoners, something I had lost sight of over the 18 months of my involvement. I slipped into the position of 'me against them'; I was pitted against the system, believing it to be unable and unwilling to change. In many ways, this approach incorporated remnants of the confrontational style which pervades the prison culture and leads to a narrowing of possible alternatives rather than the generation of new possibilities.

Finally, I departed from my usual orientation towards process and adopted the prison's end-focused approach. This meant that I missed many of the opportunities to initiate small changes, and found myself feeling trapped by something to which I thought I could not add anything positive or constructive.

In conclusion, the presentation to my peers clearly demonstrated my perception of the situation as 'hopeless'. Given this, I felt angry and frustrated by what I saw as 'their inability to be flexible' and my 'inability to create change'. This was the motive for selecting this episode as the critical incident to be analysed, because at some level I recognised that there were many opportunities within this scenario which I was failing to acknowledge and utilise.

Utilising a problem solving framework

I think that many of the constraints around the situation related to the narrow focus I took in my understanding and interpretation of the events. Bunston (1985) suggests that 'the perception of problems and solutions is shaped by one's commitment to certain theories, techniques and values as well as by personality characteristics, working style and environmental factors such as organisational and legal boundaries' (1985 p. 227). Bunston's conceptualisation of 'a problem' is helpful to me because it allows me to find myself and my values in the situation. For example, I am aware that the prisoners I work with in the prisons have limited power over most aspects of their daily lives, limited freedom, little contact with those they love, and that they live in an environment which can be harsh and uncaring. Therefore, I try to work in an open, clear and empowering manner. My ideas, my working style and the realities of prison have significantly influenced my perception of the problem and any possible solutions to it. Hence, considerable value lay in utilising structures such as peer supervision, class discussions and readings which assisted me to step outside of my constructions of the situation, which were driving my thinking in a very linear way.

Bunston (1985) goes on to say that when we work through situations such as these, we call upon convergent (that is, rational), and divergent (that is, creative) forms of thinking. He characterises creative thought processes in four phases including: preparation, incubation, illumination and verification. His concepts provide a framework for the process in which I engaged: from the development of this critical incident in a written form, to the creation of a range of possibilities to deal with this and like situations.

Using this framework, the preparation phase was characterised by the detailing of this incident as I perceived it, and the planning for discussion and further thought on it. At this point, the focus was on accessing my actual thoughts on the incident, including the underlying themes and biases which were undetected.

The incubation phase followed the group discussion and was when I reviewed what I had written and considered it from the perspectives given during the discussion. This phase produced a clearer understanding of the constraints around my own thinking and the outcome was an identification of barriers, beliefs and feelings previously implicit and therefore difficult to access. These stages are detailed in the first part of this chapter and provided the starting point for resolution of this 'problem'.

The third phase, which Bunston calls illumination, refers to the time when resources fall into place and a decision is reached. Following the peer discussion and reflection period came the time for reading and contemplating how these ideas applied to my incident. At this point I was keen to include all new ideas and approaches to the situation, including thoughts I had not previously included. The thinking around the practicalities associated with implementing these ideas as 'solutions' refers to the verification stage. Then, the ideas generated were refined into a clearer form. Discussion of these final two stages follows with details of the process from 'problem identification' to the generation of 'solutions'.

Relevant approaches utilised to provide direction

A variety of ideas and concepts were utilised in the creation of a new approach to this situation. The inclusion of radical social work theories and strategies and post-structuralism provided many ideas around possible strategies as well as offering a more liberating way of perceiving the environment and structures. Theories of psychodrama contributed significantly in the creation of flexibility within individual interactions and finally, organisational theories and sociological theories added further depth to my understanding of the system and influenced my perception of it as an entity.

The system

One of the major factors I considered in the development of constructive responses was the place of 'the system'. Williscroft (1993) categorises this system as a closed one which is inherently inflexible and not open to dealing with problems fluidly. She argues that 'in a closed system complaints generate counter-complaints ... and they appear to be circular and have the effect of fragmenting the team and causing paranoia and distrust' (1993, p 8). She adds that in a closed system '... leadership is exercised ... by being superior ...' (1992, p 11). Using this concept of 'closed systems', I was able to conceptualise the way the prison operated. Rather than thinking about the prison system in an isolated manner, I started to think of prisons as an example of closed systems. Understanding that certain behaviours, like direct confrontation, do not work well in this system, resulted in me having to develop other ways of challenging practices which I thought unacceptable.

Rein and White (1981), suggest that of all the causes of doubt within the social work field, one of the most common is the experience of the system all around acting to subvert its own end, the most obvious phenomenon being '... slotting clients into predetermined categories that reflect the needs of the agency rather that the needs of the client' (1981, p.26). This resonated strongly for me, as I felt it was true of my experience, particularly in this instance.

Jones and May (1994) argue that 'complex organisations tend to develop a large volume of rules ... which are ... fundamentally a form of organisational control' (pp.192-193). This applies to the prison context where, to make an exception to the rule in one case, places the system in a vulnerable position; for the system to acknowledge that it is fallible would leave it open to legal action from prisoners across the State. Hence, I developed an understanding that any intervention or strategy aimed towards the system altering its formalised rules would not achieve its desired outcome. In this case, a first-order change is required which involves '... a variation that occurs within a given system which itself remains unchanged' (Jones & May, 1994, p 352).

Thus, in terms of effecting change in this closed system which is geared towards self preservation at all costs, I thought the approach ought to focus on small incremental reforms rather than large scale revolutionary change (Jones & May, 1994). The 'system', when viewed as a number of smaller, distinct parts which are connected together, as opposed to an enormous entity, appears less intimidating and more flexible. This conceptualisation helped because I started to see a range of possibilities for action when I thought of the prison as made up of smaller interrelated parts.

Robertson (1983) likens the unique nature of culture in every society to the culture of every organisation and asserts that '... an understanding of that culture - which is essentially a combination of norms, values and beliefs - is important if we want to achieve change' (1983, p 63). This sociological perspective would hold that the patterns of behaviour within the prison are shaped and controlled by the culture of the establishment. From this perspective,

> *... the ability to achieve a full understanding of another culture depends on one's willingness to adopt the position of cultural relativism - the recognition that ... a culture can only be fully understood in terms of its own norms and values* (1993, p. 68).

When I reflected on this, I understood that my view of prison culture, although mostly accurate, was tainted by my judgements and comparisons with 'community culture'. My actions and thoughts were driven by the belief that prison culture was unacceptable or flawed. This starting point was unhelpful to the generation of an appropriate action plan. Therefore, I understood that the development of a plan of action needs to be preceded by a clearer, less tainted view of the culture in the prison, its norms, values and beliefs. This facilitates a deeper understanding of the people who make up the system and their motivation which, in turn, assists in the implementation of strategies for change that are sensitive to the prevailing culture.

The ecological perspective supports this general idea, arguing that '... people can best be understood through the interrelatedness of people and environment' (Fook, 1993, p. 13). Germaine and Gitterman (1980) hold that a mobilising source of change for individuals is found through their interaction with the environment. Thus, given that any plan for change will necessarily involve the officers in the system, a clearer understanding of them and their place within this culture would facilitate more positive outcomes for all concerned as well as fostering a healthier working relationship between the different components of the system.

The client group

I initially overlooked the fact that the 'client group' being serviced is varied, comprising staff as well as prisoners. This initial view resembles what Moffatt (1994) terms 'categorical' or 'dichotomous' thinking, which impedes progress. The inclusion of uniform officers as 'client' creates a freedom in terms of possibilities for further intervention.

Moffatt's suggestion that social workers may be creating constraints on how they think about the nature of their practice (p.1) is, in this case true, as my thinking acted to limit the options available and to create in me a feeling of frustration and hopelessness. This emerging perspective led to more reflective practice which is based on the assumption that '.. people grow in connectedness with others through relationship' (Davis, 1988, cited in Moffatt, 1994) and that 'knowledge is constituted through interpersonal connection rather than being developed in isolation' (Dore, 1994, cited in Moffatt, 1994). Therefore, it became clear that I should not be working in isolation and that relationship building with the officers was an important consideration in any intervention plan developed.

Simons and Aigner (1979) argue that 'satisfactory social functioning occurs when people are able to take on roles and perform them in such a way as to fulfil their needs, accomplish their tasks and realise their aspirations and values', thus, 'all human problems are seen as role problems' (1979, p. 203). This theory, which bears some resemblance to that of psychodrama, shifts the emphasis from what could be termed 'dysfunctional behaviours of individuals', which is then personalised and not particularly helpful, to a broader notion of people's role repertoire which may be in need of expansion.

According to Clayton (1993), it is '... necessary that an individual does not stay fixed in one position, but rather is assisted to develop a larger perspective and greater flexibility' (1993, p. 56). He would refer to work on the individual's role system as 'social atom repair' which essentially means '... any reorganisation or any development in the relationship of a person with the outer world' (1993, p.55). These theories on the importance of a range of flexible and creative roles helped me considerably. In relation to myself, I understood that good social work practice required that a range of roles should be in place, some of which I may not always have thought relevant. For example, the role of 'accepting companion' was an important one to develop in relation to my interactions with officers who may have perceived me as an intruder who opposed them.

The theory was also important in that it prompted me to revisit my ideas about how to work with prison officials. For example, intervention with the officers focused on encouraging an expansion of their roles with a view to developing a more flexible, confident and caring response to issues as they arise. An additional assumption here is that any positive changes to the officers' roles will have positive repercussions for prisoners in the system.

Finally, a thought which was always somewhere in my mind was that any intervention should ensure that prisoners '... have access to the resources, services and opportunities which will contribute to their well being' (The Australian Association of Social Workers, Code of Ethics, 1989). In the case of the prisoner in question, access referred to the development of a programme which, although not directly relevant for him, assisted him to have his most significant needs met, including return to a safer, more constructive environment, the recommencement of his family visits and so on. Thus, the focus had to remain firmly on the prisoner's needs and on facilitating the best possible outcome.

Strategies for implementation

Following the peer discussion and reflections on readings, I developed new ideas to address this incident.

Documentation

In order to '... help make radical ideas more socially visible and increase the possibility of their acceptance' (Fook, 1993, p. 92) documentation is necessary. A full account of the incident relating to this prisoner was written up and copies were made which were forwarded to appropriate prison officials as well as being placed on his file. Although nothing instrumental could be done to change the course of action for this prisoner, his case will be incorporated with others like it into the statistics in the final report to the Department of Justice. When the number of extraordinary cases become significant a case can be made for system-wide changes to be instituted.

Small changes

Rather than focusing on the system as a whole, identification of the crucial players or parts was helpful, with interventions concentrating on small changes, which are most achievable. In this case, although the intervention needed to take place in order for the prisoner to achieve his desired end, small changes could be made to the nature of the intervention. Utilising the strategy of 'relabelling', the program developed was not a 'Identified Drug User' (IDU) program, but rather a 'Drug Education Program' which is available to anyone in the prison wishing to apply. Hence, the documentation in his formal report and in the Classification System read that he had completed this program and had been approved by officials for transfer. The implication of this is that the Drug Education Program is now a recognised program for the elevation of a prisoner's IDU status. The inclusion of a different program has also opened the door for the development and inclusion of other programs like personal development programs. The aim will be to include a wide variety of approved programs so that eventually the stigma associated with any of them will be gone given that they are accessible to the entire prison population.

Relationship focus

Rather than isolate and remove myself from the aspects of prison that are most challenging to my values, and distancing myself from officers whose values and beliefs oppose mine, it is necessary to involve myself more fully in these aspects. According to Daniel (1992) psychodrama techniques have been utilised to gain fuller expression and encourage freer interaction. She states that 'small pieces of work enable and strengthen frightened protagonists resulting in greater courage and freedom' (1992, p. 23). Accordingly, putting time, effort and energy into building and sustaining positive interactions with officers who currently pose the greatest obstacles will result in more positive relationships. In keeping with role theory, developing a better understanding of the roles officers are in will foster deeper knowledge about their motives which will assist me in framing any future responses to them. Further, better working relationships will hopefully engender a fuller appreciation of one another, and may develop a sense of mutual respect. When the concerns of the other are taken into account, there is greater opportunity for creation of a slightly more flexible and creative response repertoire.

The unfinished

Finally, Mathieson's concept (cited in Fook, 1993) of the unfinished which refers to '... an approach which views small achievements as legitimate as long as they are kept open to change and are continually viewed as being part of a larger scale political change' (1993, p.94) is quite useful. This affirms work done, without denying the larger political picture. Thus, while a positive outcome was arrived at for this individual, attention must be paid to continually challenging the system through small scale as well as larger scale activities and interventions. This encourages greater accountability and better practice in the longer term.

Conclusion

The creation of freedom and greater creativity in the way problems are addressed is liberating. In an environment where it is all too easy to become cynical and jaded, it is critical that approaches, which are expansive and empowering of the worker, are called upon and utilised. The theories and strategies drawn upon have challenged, as well as validated, my practice beyond its previous boundaries. Working through this critical incident has reinforced process oriented thinking and added to my role repertoire that will impact constructively on my practice.

In conclusion, the use of critical incident analysis as a facilitator for reflective practice prompted me to closely examine my practice in a new and open way. Although very challenging, this was a liberating and rewarding way to improve my approach to work in a closed and guarded system.

References

Bunston, T. (1985) 'Mapping practice: Problem solving in clinical practice', *The Journal of Contemporary Social Work*, 225-236

Carter, P. (1994) 'Towards a definition for spontaneity', *Australian and New Zealand Psychodrama Association Journal*, 3, 39-40

Clayton, G. M. (1993) *Living Pictures of the Self: Applications of role theory in professional practice and daily life*, ICA Press, Victoria

Daniel, S. (1992) *Building Healthy Group Culture: A psychodramic intervention*, ANZPA Examiners, Melbourne

Fook, J. (1993) *Radical Casework*, Allen and Unwin, Sydney

Germaine, C., and Gitterman, A. (1980) The Life Model of Social Work Practice, Columbia University Press, New York

Goldstein, H. (1987) 'The neglected moral link in social work practice', *Social Work*, 32, 3

Harrison, W. D. (1987) 'Reflective practice in social care', *Social Services Review*, 393-403

Healy, B. and Fook, J. (1994) 'Reinventing social work', in Advances in Social Work and Welfare Education, Ife, J., Leitman, S. and Murphy, P. (eds) AASWWE Conference, Perth

Jones, A. and May, J. (1994) *Working in Human Service Organisations: A critical introduction*, Longman Cheshire, Melbourne

Moffatt, K. (1994) 'Teaching Social Work Practice as a Reflective Process', 27th Congress, The International Association Schools of Social Work Amsterdam: The Netherlands

Rein, M. and White, S.H. (1981) 'Knowledge for practice', *Social Service Review*, 1, 1-39

Robertson, I. (1983) *Sociology*, Worth Publishers, New York

Schon, D. A. (1971) *Beyond the Stable State*, Norton Press, New York

Simons, R.L. and Aigner, S.M. (1979) 'Facilitating an eclectic use of practice theory', *The Journal of Contemporary Social Work*, 201 - 208

Williscroft, C. (1993) 'Integration of organisation theory. *Australia and New Zealand Psychodrama Association Journal*, 2, 1-11

Wagner, R. (1989) 'Fate of idealism in social work: Alternative experience of professional careers', *Social Work*, 34, 5

4

'Just doing referral'
Creating social work subjects

Cathy Peut

I am a public servant - a social worker in Centrelink, a Statutory Authority which delivers services for the Australian Federal Government, including job seeker information and referral services and income support. For various reasons, I have never experienced the disquiet expressed by many social workers about that conglomeration of practices and conditions known as 'The State'. On the contrary, 'state responsibility' and such currently unfashionable attendants as 'public ownership' and 'public service' inspire my commitment. I came to social work from an employment background in the public sector, private enterprise and community care. These experiences may have influenced my eventual choice of social work within a public income support framework. Influential too, were my interpretations of structural sociological theories and the history and philosophy of social policy, where arguments for legislated entitlement and state provisioning, however contested, were compelling. Whatever the influences, I find most uncompelling the view propounded by some social workers that, to be in the employ of 'The State' is to automatically align oneself with 'agents of oppressive authority'. Instead, and with passion, I actively sought to do social work as a public servant.

Given this, it is not surprising that such a position involves an ongoing dialogue with a variety of dichotomies familiar within social work discourse, such as 'care versus control' and 'radical versus traditional practice'. That I do not find such oppositions either accurate or helpful may, of course, be part of a convenient fiction - a rationalisation of my role and position. Yet, the assertion that social control represents the inescapable terrain of all social work practice from mandatory settings to community action groups, from therapy to consciousness raising, is not news within the discourse either. The care/control dualism and assumptions about the alignment of these terms with so-called radical versus traditional practice, have received a certain amount of de-mythologising attention in the social work literature (for example: Day, 1981; Rein & White, 1981; Rojek, 1986; Hasenfeld, 1987; Furlong, 1990). Nevertheless, in my experience of interagency

49

practice, it is clear that, whatever the status of such issues in the Academy, they maintain a strong hold over the way many workers conceive of their own and others' roles.

In addition, student social workers on placement with my agency most frequently ask the angst-filled question: 'If you're implementing government policies, aren't you doing Social Control?' Interestingly, the policies and strictures of community-based charitable agencies, to which the same student may become conformed, are not conceived as 'Social Control'. Also not recognised as such is the local neighbourhood centre with its single young mothers program, to which the student makes referrals in the belief that, if it's not 'Radical' at least it's 'Care'. The mythological quest for a form of social work outside of the shadow of 'Social Control' distracts from more valid questions about direction, purpose, principles and strategies of practice within specific contexts. I do not contend that social work is or should be a harmonious enterprise, but that what Rojek (1986) has called 'the gladiatorial paradigm' distracts from more vital and interesting disjunctures.

Social workers within statutory agencies, especially those associated with the public social services, must often contend with a referring social worker's overt perception of us within such a dualistic framework. Interestingly, it is self-styled 'radical' social and welfare workers who make so much of this arguably neoliberal thesis of 'The State' as inherently antagonistic to 'Community', regardless of any particular set of government policies with which their referral may engage. At the very least, where this antagonistic view is obtruded into the process of client referral or advocacy, as if a blunt object is required in dealing with social workers in 'the system', the client - subject of the referral - is at risk of becoming a mere cipher for this set of assumptions.

Resisting identification with such automatic assumptions while attempting to act as a resource for clients so referred, can add another layer to social work practice in this context. Because it may be an issue for social work and welfare education, and because it is rarely, if ever, articulated from this perspective within social work practice literature, I found it a compelling theme in selecting an episode of practice for this chapter. I mention this now, in the interests of making explicit an agenda which underpins both my selection of a 'piece of work' and my (apparently) subsequent reflection on it. It is also an important aspect of the context in which my practice example is embedded.

The episode of practice involves my interaction with a 14 year old young woman, a social worker from a community-based youth refuge and a child protection social worker in a state government agency. My reflection on this practice cannot be extracted from the ideological commitments which led me to work where I do. These and the already mentioned theoretical and experiential frameworks constitute the lens through which I retrospectively compose my narration and perform my reflection. For me, the project of reflecting on a piece of work and comparing my 'espoused theory' with what might 'emerge' as 'theory in use' is problematic for these reasons. There is no pure reflective moment completely divorced from the very contextual parameters influencing the work in the first place. That is why I have started, not with the story of the work, but with some sketching in of my theoretical and ideological commitments and dominant contextual themes.

Of course, the context is also constituted by the defined role of social workers in my agency, my interpretation of this, and the legislative, policy and organisational shaping of that role. For institutional and historical reasons, social workers in Centrelink have developed specialised income support and social service knowledge. A primary focus of much of our casework involves the deployment of complex and changing social policy knowledge within crisis situations, with people for whom basic survival is a fundamental issue. ('Fundamental', but never separable from needs and issues which may not bear the stamp of immediacy, but which are no less present for that - the need to make sense of events and circumstances, to maintain dignity in the face of these and in the process of getting help...)

People who see social workers in my agency include refugees, migrants, women and children experiencing domestic violence, sole parents, people with disabilities, their carers, bereaved people, those who have lost jobs, homes, possessions, people who have never had a job, young people who are homeless, people with addictions, with unmanageable debts, with nowhere to stay tonight, no money, no food ...The list could go on. The casework role embraces counselling, referral, advocacy (within and outside the agency), assessment and, in some cases, decision-making within the framework of legislation and interagency protocols. We simplify as 'casework' this complex of arrangements, this interplay of discretion, statutory authority and responsibility, and professional considerations. From one hour to the next, any combination of these personally experienced social issues can claim the focus of Centrelink social workers. In mutual relationship with casework, our role also encompasses the monitoring of services for their impact on clients, feedback into the service development process, and involvement in community liaison and interagency activities.

In that description of my role, I have glossed over a seemingly endless variety of interactions and social issues experienced as personal problems. Why choose for this exercise the case of a 14 year old in which the primary function of my role is 'simply' to facilitate a voluntary referral to another agency – one publicly designated as authorised to address her needs – in accordance with procedures clearly agreed in a protocol between our agencies? Indeed, what could be more straightforward than direction to 'the right place'? A little information exchange, a telephone call, some paperwork to formalise the referral and some advocacy of issues important to the client. I recall social work skills manuals presenting information gathering and referral as just such unproblematic functional steps on the way to the 'real' work (such as counselling), to which chapters are devoted in micro layers. Consequently, information gathering, referral and associated advocacy can be trivialised, denied their complexity and de-contextualised. Again, it is student social workers who have alerted me to this style of theorising, by their linguistic constructions of aspects of practice as 'just doing referral'.

Selecting this example of practice then allows for a focus on these least vaunted, often patronised and yet crucial types of intervention - referring a client to another agency and actively representing the client's interests to an institution. Less regarded than community development or counselling, these practices cut across all modes of social work, and can represent a fundamental shift in the fortunes of clients. In each case, they involve an ability and willingness to 'construct' the client as a subject out of a plethora (or dearth) of objectifying details, through the use of language and regulations meaningful to the agency with which I confer. This, in Philp's (1979) terms, is to create a space within institutions for marginal voices to be heard, and is the terrain of interpretation, negotiation and influence within defined parameters. If the client - subject of the referral - is to remain central to the process, it should be apparent that, whatever the referring social worker's views about their 'social control' counterparts in 'the system', the blunt object approach will not serve. So my pet themes converge.

In order to understand the following example of practice, I need to briefly describe the legislative and policy framework informing my practice options. Dry as they are, these details will soon be animated by my cast of characters. The legislated minimum age for entitlement to income support in one's own right is 15. The needs of young people without family support, under that age, are the responsibility of state government authorities, known in New South Wales where I practise, as the Department of Community Services (DoCS). Their child protection teams are responsible for investigating and assessing the safety and well-being of young people and making arrangements for their support. Homeless young people at age 15 are eligible to apply for income support from Centrelink under Federal legislation. There is an agreement or protocol in place which sets out these responsibilities and describes the processes by which, for example, a 14 year old homeless person applying to Centrelink for help, is to be referred to DoCS for assistance. Such an interagency protocol is designed to assist young people at risk, by ensuring that the responsible agency is clearly recognised, the young person is quickly seen by them and the referring agency is advised of the outcome within a defined time-frame. The arrangements are designed to reduce delays and to avoid any confusing 'pillar to post' experiences, instead allowing us, as it were, to cooperatively accompany the young person across agency boundaries.

My involvement as referring social worker can be minimal or intensive, depending on circumstances, such as the immediate needs of the young person, their capacity or wish to speak for themselves, whether they are already 'known to' DoCS, and whether the referral is voluntary or to be made without client consent. (The Social Security Act provides for information to be released 'in the public interest' where people are at risk to themselves or others). This framework of legislation, policy and interagency protocol, its language and concepts, represents the formal parameters within which my first - and possibly only - interaction with 14 year old Mary will take shape. I will be the face of the authority which constrains her options within these boundaries - and her resource for translating them into possibilities, for rendering her visible and audible within the terms of the institutions she is entering.

All of this meaning is contained in the phrase 'protocol referral', a term which carries a certain degree of predictability, of known structure, of tidy sequences, and which enters my head as soon as I am told that a 14 year old has asked to claim a payment. That I am also told she is accompanied by a social worker from a youth refuge triggers the assumption that there is a safe place to stay and a supportive guide through the system. This is also a clue that the young person has already told her story (a potentially distressing process) to at least one worker, and so, given the possibility of telling it again to a DoCS worker, it may be less intrusive if I keep my information gathering to a minimum. I haven't met Mary or her worker yet, but as I search out the appropriate referral form, I'm forming such assumptions. As the form comes to hand, it occurs to me that such referrals have become rare in my office. The information networks of young people themselves, youth refuges and services, have disseminated the knowledge that DoCS is the appropriate agency for help if you're under 15. Many youth workers make direct arrangements with DoCS, rather than insert another layer of story-telling and further referral into the process. My initial assumptions are now feeling less neat. Once I have settled Mary and the worker, Diana, in a private room, predictability is fractured immediately. Diana looks and sounds angry and Mary bored and restless.

I've chosen these names because I've never worked with a young person called Mary or a youth worker called Diana. Location details are omitted and I don't believe there is any singularly identifying feature in Mary's story, as I relate it here. Given the power of my position as story-teller here, it is incumbent on me to make clear that, while Diana's theoretical assumptions and mode of referral and advocacy represent the recurring paradigm I highlighted previously, she is not a symbol for youth workers in general, some of whom, in my experience, depart from the paradigm. Moreover, the style of advocacy represented by Diana here, is adopted by some social workers in other arenas of practice. Diana also acts as a kind of literary device - an alternative lens through which, on reflection, I can view my own theory-practice assumptions.

How Mary's story was related to me cannot be reproduced here, for numerous reasons. If I may compress an interview of almost two hours into a few paragraphs (clearly a subjective and selective exercise), I shall attempt to describe the emergence of details which gained the status of 'relevant information', some points of impasse and decision-making, the jostling of different perspectives and purposes and the forging of tenuous agreements.

I shall not be concerned to relate a case-study narrative with an edifying outcome, since a feature which interests me is the stubborn refusal of casework to conform to the linear neatness beloved of case study writers (myself included on other occasions), where the technique (whatever the mode being propounded) triumphs in resolution. Perversely perhaps, I do not want to focus so much on what happened for Mary as a result of her contact with this cast of social workers. I am here interested in what we, as workers, made of Mary. That is, how, as agency employees, we constructed and represented to each other the subject 'Mary', from sometimes different and sometimes overlapping sources of information and perspectives, and for purposes which converged in a notion like 'Mary's welfare', but were also refracted through the distinct interpretative lenses of our respective institutional imperatives. I do not use such a phrase in any pejorative sense, nor is this observation meant to summon up images of the bureaucratic distortion of the somehow 'essential Mary' lost in the mist of social work jargon and government red tape. On the contrary, I believe such an image rests on the assumption of a romanticised and essentialist conception of the individual, a view which portrays 'free choice' and 'self determination' as if they were not always, anyway, socially constructed and contextually constrained. In this scenario, it is Diana who bears the burden of this ideological position. She didn't propound it in quite that way, however, she quickly made it clear to me that if I (presumably Centrelink) would not pay Mary enough to cover her refuge fees, that if I insisted on the 'bureaucratic red tape' of a referral to DoCS, Mary's 'real needs' would not be met, she'd be 'on the streets' and 'at risk' because 'the government' would not take responsibility. Mary would 'fall through the gaps' and become 'another statistic'.

The circumstances leading to Diana's concerns for Mary were not yet clear to me. What seemed reasonably clear was that, to proceed, we needed a framework: that could offer Mary an opportunity for speech; make transparent the constraints on choice as well as the possibilities opened by the authorities she had approached; find common ground with Diana; and allow all of us to explore Mary's own concerns. Still in the dark about Mary's reasons for leaving home, I wanted to give her an idea of the possible implications of telling her story to me. I offered to provide an explanation of how things worked, what sort of rules existed, what I could do with any information she might choose to give me, how I could support her in a referral she might accept to DoCS, or in other ways. I then suggested that, knowing more about this, Mary might wish to talk about what had brought her here. We could then all discuss the options for responding to her situation. This plan of procedure being agreed, and my explanation concluded, the plan was then ignored. Diana resumed her diatribe against 'the system', during which Mary announced she was going outside for a cigarette. I reminded her that I needed to hear from her if I was to be of any assistance. She shrugged and resumed her seat.

In the fullness of time, the following picture was developed. Mary had left her parents' home a month ago. They were, she felt, too strict. Not only did they refuse her permission to see her friends (all three years older than Mary), but they were insistent that she continue with school. She had been a reasonably successful student until recently, when she began 'skipping' regularly to meet up with her older friends. Mary was also frustrated by her parents 'nagging' her about drugs. She believed their concerns were ill-founded, given that she only ever smoked 'dope' when her friends provided it to her. What Mary felt she needed now was the freedom to 'hang with' the friends with whom she had stayed upon leaving home. There was 'no way' she would return to her parents with their rules and nagging, or to school which was boring. Anyway, she added, her parents had become 'fed up' with her and, after all, she had her friends.

Diana broke in at this point. Her refuge could not provide free accommodation, she insisted, and Mary's fees had to be paid. Adamant that her own agency's conditions be met, she continued to construe other institutional realities as insensitive and unreasonable. Happily, she appeared oblivious to the irony of this. Thinking something less coherent than this but similar, I was further informed by Diana that an avenue of fee payment already explored by the refuge had been the local DoCS. They had declined to commit to payment pending an assessment of Mary's family situation. In pursuing this issue, I learned that Mary had come to that agency's attention following the arrest of her friends on break and enter charges two nights previously. Police had searched their flat and encountered Mary who advised them she had been 'kicked out' by her parents. Following their protocols, the police had notified the emergency child protection team, who organised for Mary to stay at the refuge until an assessment was completed.

Strictly speaking, I did not need to make a formal referral to DoCS, given that they were already involved. In view of my awareness that a protocol referral would enable an official response to be prioritised and that Mary's refuge tenure was very short-term, I believed there were valid reasons for continuing to offer such a referral with my ongoing support. At the same time, aware of DoCS priorities and definitions of risk (in the family), I felt it important to emphasise the referral as related to Mary's current situation of risk and not to portray it as the definitive answer to the fee payment issue, but rather as a means to ongoing support in addressing the concerns of Mary and her parents (as far as I knew them). I did this kind of thinking out loud so that Mary and Diana could participate in the process. I suggested to Mary the possibility of my arranging and accompanying her to an appointment with a DoCS social worker with whom I enjoy a good rapport. My hope was that this would provide her with an opportunity to discuss her situation with a worker on whose professionalism and sensitivity we could rely. While I continued to feel the need for an understanding of Mary's parents' views about the prospect of her returning home, Mary maintained her position that this was irrelevant as she could stay with her friends. She left at this point to meet them, indicating that she'd think about the appointment idea and let me know.

Diana remained. It was 'obvious' she said that, whatever the case from her parents' perspective, Mary would not choose to return home. It was time for the system to react accordingly. With the option of returning to her friends a very real and risk-laden one, Diana informed me that the refuge would be providing Mary with accommodation for no more than a week unless her fees were paid. Implicit in this was the suggestion that, while government agencies can and should disregard legislative requirements, the policies and procedures of a community agency are written in stone. Valid as the fee payment issue was, I experienced Diana's refusal to acknowledge the parameters of constraint and possibility as an obstruction to dialogue about alternative courses of action. Diana also left, agreeing to follow up Mary's decision.

That same afternoon, Mary returned to the office. Her friends - out on bail - had disappeared. The flat was empty and there was no message left for her. Still startled by the turn of events, and clearly feeling angry and let down, Mary agreed that I 'might as well' arrange an appointment with DoCS to which she requested I accompany her. This was arranged to take place in two days time. Having reached this rather tenuous agreement, I asked whether she'd like to use the phone, maybe call her parents, alone or with me, or just talk more about how she saw things now. Mary wavered, hanging on the doorknob, apparently considering further talk. But this was going too fast. Still angry and unsettled by her friends' apparent abandonment of her, Mary made her exit, saying she would see me later.

The following day, I received a call from the DoCS social worker (call him Bill). He had been liaising with staff at the office near Mary's parents' home, in preparation for our meeting. Bill learned that the parents themselves had approached DoCS some months ago, requesting help in dealing with what they saw as Mary's behavioural issues. According to that office, these issues were broadly as identified by Mary herself: skipping school, mixing with older friends, some drug use. On the basis of a DoCS referral, Mary's parents had arranged family counselling, a measure Mary had steadfastly refused on every occasion. This attitude, they reported, led to increased arguments at home. Following one marked by exasperated cries of 'fed up', 'see sense' and 'give up', Mary left. Her parents notified DoCS but, concerned about the impact on Mary's younger sister, insisted that she would need to accept counselling or compromise upon returning home. This remained the situation the parents claimed they hoped for.

In the light of this information - an aspect of Mary's situation hitherto unrecognised by myself or Diana - it was unlikely that DoCS could justify financing Mary's stay in a crisis refuge. There remained, however, the possibility of a number of compromises being negotiated, and I discussed with Bill Mary's apparent confusion, vulnerability and need for sensitive assistance in negotiating these. I explained Diana's and my own concerns about risk should she maintain her current stance. Bill agreed to explore some possibilities before our meeting and I phoned the refuge to discuss these with Mary. Diana advised me that Mary had left suddenly, following an incident in which she was discovered with marijuana on the premises. Warned that another such occurrence would lead to her eviction, in the heat of the moment, Mary left, vowing not to return.

Mary's story, unlike exemplary case studies, just seems to peter out. There are loose ends, a sense of anti-climax. Of course, it's not always like that. Sometimes the issues are stark enough to fit all the agency categories, referrals work smoothly, DoCS reports outcomes - placements arranged, support accepted - half decent developments considering where things started. But text books are replete with case examples where things work and stories seem complete.

My narration is necessarily truncated and selectively focused. I wanted to highlight aspects of the process of interagency referral which point to the fragmentary, approximate, interpretive and complex business of negotiating the creation of a subject for referral across institutional contexts, especially where one agency already has another construction of the subject in the making. I also wanted to evoke the complexity of contextual layers - that context is not a static environment into which a blend of theoretical orientations and techniques are inserted. Context rather is dynamic. There are mutual and fluid relations between layers of context, with theoretical, experiential and strategic orientations and influences.

If my theoretical orientation eschews any necessary dichotomising of care and control, any alignment of these labels with the myth of some inherently radical or non-directive (dare I say empowering?) set of practices, versus some inherently conservative, directive and power-wielding version - then the episode of practice I've described could be read as a reflection of that orientation. That there is also no state monopoly on social control to be disparagingly compared with an imagined community agency libertarianism (equated with care) is also a recognisable theme in my narrative of the episode. For me, it illustrates how the 'gladiatorial paradigm' masks continuities. Just as Centrelink and DoCS contextual parameters are delineated by legislation, policies and rules of accountability for the use of public monies, so the decision-making, priorities and practices of the community-based refuge are contextualised within funding imperatives and rules of residence controlling unacceptable behaviour. In this sense, a 'continuity' masked by the care/control dichotomy is what Day (1981, p.98) refers to as 'the *fiction* of non-directiveness' (my emphasis).

Further, it is not only continuities which are masked by the 'gladiatorial paradigm'. The paradigm also distracts from salient discontinuities or divergences at the level of institutional interpretation and treatment of client circumstances - differences or particularities which I would argue must be understood and strategically engaged with in effective front-line referral and advocacy. What I earlier referred to as 'institutional imperatives' shaping the way a notion like 'Mary's welfare' is represented by different agencies to each other is an illustration of this.

The refuge, for instance, relies on limited funding (some of it government funding) and, to meet demand, must charge fees. Its residents therefore require a form of income or must be subsidised by another agency (such as DoCS). The payment of fees is an imperative validly structuring the representation of Mary's welfare as 'at risk' if this accommodation cannot be provided to her. The youth worker's focus is not, therefore, on why Mary is not able to live at home, nor on what may be alternative interventions to address her situation, but on the perceived likelihood of Mary refusing other options and thus requiring refuge-fee payment.

Similarly constrained, but using a different lens, so to speak, I as Centrelink social worker must adhere to legislative limits on payment and to an interagency protocol - institutional imperatives defining the terms in which 'Mary's welfare' will be constructed, necessitating a relationship with DoCS and their definition of 'risk'. Thus, the Centrelink and DoCS imperatives require a focus on the reasons Mary cannot live at home. We must ask: 'In what way is Mary able to be properly constituted as a subject within the boundaries of a child protection authority? What alternative interventions or supports are possible?' The DoCS worker must ask these questions from within their own legislative definitions, resource allocations and guidelines on accountability for public monies. Mary's own expressed construction of her welfare can also be seen as refracted through the lens of contextual imperatives - whether we describe them in terms of a children's rights discourse or use the language of developmental stages and phrases like 'peer group priorities'. There is both overlap and disjuncture in these different constructions of 'Mary's welfare' and, given the relations of power in which the negotiation of meaning occurs, it becomes a matter strategically and ethically, of ensuring that marginal voices (Mary's in this case) gain a point of entry into the process.

I can recognise this espoused theoretical principle in my attempt to encourage Mary's own speech and to locate aspects of her situation which would allow me to present 'Mary' to DoCS in a fashion meaningful within that agency's terms of reference. In Philp's terms, this is to create powers of speech, rights to discourse within specific institutions (Philp, 1979, p.102). The DoCS story of Mary was, understandably thus far, her parents' story. To insert Mary's voice meaningfully into that picture - to render her visible and audible within the DoCS framework – required first of all that I grasp that framework: its language, (what does DoCS mean by 'risk'?); its rules, (how much discretion exists? what is DoCS legislatively empowered to provide?); and its limits, (what contextual issues shape its priorities and use of resources?). It is in grasping this, and then listening to Mary and other participants, that I may possibly, strategically, create a subject for referral and advocacy with a voice audible (with the right to discourse) within that institution.

But what I recognise as an alignment of my espoused theory with 'theory in use' is open to contestation. In response to the above interpretation of my practice, I can hear a chorus of Dianas deriding the power plays of bureaucrats and insisting that what I perceive as strategy is actually a hopeless descent into compromise. Better to take and maintain the high moral ground. My response, of course, is that the high moral ground is also contested terrain. Furthermore, structural power is not relinquished by wishing it away or in deluding ourselves that we are not bearers of several forms of authority. The issue is how authority is used. In addition, it is not, I believe, a question of a false alternative between dogged insistence on one's own agenda and capitulation at the first hurdle. Rather, it's a more complex matter of asking who has what kind of discretion, at what level, to engage with my agenda. Policies and procedures should be open to challenge. The challenge, though, needs to be directed where the power to change resides.

I could articulate a further list of theoretical principles I espouse and see their 'footprints' in my practice example too. For instance, Moreau's principles of 'structural social work' call for workers to consciously recognise power relations by de-mythologising processes, sharing the rationale behind questions and interpretations, encouraging mutual dialogue, sharing information and offering honest choices (Carniol, 1992). All the same, 14 year olds aren't always bursting with enthusiasm to engage in mutual dialogue with social workers keen to make transparent the limits on choice - none of which add up to 'the money - now'. In any case, I can recognise my attempts to operationalise such principles in my practice narrative. However, just as readily, I hear the Diana chorus disputing this too. All that talk about transparency and information sharing, about honestly portraying options and their limits, is only so much bureaucratic obfuscation - just another means of complicating what was really 'obvious'. Of course, this begs numerous questions, such as 'obvious' to whom?

My recognition of my espoused theory is not surprising, since the theory is not a neutral tool which I pull out of a bag of tricks and use or discard at whim. Rather, it is the value-laden fabric of my interpretations and decisions, moment to moment in the work itself, and later, in my way of telling the episode - structuring it, selecting for it and analysing it. At the same time, my practice is open to multiple interpretations of its theoretical underpinnings, and Diana's is but one. These interpretations are also woven from the fabric of theoretical orientation, experience and context. In my story of the practice, Diana's perspective as a participant interacted with aspects of my context already familiar to me (such as legislation, role and workplace organisation). This is what I mean by context not being fixed or static, but dynamic. What I notice in my practice story is thus more than what I can neatly fit into the term 'espoused theory'. There are mobile and dynamic contextual relations and human interactions and interpretations that produce immediacy and unpredictability. Sometimes I experience these as opportunity (however effectively or ineffectively I use it), such as in Mary's sudden return to the office. At other times, I experience these features as frustrations or obstacles, such as Diana's explicit and aggressive projection of the care/control dichotomy onto our roles and practice possibilities.

In reflecting on my practice narrative, I have transformed Diana from the intensely committed, if blinkered, worker of the story, into a more generalised Devil's Advocate - assuming certain theoretical implications from her apparent mode of participation in the work. In a sense, this is a metaphor for the complex and creative process of referral and advocacy, the construction of client-subjects. We, as workers, become similarly constructed by each other. Motives are attributed, constraints recognised or ignored, emphasised or under-acknowledged. Theoretical positions are attributed, misinterpreted, acknowledged or negotiated. Ideological commitments are acted upon, compromised, decisive or ad hoc. We make and re-make our clients and co-workers according to written and unwritten rules and conditions, in images with which they will experience varying degrees of discomfort or ease. More or less consciously, aggressively or cooperatively, we make institutional space for speech. Theorising about referral from the standpoint of practice both clarifies and complicates relations between 'espoused theory' and 'theory in use'. However we construe these relations, we are never 'just doing referral'.

References

Carniol, B. (1992) 'Structural social work: Maurice Moreau's challenge to social work practice', *Journal of Progressive Human Services*, 3, 1, 1-20

Day, P. (1981) *Social Work and Social Control*, Tavistock, London

Furlong, M. (1990) 'On being able to say what we mean: The language of hierarchy in social work practice', *British Journal of Social Work*, 20, 575-590

Hasenfeld, Y. (1987) 'Power in social work practice', *Social Service Review*, September, 469-483

Philp, M. (1979) 'Notes on the form of knowledge in social Work', *Sociological Review*, 27, 1, 83-111

Rein, M. and White, S. (1981) 'Knowledge for practice', *Social Service Review*, March, 1-41

Rojek, C. (1986) 'The "subject" in social work', *British Journal of Social Work*, 16, 65-77

5
Introducing a culture of reflective learning in a non-statutory social work agency: An action inquiry

Nigel Hinks

Introduction

This is a case study of change. It reflects on the ongoing process of introducing a research and learning framework into a voluntary child-care organisation. The organisation comprises some 90 practice locations in England and Wales. It has undergone radical change during the latter part of this century, moving from a predominance of work with orphanages and adoption work towards a value-led approach, targeting the justice issues that impede the well being and proper development of children and young people today.

I recently opened the yellowing pages of a paper I wrote as a social work student. The concluding paragraphs of some critical reflections on my placement, working with a terminally ill man in his early 40s, made several references to a need for opportunities for learning from a difficult and poignant experience. I was drawn to my pleas in the conclusion (made long before I had any theoretical understanding of organisational and practice learning), for opportunities for learning to enhance understanding, meaning, and to give value to and respect for those I would work with.

Over 20 years later I find myself asking for similar things, and in a position to perhaps influence conditions for practitioners. Rediscovering that piece of my past helped me feel that my quest for deeper understanding and organisational credence for practice learning was authentic, and located at the heart of my values as a social worker.

My story outlines some ways in which I sought to discover meanings as a social work manager responsible for the development of practice learning. It represents something of how I embraced the philosophy of action research processes and reflective learning, and the consequent actions. It highlights tensions and dilemmas surrounding some of the thinking attributed to practice research, and draws upon sources of learning from a study undertaken with managers and practitioners. It describes how both my own and organisational learning relating to action research and reflective practice highlighted the need for further exploration of this nature. Finally, evidence of learning from the accumulated collaborative practices is detailed.[1]

Organisational context

Mine was a new senior management function within the organisation. I was to approach the task of creating a reflective learning culture as high order organisational change. It is important to recognise at the outset, the commitment and vision of the organisation to the creation of a senior management role devoted to 'Practice, Research and Learning'. This embodies a commitment to the development of services through learning derived from iterative practice. However, there is also a commitment to conditions that facilitate learning, though there may be different manifestations of these conditions within the agency.

My reflections have led me to suspend simplistic notions of linear change and actions, and the need to correlate these with planned and desired outcome. Reflective practice and learning cannot be imposed 'top-down'. Nor can it take place without a concerted understanding of how learning takes place. I felt that, to institute a true culture of learning, fear of risk and failure had to be suspended. In organisations, the top-down, mandated, mechanical, bureaucratic effort to control the direction of the enterprise is all too familiar.

Palmer (1992) suggests that such a paternalistic approach defines the limits within which change must occur. Change, or the illusion of change, takes place and goals are achieved by a rearrangement of the power of the organisation. Resistance is overcome and the resistors are punished. Fragile innovation is often overwhelmed and shaped to fit, and the outcome is a past already experienced. The so-called 'new' is not usually new—it just looks different. Those committed to real change are left disillusioned and marginalised, though the repeated cycle of promised change, frenetic activity, and disappointment may offer perverse satisfaction to some. This cycle can also be comfortable for employees fearful of taking responsibility for the creation of new ways of working together, allowing them to blame

---

1. This has involved collaboration and co-investigations with Dr Nick Gould , Reader in Applied Social Studies, University of Bath, England and latterly with Professor Susan Weil, Social and Organisational Learning and Re-animation Centre, University College, Northampton, England

those in authority. In the end, fear wins and all lose.

I was conscious that reflective practice might only be paid lip service and trivialised. I thought of it as a desirable, yet a passive and indulgent activity, seen by some as something just slightly better than doing nothing at all. I became conscious of my own doubts when embarking upon this process. I had, like many social workers, trained and practised within a field delineated into 'thinkers', 'deciders', and 'doers'. Surely change could not be possible without strong action?.

> *Reflective practice is all very well but what of performance indicators, the market share, standards, best practice, quality, value and ... the real world?* (A question posed to me in 1997).

I also found it important to address some of the existing research practices evident within the organisation. Was research contributing to learning and knowledge? Practitioners expressed a general confusion over research. This included an uncertainty about their own capacities to respond to the imperative that 'all practice should be evaluated in order to improve'. For some this was a top-down requirement for external researchers to be called upon to provide documented evidence of 'good health' or to provide a 'clean bill of health'. This felt like research as audit or for publicity purposes, which, in my view, was not likely to contribute to better practice or learning outcomes.

Robson (1993) writes about 'real-life' research' [as] '... seeking to say something about a complex, relatively poorly controlled and generally "messy" situation' (p.3). This is an account of a messy real-life situation, not least because it is far from finished as I write. Through my actions and collaboration with others, I am learning and reviewing. I have become conscious of contradictions and dissonance between my actions, desired outcomes and theory. The reflective process is both the privilege of, and a threat to, the manager, and it is an activity that has to be rigidly protected, as it is often the first casualty of busy workloads. As I write I am aware of a report from practitioners stating that they have 'inadequate resources for action research' and others for whom reflective learning remains an ideal.

It is a frustration that we can be too busy to be reflective, and hence too busy to learn. I became, and remain increasingly concerned about how learning is perceived. Perhaps the legitimising of reflective practice as a mainstream social work activity could enlighten and empower? This story offers some concrete experiences of an intervention that has enabled rethinking in motion and the embracing of reflective practice and action learning in the wider organisation.

Starting assumptions

At the outset I began with a resolute belief that my role was closely linked to the ultimate 'good health' of our social work practice; and that the organisation should have learning potential, rather than just using slogans associated with organisational learning. The benefits would be to service users and would flow from better-informed judgements and practice knowledge. A serious tension was that others made it clear that their expectations were for more 'research outputs'. I felt that I was in danger of trying to juggle the several incompatible requirements of managerial practice to be found in 'good' social work agencies.

I held firm principles from my own practice that another 'flavour of the month', would be far from welcome. I became aware that 'practice research and learning' needed to be deconstructed, as staff sought 'research data' from me and requested advice and guidance on 'doing research' and providing research outputs for dissemination purposes. I feel ill equipped to respond; these were not the functions that I believed I had been employed to fulfil. This was an early and unsettling dilemma.

I felt intuitively that this pursuit of evidence-based social work practice and action learning should not be about embracing a current fashion. It was about a higher guiding philosophy and therefore conditions were necessary to allow practitioners to enact this. This was not to become an act of acquiescence to a written definition, followed by a process of measurement or technical form of accountability, although this could have been a methodology. My pursuit of an academic partnership was, in part, an attempt to obtain some reference points, and help with the 'doing' thereafter. It may also have been a demonstration of my vulnerability or need for validation? I was looking for espoused theory in action, but also ways of effectively bridging the theory and practice void. A reflective approach helped me to see that this lay with practitioners and practice. Another goal was to show how practice in a social justice organisation can practically address the devaluing and marginalisation of people. Evidence of learning from practice that 'made a difference' appeared to me to be fundamental.

What has made a difference to me has been the strength derived from others who have enabled the struggles, and the absence of certainty, to be viewed as positive opportunities. I felt that I had to personally unlearn many of my preconceptions about research and theory. I learnt that I needed to counter isolation and to find allies. Despite warnings about the pitfalls of academic partnership, I believed that positive collaboration was possible. This story also identifies some details of how creative 'learning partnerships' were made possible.

Just as the philosophy of the learning organisation is that learning is not limited to training events or courses, but is a set of processes located within the organisation, I became aware that the reflective learning paradigm is viewed as a process of purposive engagement with practice. I wanted a collaborative engagement that got people out of the university, yet was rigorous and credible and met other key factors; not least that it was affordable and that it could deliver and be responsive. In 1998 I documented some personal assumptions and dilemmas:

- 'Research' (in practice) is not homogenous (and exists without any agreed definition) despite tensions and forces seeking to make it so, or trying to impose a particular research perspective or definition. It's definition, or definability, lies at the heart of my inquiry.
- Organisations gather up 'credentials' particularly as they reinvent themselves, as was the case at the time within statutory social work agencies in the U.K. If 'evidence-based' practice is a measure of this, could it result in superficiality, and the paying of lip service to practice research and reflective practice? There were definite benefits to be had for organisations 'embracing research'. I was responsible for something currently perceived in the general social-work world as desirable and increasingly as a constituent part of any worthwhile social work organisation. There was, therefore, currency to be had from even a tacit observance, or a 'signing up' to this movement. Such descriptions gave rise to differences and interpretations that needed to be examined inclusively. After all what happens after we make the statement 'we believe in reflective practice and learning?' Does anything change implicitly? It is not about talking 'reflective learning' and was this a failing of it as an abstract and non-productive activity? How could this be changed?
- I held (and continue to hold) an optimistic view of practice and practitioners and recognise that many are seeking positive outcomes and creative solutions. I had practised as a social worker and social work manager for 26 years. Alongside this was a belief that practice research could enable improvements in outcomes for children and young people, as practice tussled with the tensions and dilemmas between quality service-provision and practices that empowered and changed root causes. This identified the need for the research but also for something to take place to both disseminate that research, and enable learning and knowledge to effect change. These things were not necessarily synonymous. I feared that we might end up with more published outputs, more publicity events and launches and precious little change.

These issues were also real tensions already encountered. On the one hand there is no deviation from the sound belief that 'research-based practice' is a necessity. What is not so axiomatic is how that is characterised, given a wide interpretation of what constitutes 'research' and, specifically, how research and its outcomes are validated. This remains a tension. Some flip charts from a practitioner event made the point graphically, 'research gives us the willies'; 'it is for experts'; 'We are not sure when we are doing it'.

Reflective practice

I was driven by a desire to learn more about the organisational impacts of reflective practice. Not so much what it is (I had been introduced to Fook et al, (1994)), but how could I actually make it a reality?

I revisited the dilemmas. They were not lessening.

- The tensions associated with the role being, or perceived as, a 'research and development manager', where research is the primary source for publication and public relations; or the means by which we make claims as an organisation.
- Action or practice does not necessarily mean learning.
- I was aware how the 'real-world' constructs of research put forward by Robson (1993) and others could easily become rhetoric. I was aided by a belief that the proliferation of research activity was not my primary purpose, and was stimulated by the work of those who appeared to challenge this notion. The consequences of learning from research and its application to our practice were however my priorities.
- If we could determine how practitioners were applying theory to their practice settings and how successful practices are being replicated, taught and learned might we have the beginnings of an understanding of evidence-led practice beyond the purely technical or superficial? Might we have arrived at a level of organisational expertise?
- My experience was that research was perceived within some social work and academic circles as an end in itself. Research alone never changed anything nor improved the lot of those in need. Something is needed in order to transform information, however generated, into knowledge. Consequently the study needed to reflect upon the outcome of social work expertise, i.e. the impact of social work expertise, exemplified by its capacity within an organisation to make conscious and conscientious use of theory and knowledge from research. The process is incomplete without further dialogue upon the relationship between theory, practice and how practitioners learn.

In search of collaboration

I set off then in search of a collaborator. This required some persistence. A process unfolded that took my initial starting presumptions and together, through dialogue over time, these took on a whole new substance.

My own reading and assumptions led me to make contact with a co-editor of a publication (Gould and Taylor, 1996), Dr. Nick Gould at the University of Bath. There was no written specification and we agreed to discuss the ideas. I recall meeting Nick in his office at the University and recording then:

> *[it] had already been a process and a half to have identified a 'champion' through a publication, tracked him down with an idea, and to have begun a series of dialogues around the subject. This could still come to nothing.*

Could this mean loss of control of my ideas as the academic, who could regurgitate them and offer them back to me as something unrecognisable, claimed them? A criticism of traditional approaches to research is that the findings are appropriated and reinterpreted by the researcher. Indeed there was sufficient evidence that this was a model we needed to change (I was hanging on to thoughts about a 'radical collaboration'). However, the risk remained. If I was to conclude this process with an academic report or discourse, what then? How could this possibly change the result?

It was our shared view that through collaboration with the research material a shared action-oriented perspective could be illustrated and tested. After visits to me and further purposeful discourse, accompanied by exploration and testing out of each other's values and beliefs, we were finally able to put forward a framework for the inquiry. This was to locate practitioners as co-collaborators in a journey of discovery into how practitioners learn. It would initially involve Nick as a skilled researcher and together we would facilitate a learning event or events. The seminar was part of the research process and would provide the opportunity for dialogue. It would also allow consideration of how the messages can contribute to a perspective for action, so transcending the gulf between descriptive research and prescriptions for action.

The first collaborative inquiry undertaken was designed to explore how the conceptual frameworks of reflective learning and the learning organisation might be combined in order to examine the learning processes in specific practice locations. We also considered how these might be extended in developing the organisation as a learning organisation. As a starting point qualitative data from a sample of practitioners and managers was analysed to examine how they learned. Additionally, an assessment of how their expertise was influenced by theory and situational learning, and how this learning was adapted to their respective practice realities was also conducted.

I had made a discovery. The formulation of research questions was recursive and not linear. I found there were several starting points and cycles of discovery. The identification of good research questions led to the few that could inform, as well as becoming informed by, a continuing dialogue, and then the 'doing' of it. This represented a reality of this sort of inquiry and led me to an early examination of appropriate practice methodology. It seemed clear to me that to attempt an analysis by way of the more technical measurement, such as surveying attitudes to research and learning, at different points in time, would be limited. This insight highlighted how research collaboration had often taken the form of a shopping list where a specification was issued and a response was forthcoming, with the parameters of the process being dictated by the amount of money available. Thus for me the potential value of inquiry and co-inquiry into the substance of the issue was demonstrated.

The 'different approach' I now espouse is underpinned by the importance of exploration. This does not mean the surrendering of our needs or ideas to academics. A framework for discreet enquiries *with* practitioners and managers, not *on* them, and involving the immense benefits from academic collaboration, was underway.

Constructing the inquiry

What followed was, and is, both an intervention and journey. My objective was to understand and establish conditions required for staff to become reflective practitioners, operating within a social justice organisation. My realisation had been that it was not research itself that was the focus of my attention. Research was an 'output', a method, and not an end in itself. The real mission was about how practitioners could be assisted in their learning.

To research was not an end; what practitioners were capable of doing with, and through inquiry into practice was. Different things became apparent and visible as part of the exploration. The potential for learning conditions to influence this exploration was one primary realisation. Consequently a question in our research planning was how far the organisation was in fact a 'learning organisation?' I had now dropped the reference to 'research' from my designation and assumed responsibility for 'Practice Learning'. A small step but something of a breakthrough. If little else it allowed me the opportunity to explain why I had done this. It provided a clearer identity and addressed the pressures to construct a 'research unit' (despite the fact that I operated alone) that could purvey research outputs for a range of organisational purposes.

Through the academic collaboration I became conscious of the need for learning organisations to achieve a level of integration between rigour and utility. Tsang (1997) suggests that inquiry should begin, not from normative or prescriptive theory of intervention but, from empirical, grounded research on the basis of which prescriptions can be made (Gould, 1999). This in turn can be the basis for a further cycle of inquiry, to study the outcome of implementing those prescriptions within an organisation. I had now begun to visualise my role more as a process, and myself within that process as a facilitator of learning through action research and inquiry with staff with the ultimate aim of reaching a shared understanding. This would require changes in behaviours, in how we operate organisationally; and not least in my own and in colleagues' management behaviours. The latter would become a focus for a subsequent collaboration.

The reflective practice inquiry

There was to be an immediate benefit from the study being undertaken in a manner that enabled regular dialogue and discussions with the co-researcher. Findings were not something to be provided in a report at the end of the process. Through exchange and reflection came learning and the capacities for change. Listening to practitioners emphasised the difficulties they encountered with the action research directive, as they experienced it. I realised the need to further test the basis and substance of the requirement that projects should be reflective, and models of action research, and the meanings attributed to this methodology.

Early indications from the qualitative study underway with practitioners supported the view that the method and content of this directive was a cause for concern. Managers stated that they found it restrictive and practitioners asked for clarity, and explanation ('What is action research and how do we know when we are doing it?' Is Action Research the latest top down imposition, and if so, tell us what it is and how we do it?').

The interviews revealed that at all levels there was an awareness that action research is important, whether as part of practice learning or as an element in the wider strategy of evaluation of projects. It was also evident that people understood that it had become a standard expectation within the organisation and should be incorporated within all project developments. However, this seemed to be giving rise to two tensions. The first was that most writers appear to see action research as a 'bottom up' methodology, which is predicated on the participation of practitioners in the construction of the method. The second was that interviewees were conscious that the conducting of action research was being imposed as a top-down requirement of projects. Of course, the two are not necessarily in conflict as the national agency could set a broad expectation, the detail of which is then provided within the local context. To achieve this, better understanding and capacity building was required. Nevertheless, practitioners and managers gave expression to a range of uncertainties around this subject.

Other staff expressed confusion as to what constituted action research, and what was expected. Managers expressed the view that they felt the organisation's direction that the methodology be identified in practice plans and budgets conveyed to them an assumption that research was not happening, i.e. that 'the people at the top don't know what's happening'. These managers felt that the factor underpinning this, and an issue to be addressed, was that there was no method for systematic dissemination of learning from research activity.

The study has enabled insights into how practitioners understand learning within this specific organisational context, and into the range of strategies that currently exist for the promotion of reflective practice and organisational learning. All those interviewed have been given the opportunity to come together in a model of participatory research that will enable a further cycle of the research process.

The study attempts to model an approach to research that is at the heart of this culture shift. Rather than to present 'findings' by way of a finished report, participants were invited to a seminar away from their respective locations to participate in, and influence, the research outcome.

A qualitative approach was adopted to answer the questions:

- How do practitioners understand learning within an organisational context?
- What strategies currently exist for promoting reflective organisational learning?
- What changes might be made to make practice (and projects) learning organisations?

To say that the organisation is committed to learning from practice is a reflective organisation, and the existence of a learning organisation may well be 'provable' by more conventional research approaches. A study designed around some pre-intervention measures followed by post intervention monitoring might conceivably show us this? This would perhaps be the simplest and contraindicated approach. But I felt that this would mean little for practitioners and service users. What would be the effect upon organisational development of such a claim and would this validation do anything to enable the organisation to function as a social justice organisation, and to meet agreed objectives? The social justice value of the organisation is important and relevant. I hold a belief that an integral part of ensuring social justice as an objective was to achieve reflective practice. This belief has both idealism in addition to being grounded in a growing body of evidence. There is a strengthening link between reflective practice and quality practice (Sapey, Pashley, Burchell and Sherman, 1996). Another evidence-based view is that social work needs to consider qualitative naturalistic inquiry to capture the diversity and complexity of issues from a user's perspective. Most significant to the discourse on power is the idea of knowledge as power. Another facet is added to this by asking who should generate, have access to, and determine the use of knowledge in social work? DePoy, Hartman and Haslett (1999) present a model for social work founded on tenets of critical theory synthesised with principles and practices from action research. The critical need is to develop purposeful models of knowing that serve oppressed populations by moving beyond the perpetuation of dominance and privilege by, and for, resource rich groups. From this it could perhaps be argued that social workers are 'oppressed' by 'academics'. Critical theory and action research provide the basis for the development of a model to meet this need. Previously devalued groups are empowered by developing and using their own knowledge and by sharing resources and skills in an egalitarian manner. Thus service users and practitioners are empowered alike. This was one of my distant aims in embarking upon this role and the 'novel' collaboration with academic bodies. Research should make a difference to the socially oppressed and be undertaken in a way that enables practice and practitioners to inquire into what is done with, and on behalf of those we seek to serve.

The pursuit of a reflective learning culture then was, and remains a pivotal goal and not something to be 'bolted on'. Research inquiry and reflective practice could, I believed, contribute to empowerment and intrinsically address the loss of power and value where people become 'research subjects'.

I became conscious of a need to move substantially from the linear viewpoint that I possibly espoused in my initial thinking about my role. No longer can I see this process as a descriptive account of implementation, similar to a material construction. A building of different parts into a whole, whereby the researching of my 'doing' would provide a systematic account of that management process. I rapidly became aware of the incremental and reactive characteristics of the management process. It is a fallacy to believe that when the whole is created the change is finalised and, (in this instance) that we will have an organisation in accord with reflective social-work practice. My experiences have highlighted that to attempt such an objectivist account would be at best impossible to achieve, and at worse, substantially false. The doing will be the knowing. This though has to be set against the need to deliver and not to be accused of 'navel-gazing'. Until the desired pivotal value is established a perceived 'need to deliver' may constitute an impediment to the achievement of reflective practice.

Emergent findings and learning

The following findings have been disaggregated from the emergent data. I was involved in the sharing of them with practitioners within a reflective learning seminar and they were revised accordingly.

- Responses to the invitation to identify how practitioners and managers learn from practice indicated that reflective learning was integrated within their own spheres of activity, and reflected diversity and quality. Practitioners were conscious of learning as something that was desirable for the continuous development of the service, and as part of professional development. It was clearly indicated that any consideration of the organisation consciously building a learning organisation should acknowledge that a significant level of purposeful learning activity was already taking place. This was a positive and optimistic realisation.

- The question of how the individuals conceptualised the process of learning from practice produced a range of discursive answers. This indicated clear distinctions between the practice regarding what might be understood as the different learning paradigm. This is not to suggest superiority of models, but to identify the emergent distinctions.

- The primacy of the team as a critical context for learning emerged from the interviews. Some aspects of this team working were identified as perceived opportunities for learning. Individuals cited presentations within team meetings, sharing learning from external events, co-working with team colleagues as well as inter-team learning from secondments and attachments. Managers were also aware of the impacts of organisational variables, which could inhibit the culture of learning within a team. For instance, one manager was able to identify examples of teams where there was an established routine of using observation, etc. as a stimulus for learning.

A manager stressed the importance of 'culture' within the team, i.e. the development of learning-in-practice strategies independent of individuals within the team. This insight is significant because it became less to do with charismatic leadership style, and more about established organisational   behaviour.

Practitioners were also frank in their judgement that just because a team met did not mean that learning was taking place. It became important to ensure that there were scheduled team opportunities, which would be more learning-orientated. Conversely a premium was placed on opportunities for informal contact within which reflection could take place. This resonates with findings within the learning organisation research that office locations and layout should be such that staff meet frequently by chance and communicate informally.

Environment and opportunity for reflection are important conditions for the facilitation of organisational learning.

- It is a platitude in social work that the wheel is continuously reinvented because developments in learning and new knowledge are not effectively disseminated. This is a common concern and encountered routinely by practitioners.

Practitioners were aware of the potential transferability of skills or knowledge and on some occasions this was linked to the value-base of the work. The second dynamic was that when workers were researching and learning about areas of work, which were authentically new, then contact and information exchange with external networks could be critical in the achievement of learning. Some talked of the struggle that practitioners have to make the space and time, and to develop their confidence and to write up their work for dissemination.

The principle of learning from mistakes emerged strongly from the interviews, although this was identified as more of an anxiety. This had interested me for sometime. I had entered into an exchange with a company who claimed openly of a capacity to 'celebrate mistakes'. I was fascinated to see that this was a substantive claim and a value related to learning conditions. My fascination was perhaps associated with my own experiences of functioning in a critical and adversarial interface. It remains a matter of some fascination as:

> *Mistakes and setbacks are elemental features of development and learning. It is the way in which organisations respond to normal features of the modern world and the lessons learnt from the experience that qualifies them for the title 'learning organisation. (Dale, 1994)*

This was not derived from an expected perspective. It was not the case that experimentation was too difficult or unethical, but that experimentation was an important element of learning which was conducive to the improvement of practice. This was perceived as having two aspects: the necessity of the organisation owning and being open to learning from unsuccessful activities and the importance of allowing the local autonomy necessary for risk taking with new ventures.

- A number of participants in the study had comments to make about the technologies which support learning and how these are embedded organisationally. In the contemporary climate 'technology' has tended to become equated with new information and communication technologies. The Internet was seen as a rich and developing source of information and as an extension to effectiveness, but this again required ready access. This resource could include a directory of expertise, and facilitate contact between individuals working within specialisms.

Similarly, a database of ongoing and completed projects could both enable dissemination of learning while mitigating against 're-invention of the wheel'. This has since become a focus of my attention and resources as we prepare to introduce the technology and expertise for practitioners to collate and engage with evidence from practice, and reflect on the learning from an Internet pilot study at the same time. This study has also taken the form of an action learning collaboration with another University and I have become aware of the richness of opportunity available from this model of collaboration.

- It has been identified that the learning organisation is more than the sum of the individual's formalised training which people either select or are put forward to undertake. At the same time it is clear that individual development has an organisational context, and a majority of the interviewees had views about the relationship between their personal learning needs and opportunities for staff development. Under this can be cited a number of issues which range from practice teaching of students to equal opportunities policies within the organisation. Some practitioners felt that the organisational emphasis given to practice development and learning would be enhanced if there was an improved career structure for practitioners which rewarded expertise which was produced through learning, thereby removing the feeling that individuals could only achieve career progression by leaving the organisation or by moving to a career in management.

Conclusions and outcomes

This study and subsequent reflections explored meanings of learning with staff and how that learning was being supported (or otherwise) by the organisation. It was reported that one of the most striking aspects of the research was the enthusiasm and willingness of people to participate in it. It is clear that the possibility of learning and developing is significant in providing motivation and in increasing the interest held by staff for their work. This may not be so startling if it is considered that several of the benchmarks for learning organisations indicated in the literature are part of the evolution of social work, amongst these being teamwork and an understanding of systemic models of change.

Those interviewed were able to identify a range of activities already in place, which promoted learning from practice and service development. These interviews and the reflective seminar event specifically attempted to elicit views of how the organisation did or did not support their reflective learning from practice. Some features of the responses were very positive, indicating an organisation moving positively towards aspects of being a learning organisation. The interviews also suggested areas for change or improvement, some of which have been the subject of further reflection and dialogue.

This study was not an audit or evaluation. It has enabled my reflections on my espoused theory of learning. I have recognised that approaches to learning are produced through the history, context and organisational structure of the practice location, and that contrasting paradigms can co-exist within the wider organisation.

I discovered that there have been rich findings on evaluation and 'action research'. Attempts are now being made to incorporate structured evaluation and action research routinely into practice and its development. Sometimes this is being undertaken internally, sometimes in partnership with external partners such as local universities, which this study has shown can indeed be fruitful and wholly collaborative. There does seem to be a commitment to see evaluation and action research as one of the inputs to reflection upon practice.

In 1998 a written plan was issued by the management team that stated that *'all projects are to be constructed as "Action Research" projects and all our work is based on a process of reflection and learning'*. Although this organisational imperative allowed a valuable foundation stone it was obvious that the imposition of a model was no guarantee of its success; certainly no guarantee that there would be learning. Without the necessary conditions it too could be relegated to the shelf along with traditional externally commissioned research reports, restored to the organisation and shelved. However as a result of this ongoing collaboration and reflective learning this edict was revisited and a revised statement of action research principles has now been made available:

> *[The Management Team] want to see our practice develop on the basis of evidence gathered from our experience and learning put alongside what we learn from others. This is why we have said that all projects must be constructed as Action Research projects. It has been easy for us to say this but much harder to work towards common and meaningful understandings about just what Action Research is, and how it is undertaken.*

We have reflected further on this, and, considering feedback and learning from projects and managers, we offer the following suggestions which may assist staff in developing their own understandings about how their work can be based on a continuous process of reflection and learning.

The outcome of reflective practice should stimulate new forms of management, organisational and social learning within the Division and Society. How we enable and support learning from practice also needs to be continual and itself the focus of reflection.

Staff will be encouraged to develop their own application of principles and practices associated with action research, and other models of learning from practice. We would expect to see the following characteristics in the way projects are pursuing their continuous process of reflection and learning:

There should be a transparent, conscious and explicit process of reflecting critically on, and learning from, experience and practice.

This would include the starting assumptions, models, beliefs and values embedded in plans and actions, in addition to the intended and unintended social and systemic effects of these:

- The reflection and learning should be recorded
- The process should be ethical and participative, inclusive of children and young people
- It should link practice and theory and be influenced from research and learning
- It should be measurable and be able to be communicated and illustrated in terms of processes and outcomes
- It should be through a process of inquiry carried out with people not on people
- It should involve challenge and change to those involved and to the systems of which they are a part

We believe that our continuing desire to be concerned with social justice will be served best by having processes in place which encourage our staff to reflect on their experience, and to develop their practice on the basis of reflection'.

There is no suggestion of complacency but the management imperatives and the identification of conditions necessary for reflective practice are now assembled within a wider organisational imperative (corporate plan) that states:

We will create a learning environment based on shared access to information and knowledge across the organisation, and which acknowledges all experiences as part of the learning process, including failure.

References

Dale, M. (1994) 'Learning organisations', in Mabey. C and Iles. P (eds.) *Managing Learning*, London

DePoy, E., Hartmann A. and Haslett, D. (1999) 'Critical action research: a model for social work knowing', *Social Work*, 44, 6, 560-568

Fook, J., Ryan, M. and Hawkins, L. (1994) 'Becoming a social worker:

Educational implications from preliminary findings of a longitudinal study', *Social Work Education*, 13, 2, 5-26

Gould, N. and Taylor, I (1996) *Reflective Learning for Social Work*, Arena, Aldershot

Gould, N. (1999) *A Pilot Study of Reflective Learning as an Organisational Process in Children's Society Projects*, unpublished report

Parker Palmer (1992) 'Divided no more: a movement approach to educational reform', *Change Magazine*, March/April,1992

Robson, C. (1993) *'Real World Research*, Blackwell, Oxford

Sapey, B., Pashley, G., Burchell, D., and Sherman, C. (1996) 'An investigation into the appropriate means of assuring quality in the delivery of social work services'. *Social Services Research*, 1, 15-23

Schon, D. (1995) *The Reflective Practitioner*, Basic Books, London

Tsang, E. (1997) 'Organisational learning and the learning organisation: A dichotomy between descriptive and prescriptive research', *Human Relations*, 50 1,73-89

6
Dedicated to the memory of Susan

Andrew Lowth and Michael Bramwell

We remember hearing a woman friend talking about a concept that she described as growing old disgracefully, meaning that she did not want to be tied down to the expected social mores, that she wanted the freedom to be able to do what she wanted to do, as a way of expressing who she was. And in doing so she took the risk of being ostracised, condemned, or at least ridiculed. As social workers, we are taught about professional modes of practice. We are given a set of rules. We are given a clearly defined role. One of our struggles is always to work out the personal/professional boundary – how much of us as people is involved and how much do we use of ourselves when we work with our clients.

This is about a woman called Susan who had a secret. This secret was mirrored in the work that we did in each of us holding a secret. We broke some rules; we were challenged; we became unprofessional and in doing so, we became skilled, professional, and, probably, better social workers.

When we break the rules, or when we do something that we know is pushing the boundaries to the outer limit of what is considered professional practice and conduct, we tend to go underground. We hide what we're doing for fear of being ridiculed or of being considered unprofessional. Words like 'over-identification', 'unprofessional', and 'over-involved' are often used.

I, Andrew, worked with Susan for nine months in 1996. When I left to work in another city, Michael became Susan's social worker/counsellor. This is our story; it is also Susan's story.

As social workers we get few opportunities to reflect on our practice in a collegiate and/or supervisory context. Even when we do get these opportunities in supervision, we do not often use those professional relationships when confronted with our flaws, or when there is the possibility that we may be breaking the clearly defined rules of professionalism. This is even more unlikely when there is little support or trust within either the supervisory or collegial relationship.

Andrew's story

I had been working as a social worker at 'The George', a major teaching hospital, in the infectious diseases (ID) unit, for a very short time (two weeks) when I received a referral to see Susan. The referral was for psychosocial assessment and assistance with housing issues. She was evicted from her housing in Rosebud with her boyfriend and she wanted her bags back. Her boyfriend had disappeared; the police wanted him on drug related and break and entry charges. I received the referral in the weekly ward meeting where people's histories, medical issues and other matters were discussed. I remember Susan being introduced as problematic, with a difficult relationship to health services, because of her perceived manipulation for prescribed drugs. It was stated that she was a drug abuser and an injecting drug user. It was also stated that she had been involved with a man who was violent. The registrar stated that Susan had been HIV-positive for eight years, having contracted the virus as a sex worker in Kings Cross in Sydney. It was also stated that Susan had been thrown out of her family of origin at the age of 11. Susan was then described as having a history of being a sex worker and heroin addict from an early age who had contracted HIV as a result of her lifestyle. It was stated that we needed to be careful with her because she was manipulative, a drug seeker, and tended to cause what is known as 'splitting' between staff.

I remember going to see Susan. She was sitting in bed. I remember seeing a woman with long brown hair, who looked sick. She was very skinny, she had sunken eyes, she looked withdrawn and sad. I remember introducing myself as a social worker and she looked at me like you know 'fuck off, get out of here'. I remember thinking 'I will need to be really creative to hold this woman here'. I could sense that her experience of social workers was really awful and not positive at all.

I was conscious of what I had heard in the team meeting – 'manipulative and troublesome' – so I felt somewhat guarded, but after a few minutes I found myself thinking 'I like you', and I think she sensed that I did like her. I remember thinking something like 'if I'm cold and if I put into practice what I have been taught about professional boundaries and give nothing of what I am as a person I will have lost her straight away'.

'The George' ID Team was very new in a newly configured ward (7W). It was the largest HIV Unit in the state with a capacity for 35 inpatient beds. Most of the beds were shared spaces unless you were critically ill. I remember seeing Susan in a 4 bed bay. I was aware that I was not going to get anywhere with Susan unless I could take her somewhere on her own.

To run smoothly, a medical ward like this has needs to have things ordered and orderly. Some of the people whom we were seeing had lives that were not ordered or orderly and immediately they were at odds with ward culture and there was tension between caregivers and the people being cared for. The team wanted them to be a certain thing – and often times those being cared for could not meet those expectations. I remember suggesting to Susan that we go downstairs and sit out in the garden and have a cigarette. And she said 'do you smoke, love?' and I said 'yes – but don't tell anyone'. When we got downstairs, she asked 'you got a boyfriend love?' And I said ' it's not for lack of trying darl'. I remember us sitting around the back of the hospital near the fish pond – a really quiet area, and we sat there and had a couple of 'ciggies'.

I remember asking her a question like 'Tell me about you'. Straight away I realised she was used to hearing about other people talking about her life in negative pathological ways and that she had begun to accept that this was a true and accurate account of her life. I remember thinking how easy it was for us and her to accept this account. The thing that struck me was how much she disliked herself and what she had become and yet she couldn't see any other way of seeing herself. This is when I first heard of Susan's secret.

It was like she was writing the final chapters of her tragic story and everyone around her was playing a part in writing those chapters. When we finished our cigarette, we went back upstairs and I sat in the nurses' station to write a note in her medical history and several staff members asked whether I had just seen Susan. I said yes and I remember the response of those staff members being somewhat similar to what she had said about herself. They had talked about her being difficult, and essentially I got the impression that they saw her as a 'drug fucked junkie' who was really hopeless and useless and that it wouldn't have mattered what we did, it wouldn't make any difference.

I got the firm impression that I shouldn't waste my time on someone so useless, as she would just continue doing what she always did. I remember walking down to my office and sitting in my room and thinking how can I work with her? Can I do anything to make a difference to her life or am I just going to be another social worker, health professional, who listens to her story, reflects back to her, assists her to get a roof over head, inadequate as that might be, makes sure she has some money and walks away? I could not sit comfortably with that. I wanted to – Susan had a soul – I could see that straight away. I remember thinking and talking to Michael about this. How could an 11 year old girl survive the street of Kings Cross, heroin addiction, abandonment by her family, the violence she had frequently experienced in relationships, and survive the rejection by the services around her? I realised at that point that you can't do all this unless you have something special.

So I went back upstairs and asked her: 'Susan, tell me how you have survived this, tell me what makes you continue living?' She looked at me puzzled, as if to say 'no-one has ever acknowledged that I am more than a victim and a loser; that it is fucking hard to live through this and I continue to do it'. I knew my way in at this point was not to see her as a victim or a tragedy but as a woman with an enormous amount of strength; someone who had an enormous lot to offer and someone who could teach us about survival.

Susan's experience of health professionals and other carers throughout her life was less than acceptable. Susan had an expectation of what she believed social workers and other carers could offer and Susan had learnt to tell her story in a certain way and to be listened to in a particular mode/style. She was giving them what they wanted. I came to call it the 'poor me story' – the victim. And what happened with that story was that it went from Susan to the worker and was then forever documented on her medical history. I don't believe people knew what to do with that story. So it became easy to provide for the practical: good social work tasks like housing and finance.

How did we know that we were not doing more damage by pushing out those boundaries to the outer limit? Why were we so sure that it was OK? For me, I knew that in this situation, if I had hidden behind the mask of professionalism, I would not have learnt so much about myself personally and professionally nor would I have ever been invited into Susan's life.

For me, I really needed to believe that there was a possibility that things could be different for Susan – I needed to believe that there was the possibility for change, and that it wasn't going to come about through our continued indulgence with her victim status. There was also a recognition in ourselves of our own flaws - we were readily able to identify with the flawed part of Susan. We also carried our own emotional baggage.

One of the most significant influences in the way that I have begun to practise social work in the last four years has been the writing on what is labelled the 'us and them construct' (Devine et al, 1999). Working with professionals entrenched in the medical model at 'The George' at this particular time, it became obvious to me that the treating team saw themselves as different, as better, as distanced from the client group, because they were not HIV positive, they were not using drugs. Because of this the 'other' became the deviant, the outsider. I found myself the most angry I have ever been in social work practice and my anger was about how I perceived these people's lives were being constructed. It was important for people in that Team to construct these people's lives as 'the junkie', 'the sex worker'.

I became one of 'them' most definitely at the time that I read in the medical history of a client I was working with that he was a homosexual – I realised at this point of the 'pathology' of the term and I also lost my status as one of the 'normal'. I remember challenging the psychiatric registrar who introduced this '26 year old homosexual man' that the notes should be signed by a '36 year old heterosexual man'. My practice changed forever at this point. I began to understand the power that is generated by the way we construct people's lives. I don't believe that not putting a needle in your arm or not having sex with a person of the same sex means you can stand outside and judge.

It was at this time I met Susan and felt strongly that her perceived deviance needed to be challenged. It stood in the way of us being of value to her. I think in looking back that Susan had not engaged with services easily as she was reminded of her deviance so readily and easily. So how could I be different to the others? How could I treat her like a human being? How could I show her that I also knew what it was like to be deviant and show that I cared, whilst maintaining the professional face of social work?

I wanted to be different towards Susan because I liked her. I wanted not to be another cog in the wheel. I wanted to prove to her that I was a person in my own right who could care about another person and that I realised that the only way I was going to make a difference in her life was by engaging with her at a personal level. I had to give something of myself and I wanted to give something of myself.

I think there a few times in my social work practice that someone's marginality and the rift between 'us and them' becomes so indistinct as was the case with Susan and myself. I felt like there was something of Susan in me – her being perceived as 'the other', 'the disgusting' and also the fact that she had only been given lip service also struck a chord with me.

I think I had just begun to recognise my own sense of being marginalised in my community, and I was relying on people who really loved me and saw the goodness in me in the same way. I realised I had people around me who loved me as I was. Susan did not have those people but she continued to survive. I identified that the gap in her life was to acknowledge the good in her, to accept her as she was.

The focus of my work with her was to challenge how the Team saw and perceived her and to get them to see what I was seeing. In doing so I also wanted to get Susan to see that there was something good about herself and that she did have this enormous strength. I had conversations with her where she would start by saying things like 'every man I meet bashes me or only wants me for sex or wants to get my pension to buy heroin' and I would respond by saying things like 'so why are you still here?' I remember she talked about friends who had all 'gone' (taken overdoses) – she was the only survivor.

I remember reading the medical notes before visiting Susan and reading the psychiatric registrar's report that described Susan as having a borderline personality disorder with sociopathic traits and that she was not too sure of her sexuality. It was later that I found myself challenging this male doctor's construction of her life. My challenge came after a discussion with Susan where she described what questions he had asked her and how he had made her feel. She said that he had made her feel disgusting, and she had asked him to leave as a response to this. I believe that in response to his anger towards her he then needed to make sense of her life for himself. And in doing so, he presented her as 'deviant and mad' so that he remained 'sane and normal'.

My view of Susan was as a person. One of the issues as a gay male social worker working in the area of HIV is that sometimes our boundaries become blurred and that is because to work in this area is not only a professional occupation, but a personal commitment. Because it is both, the boundaries do become blurred. Susan's experiences of men, her father, her brothers, her lovers had been very poor as they took advantage of her, abused her, ridiculed her difference and never celebrated what she was. I came along and didn't hurt her, didn't want anything from her and began to celebrate her life and would share that celebration with her.

As Susan was requiring medical care, the view of Susan and her life was within a very strict clinical medical context. Susan had a secret that became the focus of medical interest. For all of her life, she kept this secret from all those around her. Because of this secret, the medical team that worked with her became quite voyeuristic and at times intrusive. Susan chose not to tell us about these aspects of her life but the medical team seemed to be preoccupied with them. She had become both an oddity and a commodity – something to look at and talk about. This secret seemed to be the greatest difficulty for Susan and she just wanted to be seen as a woman with HIV. I never asked questions about these aspects to her life because I didn't believe they were as important as what she wanted me to see her as. I believe one of the major reasons why she trusted me is because I didn't see her as a 'freak show' but as a gentle caring woman, who was funny and insightful and who could tell me more about people who perceived themselves as the 'normal and sane' than they themselves could recognise. She had a wonderful insight into whether people really did accept her and respect her. She would pick up very quickly whether someone was preoccupied with her secret, rather than with her life.

Michael's Story

I first met Susan as part of a handover when Andrew announced his departure, and in my new role as a HIV palliative care counsellor. I had a lot more organisational freedom than Andrew and generally saw Susan within her own home unless she was an inpatient of the hospital. I saw Susan on a fortnightly basis for the first 12 months and then it became weekly in the last eighteen months of her life. Bereavement follow up and a palliative care role continued with her flatmate/friend for a further 12 months after Susan's death and ceased when Mary died of AIDS and a broken heart.

Susan was keen to work with another gay man and had expressed her desire to work with me fairly articulately to Andrew. Andrew and I met with Susan together and I was assessed for my 'suitability'. Over the next few weeks she quizzed me or shocked me or attempted to frighten me with her stories. These stories were essentially of her past – her life on the streets, her use of non-prescribed medications, her family of origin. Part of me was very intrigued by Susan – she had lived a life so far removed from my sheltered experience that I was drawn to her in a voyeuristic manner. Part of me also wanted to show Susan that not all men were bastards and that there was another model of being that was not abusive, destructive nor dangerous. There was also another part of me that was strongly drawn to both her vulnerability and her strength.

I also had a hard act to follow – Susan and Andrew worked well together and there was an existing model of a therapeutic relationship that they had developed. Although Andrew and I worked well together, my relationship with Susan was likely to be different because of who I was and what I brought professionally to our contact. My brief was also focused on the complexity of palliative care issues and HIV within the context of both an acute treatment facility and within her own home.

Susan challenged the very core of my social work practice. She pushed every button, challenged every boundary and exploded my idea of what a 'good' social worker was. And she had known a few social workers, counsellors, psychiatrists in her time. The easy parts for me were the solution focused interventions required that were classically social work. (An example of this might be the locating of appropriate housing for Susan – there were two house relocations in the last two years of Susan's life. Or negotiating with creditors around outstanding bills.)

The hard parts of social work practice for me were in managing my feelings for Susan and how was I going to negotiate these feelings when she died. I was very aware that these feelings detract from my practice, but should enhance my work. It still amazes me that for experienced practitioners like Andrew and me, she has had such a large impact on our practice. Her influence still challenges my work as I take time to reflect on what I am doing and why.

Susan was a client, who had my home phone number, knew the name of my partner and liked to hear gossip about him, and knew my vulnerabilities fairly quickly. She also had a great capacity to love and show care. She never abused or exploited her access to me – not even when she was very sick and dementing.

Supervision around these issues became fraught with difficulties – more for my supervisor than me. On reflection, I'm not sure what I would do if I had been supervising a worker like me at that time. I believe in many ways I may have acted out some of the behaviours and responses that were essential to Susan's survival and mirrored them in my own professional life. What I was doing was learning about professional survival. I also knew that as Susan trusted me with her life/death and her secret, I could trust Susan with things of much less importance such as how to contact me and what my relationship status was. Working with Susan created tensions and dishonesty in my relationship with my supervisor for which I take responsibility. I was worried about how my actions/practices may have been interpreted. I should have at least attempted to discuss the practice issues with my supervisor. I chose to maintain a secret and only felt safe in an ongoing dialogue with Andrew.

Susan fell in love towards the end of her illness – this man showered her with gifts and filled her heart with love. For those of us watching, this love affair filled us with dread. Susan was cachectic, vague and seriously ill. We became quickly aware of why he was interested in wooing her – again a man was going to use her, exploit her and then when he had grown sick of her, leave her. It soon became apparent that this man was interested in Susan's secret. As a person involved in Susan's medical and psychosocial care, it was very difficult to allow Susan to lead her own life and trust in Susan's ability to manage the situation.

And we did underestimate Susan's life experience and her ability to manage her life. She was heartbroken but she managed that. Better than that, when she was flushed with love, she was full of life, humour and *joie de vie*. It was a wonderful time for all of us, despite our fears. Tasks that needed to be completed such as wills and powers of attorney were easily accomplished. It was also the time to hear of her previous loves and explore the history of her relationships.

I understood some of the reasons why Susan agreed for Andrew and I to work with her. She liked men, and we were unlikely to physically abuse her or violate her in any way. We were also likely to appreciate her sense of dress and the height of her heels and her wicked sense of gossipy humour. I think she also valued the way we worked with her and trusted her ability to sort her issues through. Andrew had shifted his view of her from one of victim to that of a resilient, strong and capable woman. This shift in position ensured a greater capacity for Susan to tidy up her affairs and take control of her life/death. It also meant at times that her determination and strong will was to challenge and frustrate me when attempting to negotiate new ideas or needing to complete tasks.

Susan had a wide range of professionals and volunteer carers involved in her life. She also developed a very special friendship that developed after the demise of her latest relationship. This friend was also one of her last lover's cast offs – through their shared experience of this man they became firm friends. This flatmate/friend was also HIV positive.

Much of what we talked about was focused around Susan's impending death. She was acutely interested in what happened, how it happened and the minute details required in organising a funeral/party. I spoke of the freedom that is now associated with the rituals surrounding death and she and I agreed to explore the lot. Part of this resulted in my privileged accompaniment of Susan and Joan (the co-ordinator of 'Sunnybank', a supportive residential facility for HIV positive women) to check out the church she had chosen to have her funeral service at and the nearby cemetery to check out the suitability of her proposed final resting place. During this bitter sweet trip, we talked and laughed and cried.

It was something I probably would not have done with many/any of my other clients. It was a big 'ask' that we all did and I think we were all up for the task. The strength to do this came from the very frail but resilient Susan. On this trip, Susan also requested that Joan take a key role in the running of the Service. In remembering how we all agreed to plan and check out Susan's funeral, I think it was Susan who ran with the idea when I proposed it and challenged us to execute it.

So what was my role with Susan? And how did she push and challenge these professional boundaries so successfully? How or why did I allow her to challenge me to rethink my practice? And what I have learnt from the experience?

One of the things I do know is that there was a heightened intensity to our relationship so that when she did die, I felt sad and still miss her to this day. One of the reasons I am able to remember Susan's story so well, is that she has had an impact on me both personally and professionally. Other clients have had an impact but not in the same way that Susan did. Andrew set up the relationship with Susan; I was lucky to be able to assist in Susan's end of life issues and walk with her through her journey to death.

Susan decided that she wanted to control the time of her death. She developed a plan and worked out who could assist with information, medication and support. She was quietly resolute in her plan. A referral was made to a psychiatrist to assess her mood and ability to make competent decisions. This assessment was completed and written up – and left on her medical history should anybody question her request for death. It was Susan's concern for the health professionals in her life that prompted her decision to seek the assessment. She wanted to safeguard our legal status should her death be questioned, or investigated.

She had been stock piling her morphine, methadone and other pharmaceuticals. She also did not disclose the location of the hidden medications. I wonder whether Susan remembered where they were too as her memory was getting worse.

Susan was dementing, was very frail, nauseous, in chronic pain and smoking plenty of 'bongs'. There were suppurating ulcers on her gums that inhibited her ability to eat or wear her dentures. Her diet was appalling – drinking her 'Ensure Plus' and a wine every now and then. Most of her diet consisted of pain killing medications and marijuana. All other medications had been ceased by Susan. Occasionally, she would restart the medications after urging by some of her doctors but more often than not she took her drugs sporadically.

A visit to Susan sometimes resulted in leaving the house feeling a little stoned. She would be puffing on 'bongs' one after another and smoke would fill the room. It became a joke between the district nurse and myself that each visit to Susan ensured our fix of dope for the week and gave us both a healthy appetite. Susan became forgetful of the time and would forget when she had had the last bong – and go through a heap of dope and expense in purchasing it. Other needs such as food and payment of bills became a little tricky. A lot of the burden of care fell onto her flatmate/friend. Mary would race out and purchase her dope, or pay the bill out of her own pension.

Hospitalisations for respite became a difficult time for Susan, causing her lots of anxiety associated with who would look after her personal care needs. I arranged with the Nurse Manager that there be two dedicated staff to provide all personal care to Susan when she was admitted for respite. This gave the two staff and Susan a time to build a relationship and for trust to develop. Susan was most anxious that her secret remain a secret – hospitalisations would challenge the ability to maintain the secret given the lack of privacy and the huge number of medical, nursing and allied therapy staff involved in her care. This very simple strategy ensured that Susan felt safe and well cared for. It also ensured that her precious secret remained safe.

Her carer/friend knew part of the secret and became guarded in the provision of Susan's care. When the entire secret was inadvertently disclosed to Mary at Susan's funeral, Mary questioned the depth of the friendship she had with Susan and struggled for the rest of her life with the not knowing.

Susan's secret was revealed to me over time by Susan. I never actively sought to pursue the secret nor attempted to address it in a therapeutic manner. I had decided early on that the secret was not important to me in the same way it was to Susan and that there was not a need to probe into the details in order for any type of therapeutic resolution. What was more important was to take Susan at face value and work with Susan in a way that was respectful of her personhood. This decision resulted in Susan freely sharing this secret with me over time and in a sense was my reward for holding her trust.

Another key person in Susan's life was Joan, the Coordinator of 'Sunnybank', a Catholic nun with an enormous capacity for love. Joan became Susan's foster mother by proxy. Susan would play wicked but harmless games with Joan and Joan would always respond with love, gentle humour and enduring patience.

Although Susan was really sick, part of me believes it was because of Joan, Mary, Andrew and myself that Susan chose death when she did. For the first time in her life, she experienced true love without any demand. It was the right time to die – it was not going to get better for Susan. And for that to occur, we did have to breach our social work boundaries and be challenged to walk some of this journey with Susan in a new way. It is my fantasy that if we had maintained our clearly defined therapeutic role, Susan may well be still alive. However in showing her our humanness and our ability to offer an unconditional love, she chose to end her life.

Andrew and Michael

In coming together to write this chapter and remember our involvement and relationship with Susan, we have also renewed our long distance friendship, received affirmation and recognition for the work we continue to do and are re-energised for our respective futures in working with people who are HIV positive.

Remembering Susan, we also mourn for her death and our loss. But we also celebrate her continuing influence in our work and our life. Whilst Andrew and I continue to have our friendship and our respective memories, Susan lives on. Every time we meet a person who is given no hope or is judged as manipulative, demanding, sociopathic or given other negative pathological labels, we will remember Susan and begin the work with the new client without that framework, choosing instead to listen to the new story and show respect for the story and that person's life.

> *If we wish to understand the deepest and most universal of human experiences, if we wish our work to be faithful to the life experiences of people, if we wish for a union between poetics and science, or if we wish to use our privileges and skills to empower the people we study, then we should value the narrative.* (Richardson in Gorman, 1993, p.255)

This honouring of Susan when we begin to work with a new client is not something that is taught through social work texts, nor is it often discussed with our colleagues. Being able to reflect on a significant clinical experience and the importance that it plays in our ongoing work has been an incredibly powerful marker in our respective professional development. We often do not allow ourselves the opportunity to reflect on those experiences that have shaped what we eventually become as practitioners.

When the two of us come together from our respective worlds, there is an exchange of details about our respective clients and it is always a sound reminder for both of us of the significance and the importance of reflection. We also lament the difficulties associated with trying to seek those opportunities that allow and celebrate the significance of the story telling. We have shared the experiences of supervising the teams we work with and realise that this model of reflection and discussion is one we both encourage in our own practices.

There is a price to this sort of work though. In writing this paper, we also grieved for Susan and for all the clients we have worked with who have died. The sadness associated with this type of work became quickly apparent when we started writing – early nights for both of us; bitter sweet reflections on some of our clients that challenged us at every level of our professional and personal being; and a gentle melancholy in remembering.

Susan's story does have implications for social work practice. It requires that we re-think how we construct our thinking regarding, and obviously the doing of, practice issues. It demands that we move away from models of care that start from the premise that people are dysfunctional or not coping for some particular reason. This is not so easy to do. It demands a challenging of some very powerful institutions like medical models and even some of the dominant social work theories and texts.

Susan's story demands that we challenge the models of care that are premised on the belief that we have the answers as provided by the traditional problem solving models. It also challenges us to truly work with the person wherever they are at and with whatever reality they choose to give, rather than the reality given to us by our colleagues, or the agencies we work in, or as coloured by our own personhood.

On reflection Susan was a teacher, she taught us many things. She taught us to be more considerate and more human in our response to those that we provide a service to. She taught us that often the answers that our clients seek are not hidden away in some mysterious text but in ourselves. The fact that we can assist so greatly by not constructing our clients' lives negatively is such a powerful tool. It also requires that we have to believe in our clients; believe that there is possibility that change can occur and not necessarily the change that we see as being right.

Susan and other people we have subsequently worked with have taught us to listen, really listen. It has taught us to celebrate people's extraordinary lives of survival. It highlights for us the importance of reflecting back to the clients and other workers that this way of thinking about our client is a powerful tool that can change the way we think and work.

Susan taught us not to be frightened of loving a client's humanity and guts and determination. And what we came to realise is that this is the core to real helping, when we can really let go of the baggage that we bring with us and we sit still and connect with another's humanity.

Bibliography

Devine, P., Plant, A.E. & Harrison, K. (1999) 'The problem of "us" versus "them" and AIDS stigma', *American Behavioural Scientist*, 42, 7, April, 1212-1228

Gorman, J. (1993) 'Postmodernism and the conduct of inquiry in social work', *AFFILIA*, 8, 3, 247-264

7
'When the labels are off'

Molly and John Harvey

The theme of this chapter is partnership as a key component of good social work practice. By partnership, we mean that between those seen by society as powerful and successful and those seen as weak and failing.

Our experience of this arises out of two separate, but related, periods in our married life, when this sort of partnership seemed to us to work particularly well. From 1963 to 1971 we lived in the Gorbals area of Glasgow, as members of a community Group Ministry, where we shared much of our lives with our neighbours in what was then regarded as one of the worst slums in Europe.

Latterly, for the past 12 years, Molly has been employed by a Scottish charity, linked to the ATD Fourth World movement, working alongside families living in poverty and in conditions of stress in areas of multiple deprivation in Glasgow.

In both of these situations, we have seen this sort of partnership actually working, often at considerable cost to all involved. We have seen how people living in poverty (the real experts on poverty), in partnership with professionals and elected representatives with access to resources and policy-making, can actually bring about change.

One theme throughout this, of course, has been the challenge to us as middle-class professionals with a 'we can fix it' approach. We have been conscious - sometimes not conscious enough - of the dangers of patronising people, of becoming sentimental, of not being hard-headed enough, and of listening but not really hearing. Out of this experience, some key issues seem to us to be:

- How can we all avoid labelling each other?
- How can we learn consistently really to listen to, and hear, each other?
- How can we build into good social work practice the essential components of value and respect each for the other?

The Gorbals Group

At this point, right at the start, it might be helpful to look at the principles and practice of the Gorbals Group Ministry, of which we were members, with our family, from 1963 to 1971. While this particular experimental approach to inner city mission from the late 1950s to the early 1970s was by no means unique, it was nevertheless important in helping to form attitudes to partnership in caring.

Gorbals is one of the old villages which form the heart of inner-city Glasgow. By the 1950s, it had gone through a 30-year period of very serious structural and social decline, gaining for itself in the process the name of being one of the worst slums in western Europe. The majority of its inhabitants were by then heavily dependent on the provisions of the welfare state; were subjected to some of the worst abuses of housing provision in both the private and the public sector; lived in conditions of multiple deprivation; and held themselves in fairly low esteem. The caring services, including both social work and the institutional church, were largely seen as alien to the area - and in many cases, of course, the professionals providing these services lived well outside the area, coming in each morning and leaving again at night. The problems of the area, which were massive, were compounded by the attitude of government, both local and national, of the time. Both of them preferred to see Gorbals as a problem which had been solved on paper by the decision, later implemented with fairly disastrous results, to flatten the whole area and rebuild it with high-rise flats. In short, the area had very little going for it, except the courage, endurance and amazing humour of the people to whom it was home.

The Gorbals Group Ministry was formed in 1958 by three young Church of Scotland ministers, who, two of them with their families, got permission from the local Presbytery to live in the area in an attempt to try a new way of being church there. Drawing on the experience of similar approaches in America and France, they sought to move away from the traditional pattern of church life, which was patently failing. They wanted to develop a new one, based not on church buildings and normal church activities - Sunday services, evening organisations, and pastoral care largely exercised through full-time ordained ministers, who usually lived well outside the area. Instead, they chose to live in the area, in housing conditions much the same as their neighbours; to share an economic standard of living similar to that of the majority of their neighbours (at the level of what was then called National Assistance); to hold no public services on Sundays, but to meet together as a group for fellowship and prayer, and to share a weekly meal together, on a Thursday evening in their homes. They sought to respond to the expressed and immediate needs of the people and the structures of the area, rather than to import ready-made activities from other social cultures within Scotland.

Over the 15 years or so of the Group's existence, its numbers fluctuated from the original five adults and two children, to over 25 members at one time. Descriptions and analyses of the specifically mission-orientated work of the Group are not germane to the purpose of this chapter; a full account of the work of the Group can be found in the biography of one of the founders, Geoff Shaw. What might be helpful here, however, is to say a word about the methodology of the Group's activities; and to look first at the Group's chosen lifestyle.

Caring, it can be argued, is both about the delivery of services and about the sharing of burdens. While, on a personal level, the balance between these two aspects of caring can often be effectively achieved, it is never easy to get this crucial balance at the level of institutions and professional bodies. There can be no doubt that in an area like Gorbals, bodies like the churches, the social services, the schools and the medical clinics, had come to be seen essentially as deliverers of services pure and simple.

It would be wrong, and unfair, to suggest that this was because the professionals involved were not caring people. The reverse was, in fact, usually the case. The imbalance seems to have arisen chiefly for two reasons. On the one hand, the sheer weight of numbers of 'cases of need' had the effect of forcing the professionals to concentrate all their efforts and energies on trying to meet them; and on the other hand, the structures and systems originally set up to meet these needs were no longer adequate to the task. Social services, originally seen as there to support families and individuals, and communities, as they worked through their own difficulties, soon became seen as intrusive agents of a remote system, the Welfare State, parachuting in to the area to try to impose alien solutions on seemingly intractable problems. And the same has to be said of the churches, the schools, and the doctors - in the eyes of the majority of the residents of the area, these were 'them', and 'they' were opposed to 'us'.

In the first place the Group sought to overcome this acute problem by the fairly simple method of taking up permanent residence within the area. We rented flats in the slum properties in the mean streets; shopped in the same shops; had our children play in the same back-courts and go to the same schools; faced the same housing and health problems; and shared in the same joys and sorrows of life in Gorbals, as the majority of our neighbours. Some of us earned our living within the neighbourhood, in factory, school, and youth work. We chose to live at approximately the same standard as our neighbours, by pooling our income, and allowing ourselves the basic rate of National Assistance to live on week by week.

The Group members were quite clear, from the beginning, that this was not an exercise in identification with the people of Gorbals. From the outside, it was at times seen as that; but it was never seen as that by the Group. For a start, the Group members possessed immense reserves, of birth, education, cultural background, economic power, and support (both internal and external), which were simply not available to the majority of their neighbours, through no fault of their own. Put simply, the Group members could - and most at various points over the 15 years did - choose to leave; for their neighbours, there really was no such choice.

Living alongside: partnership

On a visit to the Gorbals Group once, Danilo Dolci, an Italian architect, who went to live amongst the very poorest families in Sicily, and who took on the might of the Mafia in an attempt to improve the lot of his Sicilian neighbours, spoke of what both he and the Group were trying to do. He described it as critical accompaniment. The Group was trying to say one or two basic things. We are here, we said, first and foremost to seek to stand alongside you. We are not here to sit in judgement on you, either by our words or by our lifestyle. Neither are we here simply to collude with everything that goes on. We are here to support you in your struggle to be agents of change; not simply in order to change individuals, but also to seek to change the structures and systems that create the conditions in which we all have to live. We do not hide the fact that we have the option, which you do not have, to leave. While we are here, however, we wish to accompany you, if you will accept us, in your struggles and your triumphs. We wish our lives and our homes to be open to you. We hope that your lives and your homes will be open to us in return. We seek, in short, to be allies, or partners, with you, as we live together, for however long we are allowed, in this place.

This was the theory; how did it work in practice? Four examples from the Group's work over the years may serve to illustrate the sort of partnership that emerged.

The practice

Very early on, the members of the Group got involved in working with children and young people. Football teams were demanded by the local lads; so football teams were started. Out of these, wee 'clubs' formed, dependent on a large team of volunteers, crucial befrienders and partners. The 'clubs' were normally groups of boys and girls in their mid to late teens, who already hung about together; often from the same street. The Group's policy was to keep the 'clubs' small; perhaps 15 to 20 in each. A converted upstairs warehouse was initially used as a games hall; but mostly, the homes of members of the Group were used. (We, for instance, found ourselves often inundated with between half a dozen and 15 teenagers, often staying well into the night, regularly a couple of nights a week - as well as a third night using the games hall.) Today, this might be called 'detached youth work', although using the homes of the 'youth workers' is probably not common practice. It was certainly not easy; damage, and sometimes theft, did occur; and the constant vulnerability of an 'open house' has its own peculiar tension! It also provided lighter-hearted moments when, for example, children enjoyed the freedom of a large bathroom where they could be found brushing their hair with our toothbrushes. But it did create, very quickly, a sort of partnership between the Group members involved in this sort of work, the young people, and often the families of the young people as well.

The women of the area gave great support to each other, as is regularly the case in areas of multiple deprivation. Some Group members got involved very deeply with groups of local women. Two projects evolved. A group of women, calling themselves 'The Old Hens' ('hen' being Glasgow patois for 'woman') started to meet regularly in one of the group houses, for support and exploration of common concerns. One of their concerns was the need for affordable, good, second hand clothing for themselves and their children. The Group was by then receiving many consignments of nearly new clothing from some Glasgow churches; so 'The Old Hens' got together, with the help of the Group's outreach fund, enough money to rent a disused shop in the area, which they turned into a most successful Nearly New shop. They called it, of course, 'The Hen House'!

The fabric of the area - the housing, the streets, the pavements - was, by the 1960s, in an appalling state. The Group was involved throughout the whole of its life in numerous projects seeking to tackle this; among these, the start of the first Housing Association in Scotland, and one of the earliest adventure playgrounds, probably deserve mention. The example, which illustrates partnership best, however, is probably that of the Street Action Groups. These arose in the aftermath of a particularly bad storm, which swept through the area in 1967. Much structural damage was caused; and for many months afterwards, the City Council seemed to be able to do very little to clear up the mess after the immediate repairs had been effected. A group from one street, again of women, decided to take matters into their own hands; and with the help of two Group members, formed themselves into a Street Action Group. Their initial purpose was to find the means to tackle the mess in their own street; once that had been done, however, they worked with the Group members to form and develop Action Groups in other streets in the area. At the time, it could have been argued that it would have been quicker to tackle the problems directly, using the Gorbals Groups members' many contacts with the Local Authority; but working with the residents obviously proved, in the long run, far more effective and empowering.

Such examples could, of course, be classed as 'first aid', but the Group was always aware that the deeper structural and systemic issues had to be tackled. They sought to approach these in several ways. One member retrained as a Secondary School teacher and got an appointment in the local school. One member, already a trained Nursery School teacher, started up a low-cost Nursery School. Another member became a local Trade Union official. Geoff Shaw eventually became a Councillor in Glasgow City Council. All worked through the local Ward and Constituency Labour Party. As residents, they could very quickly get fully involved in these political activities, supporting the local people already there.

The greatest danger, even in writing about this from a distance of nearly 30 years, is to give a romantic, not to say patronising, picture of the life and work of the Gorbals Group. While the Group lived in the area, we maintained a strict policy of never accepting invitations to speak in public about ourselves outside the area. Getting involved in partnership in the way described is, inevitably, liable to be open both to abuse and misunderstanding. Essentially, the basis of such partnership lay, the Group believed, in residence in the area, and in our efforts to share at some level in the standard of living of our neighbours, so that from that foundation trust and solidarity could be built, and things - people's lives - could be changed. The Group's members would, and did, say then - that their lives were profoundly changed.

Lilias Graham was a member of the Gorbals Group. At the time of writing Lilias is now well into her eighties. At a recent gathering she recalled that when she first came to stay in Gorbals a wee boy asked her why she lived there. Lilias, in her own words, made some pious comment about it probably being 'because Jesus wanted me to.' 'That's no what ma Maw says', was the reply. 'Ma Maw says yer a nutter.' One mother at the same gathering remembered, as a wee girl, telling her mother she was going up to a woman's house; the woman had toys to play with and gave you sweeties. 'You see and stay right away fae that wuman's door' was her mother's not irresponsible reply.

Were we all perceived as 'nutters' living in Gorbals not because we had to but because we chose to? Why had we made this choice and how did it affect our lives?

We thought we knew, up to a point, what we were taking on in choosing to live there in an 'open-house' way. What we hadn't realised was the effect a very different culture would have on us - how our middle-class values of order, control, and delayed satisfaction would be challenged - and how we would react. Feelings of exasperation, anxiety and confusion that we often had were made bearable both by our colleagues in the Group and also by the incredible resilience and spirit of so many of the people who had to live in such desperate conditions. On our own, and without the option to leave, we would not have lasted long.

Developing partnership

In the early 1960s, Lilias fell heir to a large country house near Stirling, Braendam, which she used to offer families the chance to come together in a supported environment and to enjoy in beautiful countryside a period of respite from the greyness and pressures of their life in the city. Over the years this work has been developed. Various local authority social work departments use it as a place of respite for families living with the effects of poverty, poor housing or isolation. Families have often said that Braendam is the first place where they have felt totally accepted as individuals. 'The labels are off', and there is a real partnership between staff, volunteers and the families.

Nearly 20 years later, in the 1980s, Lilias managed to secure funding for a worker for first one and then two days a week, to be a link with families when they returned to the city. I (Molly) was appointed Support Worker in 1987 and we are now, at the turn of the Century, a team of two full-time and four part-time workers. Funding is insecure, from one year to the next if we are lucky, and we often feel vulnerable about that - but the families we work alongside live with vulnerability all the time. Glasgow Braendam Link

> brings together people from all walks of life to work together in partnership with people disadvantaged by poverty and social exclusion. We aim to support and empower ourselves and each other to bring about growth and development. Glasgow Braendam Link is committed to bringing about changes in the structures of society, so that the voice of the poor is listened to, and issues are addressed.

Both Braendam Family House and Glasgow Braendam Link are affiliated to ATD Fourth World, an international voluntary organisation which, by working in partnership with them, supports the efforts of the poorest to overcome poverty and to take an active role in society.

Aide a Toute Détresse; Fourth World (ATD Fourth World) refers to the fourth estate of the French Revolution, the very poorest people, struggling to be represented in the political changes of the day. It was founded in the 1950s by Father Joseph Wresinski, a French priest born into poverty. The key word throughout ATD's work is partnership, partnership between people living in poverty, who are after all the experts, and allies who stand alongside them in their attempts to have a voice and to be heard. An example of an exciting event when the poor were not excluded took place in New York in October 1994 at an ATD Congress to investigate extreme poverty and the denial of human rights. For the first time homeless and poor people from 45 countries shared their experiences of rejection with those at the top of world government including the UN Secretary General, Boutros Boutros Ghali. Some years before several families had travelled to Rome to have an audience with the Pope. Joseph Wresinski's dream that families living in poverty would one day stand on the steps of the Vatican and of the United Nations had come to pass.

'When you get off that boat the labels are off'

These were the words used by one of a group of women to describe a week she and others had just spent living together on the island of Iona, off the west coast of Scotland. The Iona Community brings together groups from many different backgrounds to share a week of work and worship, relaxation and chores, laughter and tears. People get to know each other by name and as individuals. What they do or don't do back home tends not to be as important as who they are here and now. This particular group of women were all having a break from the poverty and stress of living in areas of deprivation in the city, They are women who are continually being written off as failures in many aspects of their lives.

But when the labels are off it's all different - a whole new ball game. People really communicate, listen, respond to each other and genuinely value and respect each other.

At the end of the week several of the group said what an amazing experience it had been to live together, to share meals, to clean loos and to have both fun and serious discussion with people like doctors, teachers and social workers - people they usually only met on the other side of a desk in the parent/teacher, doctor/patient, social worker/client relationship. 'When you get off that boat the labels are off.'

The really exciting thing was when these same doctors, teachers and social workers said what a privilege it had been for them to meet people who had such a struggle in their lives, people who they very rarely had the chance to meet in anything but a professional relationship.

'When we got back to Glasgow the labels were on again.'

At Glasgow Braendam Link, at Braendam and at ADT gatherings we try to make sure that the labels stay off. To come to Braendam from the city where you are continually being written off as a failure in all aspects of your life and not to be judged but to be warmly accepted, listened to and valued is an experience of deep significance. 'People really listen to you and care about what you think.' Likewise, when they return to Glasgow, this feeling of acceptance can continue. Glasgow Braendam Link matters to families because it gives them a voice and a chance to speak out.

I always feel like a person when I go along there ... I feel as though I grow two inches walking along to the (Glasgow Bracndam Link) flat.

To be quite honest with you the group is the only place where I can take my mask off. I've got problems at home and I've got to walk about the house laughing all the time to let everybody think everything is great, and all the time it's not. So at least when I come here I don't need to wear that mask.

Most of the families known to us are living in conditions of poverty and in situations of stress. It is hard to believe conditions like these still exist in this country ('relative rather than life-threatening' according to Peter Lilley, Minister of State for Social Security in the late Conservative administration). Poverty is of course relative and the poorest people in this country would very rarely liken their condition to that of people living in third world countries or to the poverty experienced in this country in the 1930s. Peter Townsend says that individuals are in poverty when they lack the resources to attain the type of diet, participate in the activities and have the living conditions and the amenities which are customary or at least widely encouraged and approved in the societies to which they belong. This means that poverty is not just about lack of money, but about exclusion from the customs of society. People should have an income which allows them to participate in society rather than merely to exist. Poverty is also about the lack of the basic securities in life which most of us take for granted most of the time. It is about housing and health and education and employment. It is also about choice. We all assume a certain element of choice and colour in our lives. Poverty does not allow for much of these. Day to day living for those in poverty could best be portrayed in varying shades of grey. To quote one woman, asked what she thought was the purpose of life: 'It's an endurance test - we're just put here to see how much we can cope with.'

We live in a climate of rampant consumerism where success is seen mainly in terms of purchasing power and where manufacturers of designer trainers openly target the poor because 'they have to buy their status.' So what of poverty now? We often hear that it no longer exists. It is often pushed out to the peripheral housing schemes where it is not so easily seen and where it cannot challenge the glitzy new image of our city centres, except of course when we are face to face with those who are reduced to begging - and that of course is 'their own fault'. It is easy to ignore, and more comfortable, because to admit to its existence could lead to difficult and unacceptable questions around comparative lifestyles. On the one hand we have the continual pressure to spend spend spend. On the other hand increasingly large numbers of people are living on income support, an ironic example, if ever there was one, of the late Conservative government's 'Back to Basics' policy.

There are areas in Glasgow and probably in most cities in the world where these two different cultures are living almost cheek by jowl with each other, sometimes separated by only one street, but their lives are so different they could be living on different planets, and there is very little chance of meeting across the divide. The gap is widening, the divisions are increasing and the labels are sticking well. More important, to quote Father Joseph Wresinski, is the suffering that lurks behind the facts of poverty. 'The very poor tell us over and over again that a person's greatest misfortune is not to be hungry, or unable to read, nor even to be without work. The greatest misfortune of all is to know that you count for nothing, to the point where even your suffering is ignored. The worst blow of all is the contempt of the part of your fellow citizens. For it is that contempt which stands between a human being and their rights. It makes the world disdain what you are going through and prevents you from being recognised as worthy and capable of taking on responsibility.'

Partnership: The outcomes

Partnership then, in this context, involves the bridging of the gap between people whose ways of life are so totally different they don't begin to understand each other, and it means finding ways for the labels to be off. Can these gaps be bridged, and if so, how? Is there a desire that they should be bridged, and if not, why not? What else does partnership involve?

For me (Molly) it means some points where the boundaries between home and work become decidedly blurred. People with whom I work are friends rather than clients. I receive from them as well as give to them. I am open to criticism by them, which I may not always like.

They may make decisions I consider to be the wrong ones, and I have to learn that my opinion as Project Coordinator carries no more weight than theirs - I sometimes find this a hard lesson. I also have to learn that what I may see as encouraging someone can be perceived by them as pushing. 'You weren't really listening', one woman said, when I'd persuaded her to apply for a job for which she wasn't sure if she was ready. She got the job, left it after the first day, and experienced a feeling of failure - as I did also.

A job which spills over into home life brings with it its own set of questions. These are different from the difficulties of juggling the demands of a job and a home, because the boundaries are much less clear. There is constant balancing and compromise and often feelings of guilt, especially where partners and children are involved. There is undoubtedly a price to pay - and the highest price is that of wondering if your children are getting a fair deal. In our experience of living in community and of both of us at different times doing jobs which involved our home being open others, we find it extremely hard to get that balance right.

The children certainly gain at all sorts of levels from community living, but how do we measure how they feel when it becomes the priority of the time and energy of their parents?

Our 'children' are all now in their late twenties and thirties, but it's a question that still haunts us - and it's a hard question for many people I know. Some people live this way at huge cost. Is it fair to our work, to our families, to ourselves to even attempt these jobs that merge into family life?

Partnership also involves the Director of Social Work for the largest region in Scotland coming to a Glasgow Braendam Link meeting, listening to what individual people are telling him, responding to it, being humbled and moved by the occasion, and writing to the group to tell them so, and to thank them for the meeting.

It involves Benefits Agency training staff making a video with a family member, to be used in training to highlight the need to treat clients with respect and dignity. This arose out of the representations families made, through ATD Fourth World, in a face-to-face meeting with the then Secretary of State for Social Security, Harriet Harman.

It involves two children from Glasgow Braendam Link recently representing Scotland at a children's forum in Geneva to mark the Tenth Anniversary of the UN Convention of the Rights of the Child.

It involves a volunteer befriender helping 60 year old twin sisters to read and write, and sharing their delight when they wrote their own Christmas cards for the first time.

It involves a volunteer spending time helping someone to prepare a speech for the launch of a book in London, and the woman coming home from London enthusing about how she now knew that a comma in a sentence means a pause - it wasn't going to change her life around exactly, but someone had spent time with her, and she had made a discovery that clarified something that had always puzzled her. Imagine going to London in order to discover the meaning of a comma!

Partnership can be as ordinary as sending a birthday or a Christmas card, or a wee note of encouragement to somebody who only ever receives through the mail letters of a business nature or a demand for payment of some kind.

Partnership also involves a young mother living in comfortable circumstances, offering her services to Glasgow Braendam Link, and discovering, when her marriage broke up and her life changed completely, that the friendship of these people meant a great deal to her. She had come to give, and given greatly of her time and effort, but had received a great deal more in return. None of these are earth shattering examples, but all are simple ways of the divide being crossed, simple methods of partnership.

Partnership is, of course, by definition a two-way process, and involves a certain commitment and an element of responsibility. If we invite members of our organisation to be part of the management committee, we must bear in mind that the whole concept of meetings and minutes and agendas may well be a new one. We may assume desks and files as part of our everyday life but if you haven't even got a drawer that is yours alone, or somewhere you know you can leave something in and be sure it stays there, it's not quite so simple.

If your experience is of social workers simply not turning up after you've waited all morning, or turning up two or three hours late and not letting you know or even apologising, it's hard to get the idea that if you've said you'd be at a meeting or an appointment, then other people are counting on you to be there.

We assume too often an understanding of all the jargon and gobbledegook that is spoken at meetings -'I didn't know what that meant, so I just kept quiet.'

We assume people can be reimbursed on arrival at a meeting, but don't bother to work out how they manage to finance getting there in the first place.

We invite them to join us at the pub for a drink after a meeting, and don't think of the embarrassment that might cause if they can't afford it, or if they might be struggling with alcoholism.

We pay out expenses by cheque, when many people we work with don't have such a thing as a bank account.

And yet people do manage it, despite having to rely on public transport, and in spite of all the ongoing hardships and crises in their situations: and the committees and meetings are all the better for their presence and contribution.

The power of the stories

'Telling the stories' is very important to us in Glasgow Braendam Link. Telling our stories and making sure that they are heard. If people really listen to each other, then the labels begin to come off, and the partnerships begin to form. We try to do this in a variety of ways - through straight telling of the stories, through drama presentations and workshops, through 'Let me tell you' beginnings: let me tell you about something that's happened to me or to someone I know or some situation I know about.

The Bishop of Birmingham recognised the value of the stories when he said,

> *Overcoming poverty is a matter of justice, not charity.*
> *One aspect of poverty is powerlessness.*
> *And one aspect of powerlessness is that people don't listen to you.*
> *Yet it is the stories that spell out the cost in human terms of the statistics.*

The cost of partnership

But all of this has a price-tag: it is at a cost.

One of our group once spoke very movingly at an occasion at the Glasgow City Chambers, 'and nobody knew that my blouse was held together with a bit of string, and that I hadn't got the bus-fare home.' Her photograph was in the national press the next day, posing with a well-known celebrity. We so often are unaware of the agonising and the fears to which we are subjecting these folk.

A young lad stutters and stammers his way through a prepared statement at a gathering in Glasgow city centre, a huge effort made possible by the support of the others willing him on, and afterwards says his life took off from that point as he got involved with a group of people and was accepted by them.

But sometimes the cost seems too big a price to pay. People lay themselves open to huge hurt by joining committees, attending conferences, speaking at meetings and they do it with immense courage. Rosalind Miles states that 'if children don't get what they deserve, they become adults whom no society deserves, and who no individual deserves to be.' We see all around us adults struggling against the odds, and with immense courage, managing positively to parent the next generation.

If we are serious about partnership we must continue to encourage, support and empower them in their struggle.

It is true that for us too there is a price to pay. A job, which spills over into home life, brings with it its own set of questions. There is constant balancing and compromise and often feelings of guilt, especially where partners and children are involved. The highest price is that of wondering if your children are getting a fair deal. In our experience of living in community and of both of us at different times doing jobs which involved our home being open to others, we find it extremely hard to get that balance right. It's hard, costly and slow, but for us it feels a more balanced, and possibly in the long run, a more effective way of doing social work, than any other way we know.

References

ATD Fourth World (1991) *The Wrasinksi Approach: The poorest partners in democracy*, Fourth World Publications, 48 Addington Square, London SE5 7LB

ATD Fourth World (1996) *Talk with Us, Not at Us*, Fourth World Publications, 48 Addington Square, London SE5 7LB

Ferguson, R. (1979) *Geoff, The Life of Geoffrey M. Shaw*, Famedram, Gartocharn.

Miles, R. (1995) *The Children We Deserve*, Harper Collins, London.

8
A new look at self-determination

May-Kwan Wong

Introduction

Self-determination, which has been conceived in various terms, is summarised by Weick and Pope (1988, p.10) as 'clients' right to make their own decisions, their right to actively participate in the helping process, and their right to lead a life of their own choosing. Despite the subtle differences in emphasis, each conception conveys a belief in the capacity and right of individuals to affect the course of their lives.'

Self-determination is recognised as a fundamental principle of the social work profession in the helping process. Its perpetual value in the profession is asserted in a substantial part of social work literature (e.g. Levy, 1983 and Freedberg, 1989). However, from my many years of social work practice, I feel that such literature has not sufficiently addressed the process of applying this principle to practice.

When applying the principle of self-determination to practice, I have encountered the following constraints and limitations:

- How can I work with clients towards the treatment goals without imposition of my personal values?
- If a client's final decision will eventually bring harm to her/himself or others, what should I do to resolve the dilemma?

I hope to resolve the above conflicts and re-conceptualise my understandings of the exercise of self-determination by the following case illustration.

Case illustration

In 1993, I worked in a Hong Kong outreach social service team which provided counselling services to delinquent youth. My approach was based on the theory that a trustful worker-client relationship is the main key to change.

One of my clients, 'Ah Wing', became pregnant soon after she was discharged from a girls' hostel. With my immediate intervention, a trusting working relationship was soundly built. She bore a boy a month before her 18th birthday. In the meantime, her relationship with her partner deteriorated and they separated at the end. To earn her living, she intended to work in a night club. During a session we discussed this issue and I strongly disagreed with her intentions. Regarding this as a situation requiring crisis intervention to deal with the client's financial problem, I immediately examined many contingency plans: for example, public assistance, temporary accommodation and a nursery. By taking these actions I hoped that it would save Ah Wing from the 'dangers' she might be faced with when working in a night club environment.

Ah Wing did not accept any of my suggestions and started the job at the night club soon after the session. From subsequent sessions, I began to feel that her job gave her satisfaction such as easy money, luxury clothing and dates with many powerful and rich men. These are all things she had never experienced before. Finally, I managed to draft out a contract with her, as she persisted in staying in the present job. In the contract she promised to have regular medical check-ups and to adopt safety measures against any sexually transmitted diseases; and once she saved up to about HK$200,000 (about £16,000) she would quit this job and run her own florist shop.

During these days, both Ah Wing and I were frustrated. She sensed that I was no longer unconditionally supportive to her, therefore I was frustrated as I saw my efforts become useless and I came to realise that the above-mentioned contract was unrealistic for her. It only gave us both an excuse to avoid the present situation.

What are the problems?

It is difficult to define the problems at first glance as there is a loophole in the law—an adult working in nightclub does not commit the offence of prostitution. Since Ah Wing was aged over 18 when she started working in the night club, she was legally allowed to work in such a place. This reinforced her decision because she was neither bound by the Care and Protection Order nor was she committing any offence of indecency.

On the other hand, this did not mean that she was free from judgment against social norms, even though her decision did not work against any particular social interests. Prostitution has long been frowned upon by mainstream society. Therefore, even though the Hong Kong value system is composed of several conflicting and subordinated factions in flux, being a prostitute is undoubtedly rejected by the majority of people. In this case, Ah Wing was concerned about being socially rejected. In fact, she understood that her decision would not be morally accepted by society, but she chose to ignore the more socially acceptable route of social services.

What was my role as a helping professional? It is worthwhile to examine the following questions before the helping role can be identified:

- How did Ah Wing perceive the impact of social norms on her?
- What were Ah Wing's beliefs and how did these influence her decisions?

Obviously, there was a disparity between the moral values of Ah Wing and mainstream social norms. The client justified her decision by reference to her need to fulfil the breadwinner role. As well, in her family context, she was socialised to 'dress up' her decision in socially acceptable ways—both her mother and her peers accepted casual sex—she belongs to a sub culture deviant from mainstream society. Also, her behaviour was reinforced by what she gained from the job: the unexpected delights of a luxurious life and having numerous boyfriends. All of these seemed to her to be an extraordinary adventure. She believed that the benefits she received outweighed the risks. Clearly, the material pleasure and temporary psychological fulfilment gained outweighed for her the 'harms' both from moral judgment and social rejection. Again, it is obvious that the client's decision was both accepted by herself and by the subculture. This explains why she did not regard this as a problem or felt shameful. Therefore, I felt that I should have given more respect to her decision, because of her intrinsic right to lead her own life.

From another point of view, it was mainly my problem because Ah Wing's decision was contrary to my value system. Thus, it was my responsibility to distinguish my role in regard to the client's self-determination. I had managed to keep up regular interviews with the client even though she understood my disapproval about her job at the night club. This indicates that Ah Wing still trusted me and needed some service. From a professional point of view, it was my responsibility to encourage the client to be fully self-determining in defining and solving her problem. Nevertheless, both Ah Wing and I were, at that time, trapped by the so-called 'good worker-client relationship'. Thus I was too emotionally involved and not aware that my own value judgment might be imposed upon her. This explains why I felt frustrated when she did not adopt my advice. Sometimes, social workers cannot stand back and be non-judgmental, especially in such outreach settings where clients come on a voluntary basis, and where a successful building of the worker-client relationship is believed to be a primary key for motivating clients' changes. Clearly, it is difficult for a social worker to balance subjectivity and objectivity in her or his practice. Nevertheless, no one promises that social work is easy. It is useful to bear in mind that a good worker-client relationship does not guarantee a client's adaptation to the social worker's suggestion. Such a guarantee is both unrealistic and unethical because it may abuse the relationship. Therefore, how to maintain a good balance between a workable level of emotional concern and the practice of 'self-determination' has become a crucial challenge to me.

First of all, it is necessary to clear up the confusion which may arise from the disparity between the client's value and mine. Biestek (1975) suggests that

> *the caseworker, especially when he (she) is of a different religion than the client, must respect the conscience of the client and help the client make choices and decisions which are within the boundaries of that conscience.* (p.30)

It is understood that the client may come from a different social class which has its own subculture and system of values. The client's own value system should be accepted, not because it does or does not conform with the social norms, but simply because it is the way for the client. Therefore, it is crucial to avoid any imposition of personal values upon the client.

Conflict between client self-determination and the client's welfare

At first glance, it is unquestionable that I should respect the client's choice because she owned the right to lead her life. But what created difficulties for me was that her decision, through exposure to both moral and physical dangers, might eventually bring harm to herself and her son as well.

First of all, since she was not well-acquainted with the serious consequence of promiscuous and unsafe sexual activities, she was at a high risk of contracting AIDS or some other sexually-transmitted diseases through frequent sexual relations with strangers. Besides, those engaged in prostitution are often exposed to lifestyles characterised by drug addiction, casual sex and gambling. Regarding the client's vulnerability and a lack of social support (she had just separated from her partner), it is possible that she might engage in such a life style and this might damage herself both physically and psychologically. In such a situation, the primary thing that I believed I should do was to enhance Ah Wing's understanding of such risks and to work out a strategy of harm minimisation. This will be further elaborated later.

After all, as Weick and Pope state, 'self-determination does not guarantee clients' behaviours that will meet professional or social norms of acceptability.' (1988, p.12) It is clear that social work is not always a tool of social control. Ideally, according to self-determination principles, there should be neither any imposition of my moral judgment on the client nor any direction of her behaviour purely in accordance with the social interests. Sometimes, a client may make a decision that may be regarded as unwise or immoral. Yet, this is her own decision, provided she is not causing harm to others. In summary, the principle of self-determination is to provide a 'moral constraint' upon social workers. As McDermott states, the client has a right 'to go his (her) own way not because it is constructive, good, or socially acceptable, but simply because it is his (her) own.' (1975, p.132)

In a similar vein, my respect for the client's right in making her or his own choice is highlighted by Perlman in her statement that, 'the problem-to-be-solved or the question-to-be-answered must be recognised, felt by the person who faces it.' (1975, p.75)

According to this approach I should recognise that the client possesses her unique interpretation of the situation and hence, I should avoid any imposition of personal values upon her. After all, it is the client who has to face, experience, and define the experience and learn from it; my role is to assist her in evaluating and integrating the experience to become an empowering part of her life.

In the meantime, the interests of her child also called for my concern. As mentioned, she might not recognise the harms that her decision brought to her and her child. What particularly drew my attention was whether Ah Wing has considered how her child might be affected.

Since Ah Wing was separated from the child's father, she took up the parental responsibility alone. Therefore I questioned to what extent the child would receive appropriate parental care. I did not intend to be judgmental if she might be neglectful of her parental duties. Since her son was still an infant, the crucial question is how could she perform her mothering role in a single family setting. Instead of depending on public assistance, Ah Wing insisted on earning her own living. She was obviously occupied by her job. Usually she left home for work at evenings and did not return until midnight. The care and safety of her child is worth a further examination. Although there was not any sign of reckless disregard for her child's safety, Ah Wing might need assistance to arrange a quality baby sitting service for the child.

It was necessary to consider how to assure a nurturing environment for her child's growth. This brought such matters as his physical growth condition, psychological needs and positive pre-school education opportunity into consideration. They were not the only responsibilities a mother should take, but also it is important for her to understand that a nurturing growth environment could facilitate the child in breaking through vicious cycles of being chronically poor, chronically disenfranchised and marginalised.

Further, the dignity of the child should be respected. Even though it is too early to determine how her son would feel, Ah Wing was encouraged to envisage how he might feel when old enough to understand how his mother earns a living.

Although Ah Wing's right to become self-determining is acknowledged, she should also behave in a socially responsible manner. Clearly, she should not wilfully abuse the right of being self-determining. It was important for her to understand that her self-determination should not be made at the expense of her child's interest. This calls me to resolve the conflict between her interests and that of her child in a socially responsible manner. Under no circumstances should the principle of client self - determination connote a 'selfish' determination.

The roles of social worker in client self-determination

From my case illustration, I will now discuss the practice roles and strategies.

Leaving the client in control

As Levy states, 'the social worker always has the ethical responsibility to honour, to preserve, and to facilitate the client's self-determination.' (1983, p.905) Being a social worker, I assisted the client to be fully self-determining and to have a sense of control over her situation. The following analogy described by Biestek explains my role as social worker in actualising the client's self determination:

> *To summarise the role of the caseworker in a figure of speech, the caseworker opens doors and windows to let in air, light, and sunshine, so that the client can breathe more easily and see more clearly. The aim is to help him (her) to gain a better insight into his (her) problem, and develop strength to help himself (herself).* (1975, p.22)

Further, Bernstein explains the role of social worker in fulfilling the principle of client self-determination: 'each client needs our best diagnosis in terms of where he is and how far he can go.' (1974, p.110) As I am now convinced of the importance of client self-determination, my response is to develop the following new strategies:

Respecting and working with the client.

A mistake which I may make which hampers the actualisation of self-determination is that, consciously or unconsciously, I may take up a superior status which signifies to the client that I know best. This phenomenon is explained by Weick and Pope who argue that:

> because the social worker's education emphasises a knowledge base to be used in professional practice, it is tempting to assume that the client's knowledge about his or her situation is inferior to that of the worker's. (1988, p.12)

This reminds me that my position is one of acting as a tool for enabling the client's self-determination, to co-work with her in partnership. Most importantly, I need to remember that my professional knowledge which is based on my subjective interpretation of rational training and objectivity, under no circumstances, is superior to the client's subjective and unique experience of the situation.

Assessing and interpreting the problem.

My assessment and interpretation can help Ah Wing to see her problem in other ways. This calls for a reframing of the situation with the client and it is essential to foster her capacity for decision-making. Nevertheless, people are emotional beings, and clients may occasionally find it difficult to see themselves and their problems in other ways. Supported by the trusting relationship, I must help Ah Wing to work through new ways of seeing her situation. Furthermore, I find the following questions are worth noting during the intervention process:

- Are there any possible alternatives re the available resources?
- What is the significance of each choice?
- What are the evaluations of each choice?

Through answering these questions, it is hoped that the client will become aware of pertinent resources. (Biestek, 1975, p.21)

Realising the fantasy of the client's self-determination.

Client self-determination may only remain a day dream if it cannot be actualised. As emphasised by Soyer, 'caseworkers must always represent reality to their clients, and the literature stresses the importance of realistic goals, with the assessment of what is realistic being based on sound diagnosis.' (1975, p.56) Therefore, it is a primary responsibility to give a realistic meaning to my practice.

Freeing the client from fear and tension.

Unfortunately, Ah Wing was similar to most social work clients: she came from a lower social class that is being chronically labelled, stigmatised and suppressed. As Perlman describes

> *[they] have not had the life-experience of continuity and support in finding and*

knowing themselves and having freedoms to choose. They have been denied these freedoms....The chronically poor, the chronically sick, the chronically outcast have rarely been self-determining....The 'right' to self-determination seems all but incredible to them, and indeed it is all but non-existent, so narrow is the margin of their possible choices. (1975, p.74)

In short, the clients described above are those victimised and disenfranchised, and in order to maximise their self-determination, there is a need to make them aware of their own rights. This involves helping clients to take their first steps towards empowerment, towards developing a sense of control over their situations.

Before reflecting on the case, I was not convinced that a trusting worker-client relationship was essential to the therapeutic goals. But now I am sure of its importance, that the client's trust in me can support her in terms of striving for her own rights. In return, my acceptance of the client, the identification with her and the emotional support I provide can motivate her to work through many difficulties encountered during the helping process.

Learning from self-correction.

Life for most people is rather uncertain. Both the client and I should prepare ourselves for the possibility that the anticipated outcomes may not turn out as expected. When this happens, it is important to question whether my knowledge base is sufficient to enable a complete assessment and to indicate what action is best for the client. (Soyer, 1975, p.61)

Sometimes, it is the fickle nature of life that failures are inevitable and that life is out of our control. As Weick and Pope state, 'some events that are painful and debilitating at one time may eventually be the catalyst for the future growth and self-awareness.' (1988, p.16)

After all, as Soyer states, 'they succeed and fail and through success and failure they learn.' (1975, p.61) I think this statement best describes the client as well as myself. 'Self-Determination' means allowing the client to gain self-growth through the process of self-correction. Her right of learning from trial and error should be respected, and it is my obligation to support her, without hurting others, to obtain her unique life goals as fully as she can.

Re-evaluating the roles of social worker

We recognise that social workers play an important role in promoting client self-determination. The question is: 'in what ways do social workers perform in accordance with professional ethics?' Clearly this question is worth further discussion.

According to the Code of Practice constituted by the Social Workers Registration Board of Hong Kong (1998), social workers are supposedly to believe that 'individuals have the potential to develop, and, thus accept a responsibility to encourage and facilitate the self-realisation of individuals with due regard to the interest of others'. The above-mentioned quote appears conceptually simple. The crucial problem is that, wonderful as it may seem in theory, promoting client self-determination is difficult to manage in practice.

Referring to Ah Wing's case, little was known about the justification of her choice.

It is worth noting that Ah Wing was frightened to speak for herself. She did not realise that she had potential for change. She might be afraid of taking responsibility of decision-making, or she might not receive sufficient support and encouragement. It was my responsibility to let Ah Wing articulate her needs, without any constraints. Unfortunately, both of us might be trapped in such a misuse of power and authority. Because of my educational background, my professional knowledge, Ah Wing's trust in me and so forth; I might have unwittingly taken on an authoritative role in the worker-client relationship, particularly when I believed that I was responsible for 'helping' those who were in need. I should have been chronically suspicious of whether I abused my power and authority over her.

Re-thinking social relations within the organisation

Let us now discuss another question which I feel is worth investigating, 'how does the employing organisation construct my practice?' Reflecting on Ah Wing's case, I was too focused on evaluating myself as a professional agent, I became the only culprit in the above-mentioned ethical struggles and dilemma. I did not recognise that the employing organisation, to a certain extent, fettered my practice. Social workers in the organisation I work for, are supposed to work independently. Nevertheless, under the influence of so-called 'enhanced productivity practice', social workers may not admit their needs for professional support from colleagues, lest colleagues infer that they have shortcomings as social workers. Indeed, I felt that opportunities for unconstrained dialogue among appropriate colleagues were rare. I was afraid to discuss freely my own difficulties and dilemmas because it might show my weaknesses to others. A similar situation is observed by Rossiter et al (2000, p. 20) who argue that, due to funding cuts, social workers do not feel sufficiently secure to engage in honest dialogue. Strategies which bring more ethical outcomes for their clients are then obstructed.

Clearly, in such a constraining environment, social workers are denied colleagues' support. Hence, they cannot break through practice dilemmas and learn from their experience. The growth of professional knowledge is hindered. Social workers are trapped in such vicious cycles leading to a lack of confidence. Therefore, in addition to reviewing my own value systems, this also requires me to be a whistle blower in calling for freedom to discuss dilemmas among colleagues within the employing organisation. Rossiter et al (2000) call for a shift to a postmodern account of ethics and to the belief that 'such (democratic) communication is crucial to a postmodern conception of ethics where local, particular, historical, and contingent dilemmas require a constant process of argumentation and interpretation' (p.22), I believe that, through re-examining the deeply internalised structures of power, democratic communication within the employing organisation can be promoted.

Minimising Potential Risks To the Client

As discussed previously, Ah Wing exposed herself to physical and moral dangers which might cause her fatal harm. I felt that I needed to take immediate action to stop such potential harm. The harm minimisation approach was particularly important in case Ah Wing later wanted to change her current way of life. With harm minimisation strategies in place, she could more easily change her life style at her own choice.

Taking a harm minimisation approach, I therefore, should have adopted an educative role to alert Ah Wing to the physical dangers she might face and to trigger her awareness of her health risks. Further, Ah Wing should have been encouraged to adopt effective safety measures against sexually transmitted diseases. Recalling the agreement we had made earlier, I should have continued to implement the plans with the client by developing her own way of thinking about how it could benefit her. This should have included my working with the client about timing and means, at every stage of the course. As mentioned above, regular interviews with the client were maintained, and the sessions should therefore have been focused on keeping an eye on how the agreement could be implemented successfully. Such skills and strategies as decision-making and reinforcement could have been used.

Conclusion

In this paper, I have shared my difficulties and thoughts in working with a client who chose to work as a call girl. The discussion mainly focused on how I could have put the principle of 'Self-Determination' into practice. To sum up, I find that it is important to:

- Start 'Self-Determination' where the client is.
- Review my role as a social worker.

- Be aware of my personal values and avoid any imposition upon the client.
- Help the client to recognise the importance of harm minimisation.
- Motivate the client to be self-determining in line with her parental responsibility.
- Review the value of a 'good therapeutic relationship', and
- Recognise the ways the employing organisation constructs my practice.

Previously, I focused my effort on helping the client by an exploration and exploitation of the existing social welfare services. I am now more conscious of questions such as: how did the client define her problems and needs? How did she perceive the impact of social norms on her? and, What were her beliefs and how did these influence her process of decision-making?

Before the problem had been defined, it would have been worthwhile to examine how the subculture she belonged to influenced her values and beliefs. It is crucial that the social worker's personal values should not be imposed upon the client—particularly in a helping profession such as social work. Sometimes, we unconsciously regard ourselves as the guardian angels of our clients. But what may happen is that we play the role of social control agents, which may unwittingly bring harm to the client later on.

Last but not least, I am inspired by the radical case work perspective (Fook, 1993) in understanding the case. My client was chronically underprivileged and thus, her empowerment became another crucial task. I was too focused on the conventional casework approach and hoped to fit the client into the existing services but ignored how her problems had been socially attributed. It was the client's self-determination which was primarily important to her, and therefore to me.

References

Bernstein, S. (1974) 'Self-determination: King or citizen in the realm of values?', in *Toward Effective Social Work Practice*, MSS Information, New York

Biestek, F.P. (1975) 'Client self-determination', in McDermott, F.E. (ed) *Self-determination in Social Work*, Routledge and Kegan Paul, London

Fook, J. (1993) *Radical Casework: A theory of practice*, Allen and Unwin, Sydney

Freedberg, S (1989) 'Self-determination: Historical perspectives and effect on current practice', *Social Work*, 34, 1, 33-37

Levy, C.S. (1983) 'Client self-determination', in *Handbook of Clinical Social Work*, Jossey Bass, San Francisco

McDermott, F.E. (ed) (1975) *Self-Determination in Social Work*, Routledge and Kegan Paul, London

Perlman, H.H. (1975) 'Self-determination: Reality or illusion?', in McDermott, F.E. (ed) *Self-Determination in Social Work*, Routledge and Kegan Paul, London

Rossiter, A., Prilleltensky, I. & Walsh-Bowers, I. (2000) 'A postmodern perspective on professional ethics', in Fawcett, B., Festherstone, B., Fook, J. & Rossiter, A. (eds.) *Practice and Research in Social Work: Postmodern feminist perspectives*, Routledge, London

Social Workers Registration Board of Hong Kong (1998) *Code of Practice*

Soyer, D. (1975) 'The Right to fail' in McDermott, F.E. (ed) *Self-Determination in Social Work*, Routledge and Kegan Paul, London

Weick, A. and Pope, L. (1988) 'Knowing what's best: A new look at self-determination', *Social Casework: The Journal of Contemporary Social Work*, 69, 1, 10-16

Weick, A. and Vandiver, S. (eds) (1982) *Women, Power, and Change*. Part 4. National Association of Social Workers, Washington

9
Shifting positions:
Making meaning in social work

Narda Razack

....we can never fix meanings; they are deeply contextual and shifting, endlessly taken from other meanings which are taken from others, and so on. There are a range of historically and culturally specific possible meanings, so researchers/ thinkers can never get to the final, 'real' meaning or structure of a society or action or text. (Jones, 1997, p.265)

I work from the conviction and acknowledgment that personal reflection on the conditions, past and present, out of which our discourses and knowledge are produced is crucial. The version I give is ... how I as an individual within all my other locations (educational background, colonial past, employment) have processed and constructed the knowledge that I give as history and analysis. (Musisi, p.131)

I begin this chapter with a brief narrative of my personal, professional and intellectual disjunctures which map my trajectories as a scholar, and which help to make meanings for me in social work. These disjunctures result from my shifting positions and roles within social work which allow for engagement and 'discursive strategies' to question what is known textually, in practice, and in my body.

I entered social work circuitously. Twenty five years ago my first child was born with various health problems and he had to be transported by ambulance to a big city hospital for tests and surgery. We immediately became consumers of the 'helping professions' in a more intense way. While in the hospital he was diagnosed as a rubella baby and after days of anguish we were informed that his medical problems were treatable. We received scant information throughout this ordeal and we were never approached by social workers to discuss the trauma we were facing as first time parents. After his initial medical problems were treated, we realised that he was deaf and soon after we began meeting with teachers, specialists, audiologists and other health professionals. After these initial painful events, we joined parent support groups and entered the world of deafness as outsiders - that is, knowing deafness vicariously.

A few years later after the birth of twins, and continued links with the deaf community through parent associations and the education system, I decided that I wanted to be a social worker. I had worked previously as a health care professional. Undoubtedly, this decision was enmeshed in the benevolence of caring, but I also wanted to be politically active since I had personally experienced and observed several loopholes in the system around disability. Deafness is considered an invisible disability and communication approaches and educational choices are highly politicised. Parents are viewed by the system as either being compassionate and understanding or deviant trouble makers not acting in the best interest of the child. These attitudes hold true for people with other disabilities and their care givers and families (Swain and Cameron, 1999).

Entering university for a first degree as a mature part-time student posed difficulties, and I was challenged. First, all of my prior schooling was in my country of birth, considered a 'developing' country. Second I was a mature student. Third I was visibly different. These differences were overwhelming for me because of my lack of knowledge of the culture of the academic environment, my shared responsibility for twins and a deaf child, all pre-schoolers at that time, and other family responsibilities. I do not state these difficult locations as being unique to me, but they mark my identity as I began my professional journey.

This narrative briefly contextualises my entry into social work where there was a beginning politicisation of issues around disability, the gendered nature of caring and consciousness of racial differences. The rest of the chapter highlights my shifting positions in social work as a student, practitioner and presently an academic. The narrative will be inscribed with the meanings I have made in this journey thus far through critical analyses, theory building, practice, teaching and research. I will discuss my shifting positions in terms of the multiple roles I attained, the shifting identities which result and the meanings I have constructed along the way.

Background

The aim of this text is to discuss and theorise some breakthroughs for practice which resulted from my experiences. Postmodern approaches and critical theory have left practitioners, students and academics bereft of ways to create alternative practice approaches (Mullaly, 1997; Ife, 1997). My analysis includes experiential reflections of theory formulated in action, practice and research to illustrate how meanings are produced in a processual and learning-centred way. Postmodern/post structural thinking allows us to forego linear, prescriptive and positivist practice modalities. The very nature of the dialectic of postmodernism mitigates such form.

There is a longing however for a replacement theory, a framework, a guide, in fact critical practice skills, which extend the critical reflexivity and critical theoretical approaches. Pease and Fook (1999) place theoretical concepts and frameworks developed from their multiple roles on a continuum. Their analyses were predicated on the limitations of feminism, postmodernism and critical theory on providing practice principles. Their postmodern critical theory approach provides some new direction and perspectives to ground some of the analyses of this chapter. Through my reflections, I will illustrate that although there is value and a certain comfort premised around former prescriptive models, we need to reflect on our own breakthroughs and learn ways to theorise from our experiences as they merge with our current knowledge, skills and approaches. Thus the breakthroughs will be added to our 'grab bag' of skills which inform and are informed by current sociopolitical realities, global and transnational trends. What I am promoting is an approach towards thinking critically about our individual collective histories in order to construct and redefine new meanings. Our value base for constructing theories should always be framed in anti-oppressive and anti-racist contexts which are vital to our work (Razack, in press).

Shifting positions/shifting identities

The concept of positionality, according to Burman (1989) cited in Bhavani and Phoenix (1994), is the process of constructing identifications which treat identities as produced rather than fixed, personal attributes which can potentially allow for alliances (p.12-13). It is crucial that this ongoing production of the self in different contexts creates opportunities for alliances in order to create emancipatory and transformative theory and practice modalities. Positionality is further described by Pease and Fook (1999):

> *The individual is thus constituted and reconstituted through a variety of discursive practices and changing material circumstances ... The relevance of this notion, which couples discursive constructions and material conditions for emancipatory social work practice, is that people can reconstitute themselves through a self-conscious and critically reflective practice.* (pp.15-16)

Jones (1997) discusses how the subject is constituted and formed. She believes that because we are constantly shaped and produced by and within language and meanings we are not determined by one set of meanings and therefore we can make change. These changes can be effected by examining shifting definitions of gender, different ways in which women are categorised, and through spatial analyses of position and positioning which allow us to examine how we are constituted as subjects and also how we reconstitute ourselves (Jones, p. 265). I add here the shifting meanings of race, racism and oppression which serve to reconstitute racialised subjectivities and discourse. These spaces or positions created at these disjunctures are worth exploring in order to realise how our world view continues to be shaped by external forces. When we speak of shifts and identities there is an implication that there is no unifying theory for social work, no theory base, no empirical value inherent in the profession. These notions can create dissonance and dislocation but analytical thinking and opportunities to merge present concerns and past theories will only strengthen the profession.

Brotman and Pollack (1997) describe the base of modernity on which the field of social work was developed. They discuss the more recent postmodern approaches (Brown, 1994; Leonard, 1994) and illustrate some of the dilemmas inherent in this theory for feminism and feminist practice. They call for a more progressive version of postmodern theory which would combine emancipatory politics such as feminism or critical theory. There is the notion that recognising differences can create fragmentation and also that feminism is now weakened with the voices of others which dilute its effectiveness. However, what differences and narrative allow is the inclusion and perspectives of otherwise marginalised and silent voices. To ask how we give equal time to hearing marginalised narratives and narratives of the abuser, is to denigrate and subjugate those with non-dominant status realities. Brotman and Pollack (1997) state that:

> *Social work attempts to ameliorate the limitations of postmodernism by merging them with overtly emancipatory theories (Brown, 1994; Leonard, 1994) should be regarded with scepticism. Despite the overlap between the goals of social work to value the unique 'stories' of our clients and the postmodern emphasis upon diversity, postmodernism must be viewed critically. Although it calls for the inclusion of marginalised people's 'voices,' it may promote a fragmentation that prevents any union based upon common struggles.* (p.20)

Harstock, (1990) referring to the emergence of the subject and the right to name oneself, is also disheartened with this emerging 'problematic':

> *Just when we are forming our own theories about the world, uncertainty emerges about whether the world can be theorised?* (p. 162)

Thus the marginal voice, especially the racialised marginalised voice, is not legitimised in this process.

These debates are critical to our understanding of what we do when there are spaces to make meanings in our practice. How do we merge our analysis and our thinking around marginality and voice with the traditional theory and foundation of social work? What if, in our breakthroughs there is little or no compatibility with the form? How can we then make meaning in order to reconstruct our theoretical base? What disallows us from abusing the subjective analysis of our breakthroughs and interpretation to impose the power/knowledge/knower position over our clients which would then sustain colonial and imperial practice? These are some of the deliberations inherent in making meaning of our experiences in social work.

Bhavani & Phoenix (1994) discuss 'shifting identities shifting racisms' to signal crucial areas for feminist approaches to psychology (p.5). Their approach captures and describes my thinking of how meanings continue to be created for me in social work and the impact on my identity. It is not only how my body is viewed in terms of visible differences, but more so the impact of various forces on my identity like postcoloniality, the shifting meanings of race and concepts of racism, the situatedness of class, the traditional structures of the academy, the notion of practice in agencies, the view of the client and the elitism faced in every facet of practice. What I remember clearly are the forces which gripped my attention along this journey, those areas which now mark my identity and create agency for me in my work. According to Bhavani and Phoenix (1994):

'Identity' is a word which is much used in both academic and political contexts. Its strength is that it captures succinctly the possibilities of unravelling the complexities of the relationship between 'structure' and 'agency'; perhaps one can say it is the site where structure and agency collide. (p.6)

I would like to explain what I mean by shifting positions (positionality) from two perspectives which are themselves mutually exclusive. First my multiple roles in social work inform the different ways in which I research, practice and teach social work. I will locate these experiences as breakthroughs which continue to affect my professional identities. Secondly, these concretely ascribed roles in themselves help to create the shifting positions I occupy within the profession of social work, not simply in my title but more significantly, the way in which meanings in social work are created from these positions. These meanings which will be contextualised in various analytical categories also impact on my professional identities (positions) which are informed by my gender, working class background to present middle class status, mixed race identity, able-bodied, straight, postcolonial condition and age. It is my belief that these positions affect the social work theory I embrace and my location within the profession, the type of teacher I am at present, and the resulting identities continuously being constructed. I also believe that one has to pay attention to these shifts from socioeconomic, global and transnational realities in order to recognise and relate to the power within the historical origins and present form of the profession.

Breakthroughs as a student

As aforementioned, my undergraduate days in social development studies were mixed with home and family responsibilities. I did not have access to the library because of child care responsibilities and I distinctly remember sending my papers in to be quietly put under professors' office doors at night in order to meet deadlines. Writing a final exam without listening fully to the tapes for a correspondence course compelled me to examine my inability to fully immerse myself and grapple with the theoretical knowledge base. Today as an academic I speak to students in similar predicaments, mainly women, immigrant women, and I tell them of the loss they face in terms of rigour and context of academic work which they miss when they are overwhelmed with home and away activities. Thankfully with the new age of technology, some of the dilemmas I faced then are somewhat mitigated. I have been able to view the academy as a traditional white eurocentric edifice which creates concrete obstructions for those struggling without the benefit of the powerful history of knowledge production and academic inquiry. My colonial past and British based education prepared me academically but learning the culture within this postcolonial climate posed difficulties.

What was significant in terms of breakthroughs for practice was that an immigrant has to negotiate her learning differently and map the terrain for gaining this knowledge. These contexts, including extended family and other responsibility, signify that the battle is more difficult for we have to peddle ten times faster in order to be recognised and more so to believe in oneself as having the capability to learn and to belong in a white dominated academic environment. My classroom was an almost exclusive white domain and my voice was silent and silenced. Culture, race and racism were not included in any of my classes, for we were taught about violence, abuse, poverty, community and practice for marginalised white people. I learnt white theories, and the texts were traditional and sustained the hegemony of the western, British narrative. Returning to university later on as a full time graduate student saw a surge in growth, thinking, theorising while simultaneously recognising the power of the institution and the role of dominance.

My full time status as a graduate student produced new meanings for me to understand and do social work. These understandings came about through critical incidents between other students, the professors, and the agency context in my practica. I had practised social work for approximately three years after my first degree and I felt a bit more confident on my re-entry into academia. However the culture of the environment was instantly overpowering. There were few students of colour and we gravitated towards each other. We listened to comments about the other, observed how our realities were subjugated in the classroom either as the problem client or the problem in history. In the classroom we did not deeply analyse ways in which identity was constructed from our different locations, neither did we learn the theories of oppression. I had to forge my own learning in these areas. Globalisation and internationalism were absent in my analysis and I constantly bridged the divisions of micro and macro teaching and learning. This bridging was an important realisation in my education since I could not only belong to one camp. I needed to stretch my learning to include macro/policy and community perspectives in order to understand social issues. Social justice and human rights perspectives insist upon such knowledge.

Graduate school allowed for some personal development since I used all the assignments to write and research about race, racism, culture and ethnicity for most of my courses. Sharing my personal history in the class was met with understanding and curiosity but not with a sense of urgency to change, to include other perspectives, to create an openness so that students and professors could believe in the merit of such discourse and research. My reality and learning around oppression were viewed as my 'area of study' and not important and inherent in the curriculum. A few professors included one text, an article or class session to devote to race and then we settled comfortably with the major developmental theorists. What then were the breakthroughs in practice during this period?

I realise that my learning had to extend beyond the boundaries of the classroom because the omissions would be detrimental not only to my practice but to the practice of my colleagues who would inevitably be working with diverse groups in society. I realised that the benevolence of caring was enmeshed with power and control and that learning the game of subtlety and the power of and within organisations would sustain me in the practice environment. A major breakthrough doing graduate work was to acknowledge and incorporate the wider political context of the work. On my application form I had to check one of two streams, clinical or community development/social policy. I opted for the clinical route but interacted mainly with all the minority students who chose the community development/social policy stream. The courses in the community stream touched on global politics and the impact and importance of community work were emphasised while the clinical stream allowed for absorption of theories and direct practice modalities.

Gibelman (1999) states that in the search for identity, social work is constantly hampered by the enormity of the profession because of its involvement with external sociopolitical economic forces as well as structural divisions within the profession itself. These struggles are also recognised within other professions (p.298). In locating different definitions for social work she notes the fluidity inherent in the language and discourse around the conceptualisation of theories. Specialisation within social work is inevitable as we continue to name ourselves politically. Later on, naming myself as a therapist and not a social worker was a deliberate attempt to copy my colleagues who viewed themselves as a cut above the welfare worker or community organiser. The divisions in social work education may mean that the political and global level of analysis will not be taken up in profound ways when the emphasis is on the individual in a very specific context. According to Gibelman (1999):

> *The nature of social work in the future will be affected by the influence of both intraprofessional developments and external, environmental conditions and demands. And, of course, the internal and external developments interact with each other to produce a different set of contingencies and influences.* (pp.306-307)

Johnson (1999) conducted a study to assess the nature of direct and indirect work and found that the majority of time for direct workers was spent on indirect practice, which she found demanded more skill and expertise (p.327). She states:

> *... as social work enters its second century, I would like the profession to develop a balanced theoretical and technical framework within which all of our activities are included and valued ... After all Richmond stated many years ago, the combination of direct and indirect work may be what makes social work unique.* (p.332)

It may be valuable for social work training to incorporate ways in which all aspects of social work can be valued and seen as being interdependent rather than an espousement of one approach to the detriment of one's learning and opportunities for effective intervention.

As a student, my angst in not being able to connect with the mainstream, clinical students who identified strongly with a specific clinical approach left me feeling uneasy and at times silenced in my placement setting. A split placement opportunity at a multicultural agency (Razack, Teram and Rivera, 1995) to pursue different learning was not viewed as crucial. It was recognised as my area of interest, but not clinical and therefore not highly valued or esteemed. Schneider and Netting (1999) account for these dilemmas for practitioners and educators:

> *....how do social workers balance their responsibility for addressing social issues and reform through influencing policies on the one hand with providing help to individuals in trouble on the other?* (p. 349)

Also, how do social workers strive for social justice and reform within clinical and psychotherapeutic practice?

Both my practicum experiences were engaging, threatening and challenging. The first experience allowed me to split my placement by spending some time at a multicultural centre. This experience was new to the mainstream counselling agency and therefore I was bringing new experiences and knowledge to both settings. My mainstream supervisor was clearly very knowledgeable about the intricacies of counselling but unaware of theories around culture, race and oppression which signify the lives of racialised groups. Although there was reciprocity in the learning process for both agencies, and both supervisors possessed expert knowledge, only the mainstream supervisor could complete my evaluations.

I now recognise and validate the experiences and academic training of the workers at these innovative and ethno-specific agencies where some of our students are subsequently hired. The breakthrough for me had to do with how I bridged the culture of mainstream agencies/institutions with my non-dominant status, a sustaining yet constant feature of my work. When I was present at the mainstream agency my body, my mind and my being shifted to accommodate the norms of western British thinking. When I met with the clients I tried to locate my questions, assessments and reports within the knowledge and theoretical base of my university text and learning. My colleagues intimidated me with their passion for 'object relations theory' (where analysis of race was absent), which they used with all their clients and saw the breakthroughs and fit for all through this particular theory. I felt that I did not belong to therapy, the mainstream setting or this form of 'clinical' work. While I knew about the theory and valued its meaning I was not attracted to using only one way of working with clients. At this point I vowed never to work in a mainstream counselling agency because I did not 'fit'.

There was a marked divergence in the culture and climate at the multicultural agency. One can view such a setting as flexible, loose, astructural and atheoretical. My knowledge base expanded to include the plight of the immigrant and refugee, settlement and integration, violence, torture and the constant need to respond to community issues. There were proposals to write in order to keep the agency afloat, funders to negotiate with, responses to incidents in the schools, the workplace, the media and the politicians who need these immigrant groups to get votes. I questioned why mainstream agencies were not linked with multicultural agencies and groups?

My breakthrough in practice then was to seek ways to partner both agencies. The mainstream agency invited the multicultural agency in for training and development around multicultural and cross cultural issues. Through ongoing work with the directors of these two agencies a long standing relationship ensued where the mainstream agency received core funding to work with immigrant groups in the area of violence and became more deeply involved in other cross cultural work. At this time culture, ethnicity and multiculturalism were the key words being utilised. Words like race and racism were seldom mentioned, and, in retrospect, I was afraid to use these terms with my supervisors and other workers.

I had to create and maintain an identity within a mainstream organisation which demanded assimilation ... difference counted when you attracted the 'other' but within you had to produce the knowledge of the master in order to be recognised as authentic. Some of these experiences of authenticity as a practitioner emerged clearly during my other practicum experience. My supervisor readily stated his lack of knowledge around diversity. It was not an apology, simply one of disinterest (Razack, in press). When I shared the process and approach of working with a refugee young man and I reinterpreted his narrative with my supervisor, I was made to feel in no uncertain terms that I was not 'doing' therapy and my work was not as authentic and rigorous. What he meant was that doing therapy with white clients around relationships or family issues would then allow him to work with the theoretical knowledge he was accustomed to so he would maintain his powerful position of the knower. He succeeded in intimidating me at times but I became strengthened as I observed his discomfort around difference and his gaps in knowledge around oppression.

These incidents have fuelled my insistence of narrative and voice scholarship for those on the margins. Legitimising one's story can create the catalyst for empowerment and change. Beattie & Randell (1997) discuss the need for social workers to read the powerful stories written by refugees in order to 'anticipate the needs of people whose experiences have included turmoil, flight, internment and relocation' (p.4). The true meaning of social work continued to be shaped from these experiences and I became convinced that the narrative was critical to practice and the voices of the marginalised had to assist in making change.

I conducted my research for the thesis component in graduate school jointly with a community development/social policy student of colour. We decided to interview and write about the experiences of professional immigrant women. The literature during the eighties focused on working class immigrant and refugees (Warren, 1986). Undoubtedly this topic emerged from our experiences of marginalisation within the classroom and the practicum setting. Our first interview shattered us and we could not speak or make contact with each other until a few days later. We were simply taken aback by the oppressive experiences of a very articulate and experienced social worker. She described her isolation and loneliness from the point of immigration to her present position within a mainstream organisation. Her metaphors to describe her pain were astounding. On immigration she noted that 'the apartment felt like a ship with corridors.'

The voices of all the women we interviewed startled us as to our own reality and what we would expect to face as professional immigrant women in social work. The resilience of our participants in the face of abject discrimination and racism gave us the strength to resist and be heard. I am not without these thoughts and meanings today when I teach in the academy. I know of the struggles first hand and can readily attest to the way in which power and dominance are sustained.

As a practitioner

As a student intern I vowed that I would not work in a mainstream counselling agency and ironically this is where I was employed after graduate school. These agencies are highly coveted by graduate clinical workers and I felt lucky to be offered a position without the years of experience. I came to this agency knowing that I was expected to deliver in many ways. My visible presence was a bonus for the agency, that I was knowledgable about western theory and was interested in building bridges and links with the community were also critical for political and economic reasons. My breakthrough in these areas was to recognise my potential and be able to harness my strengths to build community, to outreach to immigrant groups and to make my presence felt by working at ways to be included, not only through mainstream thinking, but by voice, by knowledge of difference, by inclusion and by education. These breakthroughs are not only critical for the minority students, but for all students to be able to include a range of perspectives for social work to respond to issues around justice, inclusion and oppression.

I did not learn about theories of oppression in graduate school and was unable to fully grasp the politics of power and dominance. I knew about power in the therapeutic relationship, in supervision because of the hierarchy and expert knowledge, in the organisation with multiple layers and roles. I did not yet learn about the way in which power is organised through differences and identity. Thus my quest to fit in and be recognised as being authentic predicated my work and therefore the notion of peddling ten times as fast reared its head once again.

My breakthroughs occurred in my ability to facilitate a relationship with all clients in respectful and challenging ways despite some of the rhetoric inherent in forming clinical relationships. I knew that I could be effective working with clients from different groups because I identified with their issues and I wanted them to feel a sense of belonging coming to this white dominant agency. I firmly believe that one has to manifest outwardly and inwardly a desire to understand difference, diversity, race and oppression in order to work effectively with different client groups. I have come to realise that being a good, caring and empathic social worker is not enough (Munro, 1998; Rossiter, 1996). The double consciousness of my life and the efforts on others' behalf to view everyone as the same, a 'colour blind' perspective, deny the uniqueness of the individual and the realities of oppression in having to function in a white dominated world.

Understanding the limitations of practice and development in a social service agency were key areas. I had to realise that I could not be all things for all the immigrants and people of colour who needed counselling. Again my supervisors had to learn with me about these realities. While I gained knowledge about therapy and intervention skills I was also able to facilitate community outreach activities, partnerships and programs for immigrant women and children. The agency was open to new ideas, new ways of practice, diversity and difference although in a very additive way. The culture of these counselling agencies is so steeped in traditional voice and thinking around therapy that one can easily become intimidated which can lead to a belief of not belonging and not possessing the right kind of knowledge. I entered academia with these reflections on education and practice.

On academia

I came to academia from the community with the profound belief that there were inherent inconsistencies in social work and that there was dissonance for me in every arena. My knowledge base was rooted in my conflictual educative and practice locations. I know that values are always attached to the theory I learn and practise (Humphries, 1997). However the meanings change depending on the various contexts and growth experiences. The contradictions produced from my locations and roles demanded ongoing critical reflection and I felt ready for a new challenge to bridge community and academia. I was aware that changes needed to be made within this large metropolitan school where there is a rich diversity of students. Students had begun to show their dissatisfaction with the lack of content in the curricula around oppression, among other issues, and created unrest by writing letters and organising sit-ins for the administration to take notice. My beginning tasks as a faculty field education coordinator were to ensure that our placement sites included innovative and ethno-specific agencies, to meet student needs in terms of their learning experiences, to teach courses, and to conduct research. My prior feelings of isolation and marginalisation within mainstream institutions continued.

There is no doubt that the position of field coordinator in itself creates this marginalised status since all field coordinators are over-burdened. However, my experiences in the institution also speak of the dialectic around race, racism, oppression, colonisation and imperialism. Unsettling situations around oppression are not fully discussed. Hiring and recruitment strategies produce tensions and the traditional setting remains largely intact. This summer I was on a panel to share experiences with new faculty entering our university. Although equity policies appear fairly progressive and seem to be well entrenched, the reality of having two minority faces amidst the majority white group astounded me and I acknowledge that there may be others with 'invisible' marginalised status within the group. Bannerji (1991); Carty (1991); hooks (1994); Spivak (1993) talk about their conflictual roles within the academy. Their struggles are similar as they recognise the dilemmas inherent for those of us with insider/outsider status.

I have to be constantly vigilant in the classroom and I always challenge my pedagogical approaches. I seek material which will allow students to produce their own knowledge base and create a dialogical space through the formation of coalitions. Recently a student of colour shared how she sensed my caution in strongly naming racism and this remark has rested within me. I realise that white academics teaching anti-racism and anti-oppression will always be viewed differently since their body is not marked like a faculty of colour. I try to engage the white students to view their power and privilege through a critical democratic learning process where all views are respected and challenged. However, I do so with caution knowing the dangers of backlash.

Breakthroughs for practice are also evident in the ways in which I continue to respect, value and incorporate community within the academy while knowing that the canons of thought and scholarly work focus more on abstract and 'intellectual' inquiry. These issues continue to shape my teaching, writing and practice, and are in keeping with the merging of teaching and practice modalities for social work. I continuously question my subject location. The notion of 'peddling ten times as fast' continues in my role as a faculty field coordinator, and more so as a minority faculty member.

Critical self reflective theory and practice approaches inform my present realities. It has been important for me to reflect on my former roles in social work to build a knowledge base and philosophy for academic work. I realise that the traditional theory will be everlastingly etched into pedagogy and practice. What is imperative is that the underlying and critical analyses used to implement the canons should include anti-oppressive and anti-racist analyses and theories. These critical race and oppressive theories should be inherent in any dialogue, modality, constructs and analytical tools for social work. Social justice issues need to be understood from global and transnational perspectives in order for social workers to indigenise their practice approaches. Promoting an interlocking approach to understanding oppression (Hill-Collins, 1990) is critical for understandings of racism, imperialism, patriarchy and postcoloniality. This approach should ground our thinking when teaching in any of the critical areas for social work. As Bannerji (1991) states:

> *My pedagogic choice to teach at all, in this country, and what I insistently teach about, have something to do with de-colonisation of myself and others, my*

innermost need to fight patriarchal imperialist racism. And existentially, with my anger, to make it visible for myself, for others, to make it political. (p.9)

Theorising our reflections, responses and knowledge base to make meanings in our work is ongoing. Concepts can be intellectualised, but the challenge remains in translating these concepts into practice. If we can view social issues as global concerns then we can indigenise responses befitting our local realities. A processual learning centred approach helps us to persist in our quest for meanings and practice perspectives.

References

Bannerji, H. (1991) 'Re: turning the gaze', *Resources for Feminist Research*, 20, 3/4, 5-11

Beattie, M. & Randell, J. (1997) 'Using refugee stories in social work education', *Journal of Multicultural Social Work*, 6, 3-15

Bhavani, K. & Phoenix, A. (eds.) (1994) *Shifting Identities, Shifting Racisms: A feminism and psychology reader*, Sage, London

Brotman, S. & Pollack, S. (1997) 'Loss of context: the problem of merging postmodernism with feminist social work', *Canadian Social Work Review*, 14, 1, 9-21

Brown, C. (1994) 'Feminist postmodernism and the challenge of diversity', in Chambon, A. & Irving, A. (eds.) *Essays on Postmodernism and Social Work*, Canadian Scholars' Press, Toronto

Carty, L. (1991) 'Women's studies in Canada: A discourse and praxis of exclusion', *Resources for Feminist Research*, 20, 3/4, 12-19

Gibelman, M. (1999) 'The search for identity: Defining social work —past, present, future', *Social Work*, 44, 4, 298-310

Harstock, N. (1990) 'Foucault on power: a theory for women?', in Nicholson, L. (ed) *Feminism/Postmodernism*, Routledge, Chapman and Hall, New York

Hill-Collins, P. (1990) *Black Feminist Thought*, Routledge, New York

hooks, b. (1994) *Teaching to Transgress: Education as the practice of freedom*, Routledge, New York

Humphries, B. (1997) 'The dismantling of anti-discrimination in British social work: A view from social work education', *International Social Work*, 40, 289-301

Ife, J. (1997) *Rethinking Social Work: Towards critical practice*. Longman, Melbourne

Johnson, Y.M. (1999) 'Indirect work: Social work's uncelebrated strength', *Social Work*, 44, 4, 323-334

Jones, A. (1997) 'Teaching post-structuralist feminist theory in education', *Gender and Education*, 9, 3, 261-269

Leonard, P. (1994) 'Knowledge/power and postmodernism: implications for the practice of a critical social work education', *Canadian Social Work Review*, 11, 1, 11-26

Mullaly, B. (1997) *Structural Social Work: Ideology, theory and practice*, Oxford, University Press, Toronto

Munro, E. (1998) *Understanding Social Work. An empirical approach*, Athlone Press, London

Musisi, N.B. (1999) Catalyst, nature, and vitality of African-Canadian Feminism: a panorama of an emigre feminist, in A. Heitlinger (ed.) *Emigré Feminism: Transnational perspectives*, University of Toronto Press, Toronto

Pease, B. & Fook, J. (eds.) (1999) *Transforming social work practice: Postmodern critical perspectives*, Routledge, London

Razack, N. (1999) 'Anti-discriminatory practice: Pedagogical struggles and challenges', *British Journal of Social Work*, 29, 2, 231-250

Razack, N. (in press) 'Diversity and difference in the field education encounter: Issues and challenges of racial minority students, *Social Work Education*

Razack, N., Teram, E. & Rivera, M. (1995) Cultural diversity in field work education: 'A practice model for enhancing cross cultural knowledge', in Rogers, G. (ed) *Social Work Field Education: Views and visions*, Dubuque: Kendall/Hunt

Rossiter, A. (1996) 'A critical perspective on social work', *Journal of Progressive Human Services*, 7, 2, 23-41

Schneider, R.L. & Netting, E. (1999) 'Influencing social policy in a time of devolution: Upholding social work's great tradition'. *Social Work*, 44, 4, 349-357

Spivak, G.C. (1993) *Outside in the Teaching Machine*, Routledge, New York

Swain, J. & Cameron, C. (1999) 'Unless otherwise stated: Discussions of labelling and identity in coming out', in Carter, M. & French, S. (eds.) *Disability Discourse*, Open University Press, Buckingham and Philadelphia

Warren, C.E. (1986) *Vignettes of Life: Experiences and Self Perceptions of New Canadian Women*. Detselig Enterprises, Calgary, AB

10
Learning to practise with the tensions between professional discretion and agency procedure

Mark Baldwin

Background

I have worked as a social worker or with social workers since the early 1970s, and currently teach students on a Diploma in Social Work Programme at the University of Bath in the United Kingdom. This connects me with social work and practitioners in many parts of the profession. As a researcher, I am interested in the development of learning for social workers, and have worked with social workers in a variety of organisations. There is a brief story that needs to be told so that the reader can appreciate how it was that I came to be doing the work that this chapter describes.

As a researcher, I wanted to match my learning with my other interests and responsibilities so it seemed natural to be asking social workers what sources of knowledge inform their practice. There have been major policy initiatives in adult services (community care in the UK), and it is this area of welfare development in the UK involving practitioners at the front line in changes of policy, organisation, practice and ethos in which I have my interest. In order to provide focus, I looked at the sophisticated task of needs assessment in care management, a practice still largely carried out by social workers. In the initial stages I was influenced by traditional methods of exploration. I engaged with care managers in two Social Services Departments, using a semi-structured interview schedule to explore the questions that interested me. This part of the story is told elsewhere (Baldwin, 1995; 1996), but it is important to summarise it here as the result directed me to the more helpful approach described in this chapter.

I learnt that care managers were not practising in accordance with the new policies and procedures imposed following the National Health Service and Community Care Act of 1990. Many aspects of the policy were being undermined partly because the care managers perceived a culture that was alien to their values and motivation for social work. They were operating as 'Street Level Bureaucrats' as described by Lipsky (1980), constructing policy through their use of discretion, and more or less deliberately undermining practices which were at odds with their espoused values. Lack of discrimination in their use of discretion, however, meant that they were also working against practices which were congruent with these same values. They chose, notably, not to engage in needs-led and service user-focused assessments because they believed assessments raised expectations and that many service users were unable or uninterested in being involved in their assessments. My second area of concern was that their awareness of the gap between policy expectations and their practice created apprehension. It was my opinion that this anxiety was the result of a lack of clarity in their role. How could they know how to practise when there was a contradiction within the official documentation and rhetoric of community care (Baldwin, 1997)?

There was, however, a bigger lesson for me from these interviews. The report that I produced for the two organisations and sent to each interviewee, elicited little response. What I learnt about this method of investigation is that it excludes the people who are being researched. The people whom I interviewed did not appear to feel any ownership of the meaning I attached to their responses. Although the findings were of interest and have been published (Baldwin, 1995), they are unlikely to make any difference to the practice of those concerned.

If I was right about the undermining of policy then my insights were of little value because they did not change the practices which the research had exposed..

Later, when I investigated whether policy was still being undermined by street level bureaucrats, I had to decide whether to repeat what seemed to be a sterile exercise of traditional qualitative research, or to engage in a different approach. In searching for a new form of investigation, I came across a cluster of methodologies entitled participative action research. It was 'cooperative inquiry' that seemed most appropriate and it was this approach (Heron, 1996) that I adopted. The following are some of the key aspects of the method:

- Research is organised and carried out with those it concerns and not on them.
- It aims to change or reinforce understanding of the area of investigation for all those involved so is transformative in nature.
- The approach removes the boundaries between researcher and subject, with all involved engaging together in a process of inquiry akin to learning cycles:

- identifying issues/questions to be investigated
- developing a model of practice for all involved to follow
- testing this model out and recording the outcomes
- providing opportunities for co-researchers to reflect with each other on these outcomes in a constructively critical way
- changing understanding and future action as a result of these reflections (if appropriate) and then proceeding to further cycles of action and reflection as long as is necessary
- Cooperative inquiry is a systematic model for incorporating reflection and reflective practice in the way that is explored in other chapters in this book.
- Engaging in cooperative inquiry with social workers

When I engaged with social workers in cooperative inquiry I was revisiting my research questions about the limits to policy implementation and the role of street level implementers. Could cooperative inquiry as a research methodology facilitate reflection and action that would lead to productive learning and practice development that addressed these limitations? Also, in the spirit of cooperative inquiry as a participative venture, I wanted to respond to the interests of group members.

I started the process by making an offer to a social services department to feed back the findings from the original interviews, and to ask practitioners to question whether the findings were 'true for them?'. I then offered practitioners the opportunity to engage with me in one or more cooperative inquiry groups. Those involved in the workshops were all carrying out a care management function - assessment, care planning, monitoring and review - for adult services provision. They were all qualified social workers.

There was agreement that the original findings were a matter of concern to current social workers. For instance service users were still getting assessments of their needs distorted by resource availability. The principle concern was that bureaucratic process, along with resource constraint, was stifling the use of professional discretion, effectively 'managing out' social work as a service. This predicament undermined their role by marginalising the knowledge, skills and values of social work practice. In addition, social work as a preventive service was being marginalised by an obsession with more formalised services, notably residential care. Targeting those in greatest need was still viewed as an ineffective way of providing service as it frequently meant waiting until informal support networks fail before providing formal services in response to crisis. In this way, organisational processes often undermined professional social work practice.

Following the workshops, two cooperative inquiry groups were formed. One was a team of five hospital based social workers (hospital group), and the other (community group) was formed from a collection of social workers, most of whom were in different teams. This group numbered eight. The two groups met separately, and I was asked to facilitate them. Both groups completed eight cycles of action and reflection, as indicated above. We agreed in both groups that they should be closed, in terms of involvement by others, but inclusive, ensuring that all members were present before proceeding. Apart from one absence, every session took place and was fully attended, demonstrating serious commitment and involvement. At the first meeting there was an 'idea-storming' session, in which the potential for exploration through cooperative inquiry was noted and areas for investigation were selected. Decisions were made about action to be taken and how it could be recorded, prior to reconvening for the first reflective meeting.

We had reached a point at which the cooperative inquiry groups had been formed within the broad framework that I had set out. Although it is I, who was not the practitioner, who is now describing the group learning process, it is important to stress the democratic nature of the groups, and that the areas of investigation were chosen by them. It is interesting that the two groups chose similar areas, and that they were concerned with exploring anxiety about their practice. We noted the degree to which feelings can disrupt learning - a point noted elsewhere (Boud and Knights, 1996), and agreed that, if anxiety was not tackled, it would sit silently in the room undermining commitment to mutual learning. We also felt that a focus on practice over which they had some day-to-day control was more practical and achievable than looking at areas such as resource deficit.

The aims of these cycles of action and reflection were much the same for myself and other participants. They were interested in exploring the limits of practice development within the policy context of care management, whilst utilising their social work practice. There was, particularly in the community group, a belief that professional discretion was being killed off by the new role of care management imposed by a management agenda ruled by resource constraint rather than service provision values. I was interested in seeing how far the process of inquiry could investigate areas such as the discretionary use of professional knowledge, and, to see how the conjunction of social work skills with the new role of care management might be the catalyst for the creation of new knowledge informing a new practice. I had already noted that the exchange model (Smale et al, 1993) of practice in assessment and care management had the potential to maximise social work knowledge, skills and values in an empowering model of resource allocation. How achievable was this practice, using cooperative inquiry as the motivating force?

The Process of cooperative inquiry

The first meetings for both groups established ground-rules around group processes. We discussed the manner in which we were to relate to one another, for example avoiding personal comments, but forming a mutual agreement that problematic issues would always be raised and addressed in the group. These discussions are similar to those in the groupwork literature (e.g. Brown, 1994) where it is argued that establishing ground rules at the earliest opportunity makes it more likely that unforeseen eventualities that might block group processes will be dealt with effectively.

The principal anxiety identified as a prime area for investigation was the lack of consistency between individual team members and between teams. How, inquirers wondered, would they know what the agency's practice requirements were? This question was a surprise, given the existence of comprehensive guidance documents. What was apparent to both groups, quite independently, was that interpretation of guidance varied between individual workers and across teams. It was this differentiation that created the anxiety. It can be seen that the methodology was already helping the reflective process. Participants were immediately learning about the source of some of the debilitating anxiety that undermined their effectiveness.

Hospital group

The hospital group tackled consistency by focusing on one part of the care management procedure to investigate variations in practice. Potential service users are asked to sign a form that provides the social worker with consent to contact third parties to collect information. Consent was seen by the agency as good practice reflecting partnership. Social workers in the hospital group had found that requesting service users to sign this document was threatening, disorientating or even oppressive. When they felt this to be the case, they did not ask for a signature, even though they knew they ought to. The group accepted the value of the procedure, but were concerned about its effect. It was a procedure that involved the exercise of discretion and was thus worthy of investigation. It allowed the group to investigate the extent to which policy was undermined by their discretion.

A technique of investigation and recording was devised. Every time that one of the forms should have been completed, participants were to record the circumstances and whether they chose to exercise their discretion. They were required to justify their actions, both to themselves and to their peers in the group. This provided an opportunity to both reflect-in-action ('why am I practising like this now?') and, at a later time to reflect-on-action ('why did I ask that person to sign the form but not this one?'), in the way described by Schon (1987). The process was followed for three consecutive cycles of action and reflection. At the third meeting one participant questioned the purpose of continuing this exercise. This challenge was important for me as it indicated that the group were prepared to challenge the process of cooperative inquiry and to make it work for them. The methodology should be flexible and responsive, but participants do have to ensure that such flexibility actually operates effectively.

The result of this challenge was an informative investigation into intuition. As facilitator I asked group members how they knew when it was the 'right' moment to ask someone to sign the form. The first response was 'I know intuitively when it is right' - 'I get a gut feeling'. We deconstructed the concept of intuition, asking how the social worker knows, and where the knowledge comes from. We identified the social work theory, values, and skills, as well as the assumptions and prejudices that sometimes converge to make us practise in a particular way. It was this combination of knowledge that had been informing practice in a generally unreflective way prior to the group's engagement in the cooperative inquiry process. Every time we got to the bottom of intuition, defining it and describing it, we were still left with something indefinable, which was labelled intuition again! 'I just knew that I shouldn't push her on signing the form.' This acceptance of intuition as a valid form of knowledge, assuming this process of critical appraisal, was another important aspect of learning that we recognised had been facilitated by the method.

I described what I saw as a 'threshold technique' intuitively (at best) or unreflectively (at worst) being employed by group members. At some point they recognised that an individual met some undefined criterion that meant they could 'cope' with being asked to complete the required paperwork, and was then asked to sign the form. How did they know that they had crossed that threshold? What knowledge, what skills, were being employed to assist that decision? An exercise was developed, with a system of recording, to enable group members to go into the next action phase and engage in utilising the threshold technique. This technique, plus the recording process used in the inquiry cycles, encouraged the social workers to maximise practice with service users and to adopt a reflective approach within their work.

When we met again we were able to engage once more in the process of defining knowledge for practice - including further analysis of intuition. Intuition was believed to be integral to creativity as long as there was attention paid to the importance of reflection and critical analysis. Reflection enabled group members to differentiate the use of knowledge informed by the values of empowerment they espoused in theory, from the more assumptive or stereotypical practice that they recognised occurred if they were not engaged in a reflective process. Recognition of the dangers of assumption created worries which were tackled within the group. 'Return to experience' (Boud and Knights, 1996) was a key to this process of developing reflection-in-action. Whenever new ways of understanding were created in the group they were tested out and incorporated into behaviour that was confirmed or adapted accordingly. For all of them, however, it was anxiety-provoking to recognise the potential for discriminatory actions. Discrimination is such a negative factor in contemporary social work ethos that to identify and deal with it was very empowering. Boud also notes that attending to feelings is a key part of effective learning.

The importance of reflection in and upon action was established as a key to the maintenance of, and the continuing development of 'good' practice. The cooperative inquiry group was providing this opportunity, but what would happen when it finished? The hospital group also recognised that social work was often the only service preventing the breakdown of informal supports and the imposition of more restrictive services. How could they protect the space for good quality assessments, develop a preventative service, and ensure that they had opportunities for reflection and practice development? To answer these questions we explored the ways that supervision might establish more creative practice through providing opportunities for reflection as well as workload management. We also tested out the possibilities for mutual aid and mutual reflection. Through the cooperative inquiry process the team developed individual and collective techniques for replicating the most useful aspects of the cooperative inquiry in anticipation of its closure after the agreed six month period. An example of this, which may appear trivial, but was not to this team, was the use of a signal which was placed on their desk when they felt pressurised. Colleagues would then know to offer support but also create space and time. The team also started to move beyond the business focus of team meetings and use them in a more reflective and critically evaluative way than they had for some time.

Community group

The community group also decided to investigate a part of the procedure that could lead to inconsistent interpretation and practice. As with the hospital group this inconsistency was making them apprehensive and they were concerned to investigate the possibilities of developing practice which was congruent with both agency procedure and agreed values in social work. This group were surprised to discover that professional discretion was still possible in the new world of care management. To discover that they were using discretion unreflectively added to their anxiety. Inconsistency was thus as much to do with their own thoughtless practice as other factors outside their control. Having discovered this for themselves through the cooperative inquiry process, the group were better able to own this learning and change their practice. Over the months they explored continuously the ways in which they could bring agency policy and professional practice into greater congruence. This was another example of practitioners, engaged in cooperative inquiry, learning about the importance of critical reflection, and the usefulness of the method in achieving this collectively.

The process the community group adopted was to provide each of them with time to talk about a recent piece of work, and to question them in a supportive but challenging way which deconstructed the sources of knowledge informing their practice. The discussions were similar to the hospital group's exploration of intuition, although the influence of organisational constraints resulted in off-loading and support being more of a feature, probably because it was less cohesive than the hospital group. The cooperative inquiry approach provided them with an opportunity for the mutual creation of knowledge and understanding that was then tried and tested in practice. One member shared how he used the group to enable him to 'reflect-in-action'. He did this by asking himself 'what would the group think of me doing this, saying that?' When engaged with service users. I thought this was an impressive extension of group reflection into everyday practice.

The community group were keen to investigate organisational processes and what they termed 'buffeting' and how they might resist it. Buffeting was what happened when resource management was the dominant approach to managing their practice. Buffeting reduced their scope for professional discretion and marginalised the social work in their assessment and care planning with service users. An example of this was the reduced time workers have for face-to-face contact with service users as a result of the proliferation of procedures within care management. The community group believed (as many social workers carrying out a care management role have experienced (Baldwin, 1995; 1996) that the procedures are more geared to the resource management agenda than to service provision. Social work, a key set of skills for assessment and care provision, and for the prevention of more restrictive options such as residential care, was what they felt they could offer, and it was being 'buffeted' by managerial concerns. As with the hospital group, they did recognise that bureaucratic procedures enhance good practice and equality of access to services. On occasions this meant the use of discretion to redefine such procedures, and plan how they would defend this in the face of managerial hostility. We learnt that procedures are often at odds with agency mission statements, and this enabled them to resist managerial definitions of practice in favour of definitions more in tune with the mission statement, and social work values. This area of learning enabled members of the group to re-emphasise the helping social work element in their relationships with service users and to be more assertive with managers about the effectiveness of this.

Learning from these cooperative inquiry groups

There is much in the literature (Heron, 1996) about the validity of cooperative inquiry, and the safeguards that have been developed in these groups ensured a high degree of congruence between what is now owned and stated by me and what was agreed collectively in the groups.

Two major themes that have evolved from these inquiries take us back to Lipsky's (1980) arguments about how social workers, as street level bureaucrats, can undermine policy and procedure. Discretion and accountability are the two areas that provided the greatest learning for me. We found ourselves addressing the question of what accountability means if it is to enhance positive use of discretion rather than the more negative and tacit use which creates anxiety for practitioners and undermines policy. Participants were concerned that inconsistency could result in an inequitable or discriminatory service being provided. This would damage their commitment to social work values which seek to avoid the replication of disadvantage for service users. Accountability, in this context, is about justification of practice. To justify our practice we have to understand and own it, and this requires the sort of participative reflective learning process that cooperative inquiry provides. Through the process, both groups recognised their belief that they had little discretion and that accountability was lodged within the bureaucratic procedures was an incorrect assumption. As they increasingly understood that they were practising inconsistently, and that the degree of leeway in their treatment of different service users was largely in their control, so the process of accountability, justification and evaluation of practice became more important. The cooperative inquiry provided the opportunity for reflection, understanding and change in practice. We have seen the example with the hospital group altering the way they worked with the consent form. The community group looked carefully at how far they included service users in the assessment process more generally. 'Hearing the voice' of service users is an important value in community care practice. It requires procedures and appropriately sensitive practice to achieve it. The cooperative inquiry helped members of both groups to match their practice with the procedures, their use of discretion with accountability.

Bureaucratic procedures can provide equality of opportunity for potential service users, particularly when procedures are used within participatory relationships and not applied administratively. The groups also learnt that critical reflection is an essential element. The usual places for such reflection are in supervision and team discussion, but because of pressures of work and management style, these opportunities are not always available to practitioners. The cooperative inquiry created such an opportunity, thus exposing what participants had been missing hitherto. To engage in cooperative inquiry, therefore, enabled us to recognise two things. Firstly how important reflection is in the process of understanding and action in learning and the development of practice, but also that cooperative inquiry is an effective way of achieving this. Replicating this group approach to learning and practice development has been an important progression, particularly for the Hospital Group who already operate as a team.

The inquiry groups gave participants the opportunity to reflect positively and developmentally on their use of discretion in relationship with service users. There was an ownership of poor practice as participants reflected on their prior use of discretion and then devised methods for testing out more positive approaches, returning to reflect within the group on their success. As this iterative process of action, reflection and learning proceeded, so we learnt that the death of discretion in the face of coercive bureaucracy had been exaggerated. Intuition was seen as an important concept in analysing the use of discretion. The groups attempted to deconstruct intuition, reflecting on how it can reveal assumptions, based on prior knowledge and experience. It became apparent that, without critical reflection, intuition can dictate practice and result in inconsistency and discrimination. The groups were left with a deep commitment to the importance of intuition as a major source of creativity in practice. This is a view supported heavily by the work of writers such as England and Jordan (England, 1986; Jordan, 1984; Jordan, 1979; Brandon and Jordan, 1979).

Bureaucratic procedures shifted from being symbols of managerial excess to opportunities for resistance. They were seen as models of good practice which urge a needs-led, user-focused and participative practice which was in opposition to the resource management position favoured in managerial practice. The groups started to think about developments beyond the good practice defined by the forms, looking, for instance, at more sophisticated ways of seeking service user feedback, and considering how services might become more relevant to people from minority ethnic communities who are often denied access to services as a result of racism.

The groups moved beyond the anxieties of resource shortfall, and developed practice reflecting their values rather than managerialist concerns. It was strongly argued, with managers, that these social work values are more congruent with the Authority's mission statement of 'service' than the managerialism they were resisting. One example of this is the social model of disability (Oliver, 1996), which they felt was a key value informing practice. The use of targeting within resource management is a form of labelling at odds with the social model. Most participants had been on training courses provided by the Authority emphasising this model in opposition to the pathologising effects of the medical model.

We learnt that practice has two extremes, both of which could result in poor services. At one end is unreflective discretion leading to inconsistency or discrimination. At the other end is habitual routine, leading to unimaginative or stereotypical responses to individual need. The pursuit of balance between these two poles provided an analytical tool for reflective practice that was very helpful to these groups. Discretion can be a positive force for developmental practice if it is reflected upon critically. Collectively we learnt more about the practical worth of reflection and developed some tools to facilitate it. I was not surprised that reflection was identified as important but was pleased that it was so apparent to the groups. The creation of analytical tools that could be used outside of the inquiries was a surprise to me, and will help me in my other roles.

Group members are still left with anxieties about consistency in their practice and the lack of clear guidance from their Authority. The gap between what they ought to be doing and what they are doing is often filled by resource constraints, which pressurise workers into practice, which they know is not congruent with either policy intentions or social work values. There remains considerable pressure, some of it self-imposed, upon social workers to assess according to what is available, rather than to develop collaborative needs-based assessments with service users. Both groups committed themselves to greater use of service deficit recording as their responsibility in the process of developing responsive services, but had not had the opportunity to test this out before the groups finished. Organisational blocks to creative packages of care still exist but the imperative to develop practice and the opportunities to do so is better understood as a result of our cooperative reflection.

The purpose of cooperative inquiry is the mutual creation of owned and useable knowledge. In reflecting on these cooperative inquiries, it has been shown that this purpose can be fulfilled by social workers investigating their practice in a participative and reflective environment. Unlike the knowledge gleaned from the earlier interviews, this knowledge held meaning for co-researchers which they both owned and adopted in their practice. As street level implementers, both groups recognised that they are able to use their discretion to influence the introduction of policy. This influence can be positive or negative, but they will be unable to differentiate the nature of the influence unless they adopt a reflective approach to their use of discretion. Cooperative inquiry, as a form of active learning, proved successful in facilitating the incorporation of understanding into practice.

It is easy to be sceptical about the potential for replicating this process of reflection and practice development in organisations still wedded to coercive forms of managerialism, but I conclude that this was an experiment that demonstrated that some of the negative results of unreflective discretion can be identified and dealt with in practice. Such experiments do require further investigation, but if policy implementation deficit created through the professional decision-making of street level implementers is to be avoided, this approach is essential. Coercive management using technical proceduralism has not worked. I am far more optimistic about collaborative approaches to policy implementation. Increasing exploration of the concept of learning organisation (Senge, 1990; Argyris and Schon, 1996; Pottage and Evans, 1994) would seem to provide the theoretical context in which to locate the organisational requirements for such developments.

Bibliography

Argyris, C. and Schon, D. (1996) *Organisational Learning II: Theory, method and practice, reading,* Addison-Wesley, Massachusetts

Baldwin. M. (1995) *The Meaning of Care Management,* Social Work Monographs, Norwich

Baldwin, M. (1996) 'Is assessment working? Policy and practice in care management', *Practice,* 8, 4, 53-59

Baldwin, M. (1997) 'Key texts in community care: The analysis of discourse in government and government commissioned documents which relate to care management', *Social Work and Social Sciences Review,* 7, 2, 76-88

Boud, D. and Knights, S. (1996) 'Course design for reflective practice', in Gould, N. and Taylor, I. (eds) *Reflective Learning for Social Work,* Arena, Aldershot

Brandon, D. and Jordan, B. (1979) *Creative Social Work,* Blackwell, Oxford

Brown, A. (1994) 'Groupwork in Britain', in Hanvey, C. and Philpot, T. *Practising Social Work,* Routledge, London

England, H. (1986) *Social Work as Art,* Allen and Unwin, London

Gould, N. and Taylor, I. (1996) (eds) *Reflective Learning for Social Work,* Arena, Aldershot

Hanvey, C. and Philpot, T. (1994) *Practising Social Work,* Routledge, London

Heron, J. (1996) *Co-operative Inquiry, Research into the Human Condition,* Sage, London

Jordan, B. (1979) *Helping in Social Work,* Routledge and Kegan Paul, London

Jordan, B. (1984) *Invitation to Social Work,* Blackwell, Oxford

Lipsky (1980) *Street Level Bureaucrats: Dilemmas of the individual in public services,* Russell Sage Foundation, New York

Oliver, M. (1996) *Understanding Disability: From theory to practice,* Macmillan, Basingstoke

Pottage, D. and Evans, M. (1994) *The Competent Workplace: The View from Within,* NISW, London

Schon, D. (1987) *Educating the Reflective Practitioner,* Jossey-Bass, San Francisco

Senge, P. (1990) *The Fifth Discipline: The art and practice of the learning organisation,* Random House, London

Smale, G., Tuson, G. with Biehal, N. and Marsh, P. (1993) *Empowerment, Assessment, Care Management and the Skilled Worker,* HMSO, London

11
A casework journey:
The search for directions

Rachel Balen

Introduction

I am a white, British, woman working as a Senior Lecturer in Social Work in a British University. I teach on an undergraduate social work (qualifying) course and a multi-disciplinary postgraduate child protection pathway. My own social work practice began after completing an Honours degree in English Language and Literature in 1975. I worked first as an unqualified residential child care worker then, once I had gained the Certificate of Qualification in Social Work, (now replaced in the UK by the Diploma in Social Work), I moved into fieldwork and spent several years as a social worker in a busy inner city office in northern England. Following completion of a Masters degree in Social and Community Work Studies, I became a Team Leader before moving into child protection training and then into teaching and tutoring on social work qualifying courses.

The case on which this chapter is based occurred many years ago now, but it is a situation to which my thoughts have kept returning over the years. What I hope to do over the following pages is to describe the situation, explore the process and outcome of the work carried out and then reflect on how it illustrates the complex nature of the relationship between theory and practice. My thoughts will offer no answers, solutions or guidelines but they may strike a chord with others who work in situations of risk, uncertainty and responsibility. All names and identifying details have been changed.

The agency setting

In 1985 I was working as a team leader in a local authority social services team in northern England. The workers in the team worked mainly with cases involving children and families who were seen to require long-term involvement. As a team leader I was responsible for providing support and supervision for these workers and I also carried a small caseload. The legislative context for this child and family work was regulated by The Children and Young Persons Act 1969 (which has subsequently been replaced by The Children Act 1989). The former legislation allowed, amongst other things, for children to be made subject to Care Orders by the courts (orders which gave the local authority parental rights and responsibilities), for children to be placed voluntarily in care by their parents and for amounts of money to be used preventatively to avoid the need for children to be received into care (known as 'Section One money').

The background to the case

Pat was a single, white woman of 23 living in a ground-floor flat on a very deprived council estate. She had two sons aged six and four years and was five months pregnant. Her sons had different fathers, with whom she and they had no contact, and her relationship with her current boyfriend, 18 year old Darren, was sporadic. He sometimes 'hung out' with Pat but was more often to be found drinking and playing pool with his mates. Pat had no extended family support, her mother had died when she was fourteen and she now had no contact with her father.

Three years earlier the local authority had applied to the court for, and been granted, Care Orders in respect of both boys. Concerns had centred on Pat's ability to care adequately for her children. Examples of her neglect of or failure to protect her children were given: One child had received burns to his leg after his brother had poked a stick into their living room gas fire and the other had been found by neighbours wandering alone down a main road near their home. Following the granting of the Care Orders the two boys had been placed with foster parents for a period but they were later placed back 'at home on trial'. Negotiations with the Housing Department had resulted in Pat being rehoused into her present accommodation with regular visiting by a social worker.

By the time of my involvement this 'home on trial' period had lasted for over two years because confidence in Pat's abilities had never grown sufficiently for Social Services to feel that they could safely apply to the courts for the Care Orders to be discharged. Health visitors were concerned about the delay in language development in the younger child and the older boy did not attend school regularly. Pat repeatedly requested money from Social Services in order to buy food, she was in arrears with her rent and, in addition, her flat was described by social workers and health visitors as dirty and disorganised. She was frequently visited by local teenagers who used her flat as a base whilst playing truant from school.

Indeed, concern was now mounting about the future safety, health and development of the children because of the additional pressures that it was felt would be caused by the arrival of a third child. As team leader I knew that I would shortly be required to chair a case conference to consider whether these children should be removed again and placed back into care, in a children's home or with foster parents.

Reading the map

Along with many other social workers of the time, my qualifying training had taken place during a period when notions of poverty, community and radicalism held sway and when there was rejection of the psychosocial casework perspectives of the 1960s. One of my key course texts had been Bailey and Brake's (1975) *Radical Social Work*, with its chapters on 'Its all right for you to talk: Political and sociological manifestos for social work action', 'Welfare rights and wrongs' and 'Community development: A radical alternative':

> ... it is perhaps becoming hackneyed to repeat the criticisms... that social workers have concentrated too much on theories of interpersonal relationships instead of examining the social, economic and political sources of problems and developing alternative, relevant strategies and ideologies. (p.73)

During study for my Masters degree I had chosen (voluntarily) to read and write about patriarchy, capitalism, gender and, although I didn't really know why at the time, concepts of love.

My early years as a social worker had led me onto run-down council estates with boarded up windows and vandalised telephone boxes and into houses with lumpy armchairs and ill-fitting curtains. I had chased up Social Security payments, applied for loans for cookers and washing machines, approached charities for holidays for children and, when all else had failed and warnings had been issued but proved ineffective, had received children into care, been a party to Care Proceedings in court and placed children with foster parents or for adoption.

At first work with Pat was more of the same. I recognised the stresses and strains of financial poverty, of single parenthood, of feckless men and of oppression by societal systems. I sought to protect the children through the giving of Section One money, the acquisition of material resources and the issuing of warnings about levels of concern for the children, a route that had been trodden by previous workers. Pat responded to these efforts with gratitude and with continuing dependence, but nothing changed. Phone calls would continue to come from health visitors and housing officers and Pat herself called at the Social Services office willingly and frequently to report some further mishap to one of the children or to explain that she had run out of money before her next giro-cheque was due. I certainly felt under some pressure. If her situation continued unchanged then I would be faced with the time-consuming, requirement-laden task of finding suitable placements for the children. To say nothing of the emotionally devastating effects this would have on Pat, who so clearly demonstrated both her love for her children and her inability to parent them adequately, and on the children themselves.

Stopping at the traffic lights

The work being done with Pat seemed to have a momentum of its own. The more we tried to ameliorate Pat's material domestic circumstances, always with a warning that we could not continue doing this if there was no corresponding improvement in her management of her life and of her children, the more contact she seemed to seek with us. She appeared to make this contact in order to tell us, unprompted, about circumstances that she knew would concern us, yet no-one who knew her doubted her commitment to and love for her children nor, in turn, their attachment to her. The more she told us of things that were happening to her or to the children day-by-day, the more inevitable it seemed that plans would have to be set in motion for removal of the children. I was dreading this and it was on my mind whether I was at work or at home.

One morning I was driving to work as usual and, as usual, reached the ring-road traffic lights just as they turned to red. I probably had the car radio on and I was not aware that I was thinking about anything in particular but I remember to this day the overwhelming feeling 'We just can't do this to this family' as I stopped at the lights. By the time I reached the end of my journey to work some half an hour later I had clarified for myself both my reaction and a possible way forward.

Reading the map again

Reflecting later on what had been going through my mind, I realised that although automatically dealing with road and traffic conditions, my thoughts had been preoccupied with trying to understand what was really going on for Pat. Why couldn't she understand the gravity of her situation? Why couldn't she get to grips with budgeting, with keeping her house clean and her children safe? Why did she choose men who behaved immaturely, were often chronologically younger than her and who offered no practical or, it seemed, emotional help? Why did she keep turning to Social Services for help and to confide in when she knew what powers we had and had used before?

How different she was from me! OK I didn't have children to contend with, but I was in control of my life, managed household tasks alongside full-time work and couldn't imagine ever needing or being required to endure the support or scrutiny of a social worker. We were both women - but then, of course, I had had a very different life. One of several children, good education, stable home life, gradual independence from protective but generally understanding parents.

As my thoughts moved on to trying to imagine how an earth I'd feel if I was Pat, I think I realised how much of our social work help for Pat was founded on a stance that was essentially critical of her. We made it as clear as we could for her what she had to do, on many occasions gave her material help to 'give her a good start' and visited regularly to see how well or badly she was doing. But if I was bringing my stable home life, good education, supportive parents into my life as an adult, what was Pat bringing?

The picture of Pat that came into my mind at those traffic lights was of an isolated young woman, no parents to support her, no parents (her mother had died) to help her from teenage to adulthood. Indeed, those 'friends' she did have were the teenagers who hung around in her flat and whom she could not turn away when they appeared asking for food and a hiding place, or those teenage young men who fathered her children and then moved on. A woman who loved her children, hugged them whilst she talked to us, bought them presents with money that was supposed to be for household goods and food and knew little about child rearing. (I remembered once asking Pat whether she talked much to her younger boy - there was concern that his language development was delayed - and she had said that she didn't really because, after all, he couldn't say anything much back to her.)

I was only about six or seven years older than her, but I felt so much more grown up. In fact, Pat wasn't grown up. I suddenly saw Pat as a teenager of fourteen. Her mother had died and Pat had stopped growing up. Her friends were teenagers, her boyfriends were teenagers and Pat behaved like teenagers sometimes do. She was not very good at budgeting (and her low income meant there was no room for mistakes), she sometimes found it hard to put the needs of others (her children) before her own, and she found it hard to say no to her 'peers' (she had often said that she was not going to let the teenage school truants into her flat any more, but she was never able to stick to this.) Nor did she have the confidence or self-esteem to struggle successfully with all the systems and attitudes that made life as a single-parent woman even more difficult.

Changing direction

Clarification of these thoughts happened later, but the intervention they subsequently led to began with a recognition that what we were currently doing was not working, that we needed to protect these children and that the greatest strengths that Pat had were her reciprocated love for her children and her recognition that she needed help, even if she had not in the past benefited from the help that we had seen as appropriate. Removing the children from her would keep them safe from the dangers that were present in their home circumstances but would involve extreme and therefore damaging loss for the children. Removal would, too, lower Pat's self-esteem still further and reduce her chances of parenting more successfully in the future. She was only 23 years old - how many more children would we have to rescue in years to come? We surely needed to find a way to protect the children while preserving their relationship with their mother and increasing, rather than destroying, Pat's sense of self-worth and her confidence in her own abilities. She needed to learn more about how to be a good enough parent but first we had to enhance her ability to learn. We had been expecting her to learn, but had been busy assessing her performance rather than understanding her learning needs.

Within days of this journey to work I had applied to and appeared before the Children's Resource and Allocation Panel to request resources which would enable us to provide residential facilities for Pat and her children together. This was an innovative / unheard of request at the time, but it was the whole family, not just the children, who needed our care and support. I felt that the message Pat needed to hear was that we wanted the children to be with her and that we felt that she was worth supporting in this way.

Another red light

I had attended Panel meetings on several occasions previously. The meetings were used for social workers to present their requests for Care accommodation and for Panel members (representatives were from Social Services middle management) to match and allocate available beds in Children's Homes to suitable children. I presented the case of Pat and her children, requested accommodation for them all and was swiftly advised that no such provision existed within Social Services and that my request could not be granted.

At first I accepted that my plan was not feasible. I could only work within the resources of the department and I would have to think again. Then I realised that it was not I but those in charge of resources who needed to think again.

This time I was more strategic. I wrote a report in which I not only gave details of the circumstances but also explained the theoretical frameworks (attachment, loss, psychodynamic perspectives) that underpinned my present assessment. I considered the strength of the reciprocal bond between Pat and her children and gave evidence for this using examples of attachment behaviour and describing the emotional and physical warmth of their relationship. I gave some detail of Pat's earlier family history and explored how her mother's death had left her unsupported and without a role model at the key developmental stage of adolescence. I pointed out how easy it was to blame women (mothers) for difficulties within their families and how I felt we should be working with Pat in helping her to bring up her children as a good-enough parent.

I looked at the implications of alternative interventions in terms of financial and time costs to the department and, using relevant research on the outcomes of care placements for children, for the individuals within the family. I repeated my request for care accommodation and relevant support worker time and I mailed my report directly to the Director of Social Services. The request was granted, an unused wing of a children's Home was opened up, a residential worker was transferred and, within weeks, Pat and her children moved in.

Discussion

The purpose of this section is not to consider the appropriateness of the above plan, or to report on its success or failure. Definitions of success or failure in respect of social work interventions are in any event, complex, debatable and open to differing interpretations. What is of relevance here is a consideration of what informed the thinking processes and actions in this case and what we can perhaps learn about the relationship between theory and practice, between thinking and feeling and between the personal and the professional.

As I have already described, my social work training took place during an era when there was an emphasis on 'welfare rights', labelling and deviancy theories (Cohen, 1971; Pearson, 1975). The influence of psychology was seen by some leading writers as having *led to an over-emphasis on pathological and clinical orientations to the detriment of structural and political implications.* (Bailey and Brake, 1975, p.1)

This meant that I brought to my practice an espoused theory which included a value base concerned with ameliorating the material poverty of people's lives and with acting as the advocate of the powerless within and against the structures, organisations and bureaucracies which oppressed and disempowered them. I was very concerned not to pathologise the clients[1] with whom I worked. At the same time of course, I also had a clear responsibility to protect children from harm.

In considering Pat's situation therefore, I initially embraced a framework of explanation that was premised upon an understanding of the effects of poverty and deprivation and in which I was seen and used by my own agency and others (Housing, Health, Social Security) to

control circumstances and behaviour, as a regulator of conflict. (Rees, 1975 p.73)

In doing this I was 'reading a map' (Milner and O'Byrne, 1998) that had already been selected by those who had worked with Pat previously. At the time I do not think it occurred to me that there was a choice of map to be made, but in any case the perspectives and values offered to me during my training would have caused me to justify the route I was taking:

> However simple or complex a case may appear, the social worker will be involved in interpreting the problem, the service required and the resources available. On some occasions his [sic] response may be routine, relatively automatic. On other occasions he may feel that he has neither the knowledge nor experience to cope, or he may be faced with a conflict of interests, or he is expected to do x and y when he only has resources a and b. In each of these situations the social worker is likely to rely on those models of explanation with which he is familiar. In this respect theories become a source of influence; they raise certain questions in the mind of practitioners and make it difficult to raise other questions, to seek other answers. *(Rees, 1975 p.73)*

In Pat's case then, it can be seen how the 'radical social work' agenda had influenced both the explanation given for her circumstances and the intervention route subsequently followed. What is of equal importance to note however, is that the perspective behind this explanation was not one that was clearly articulated, in either case files or verbally in planning meetings, nor was it one that had been shared explicitly with Pat herself. This lack of clarity made it easy for the worker (me) to respond to such a complex and demanding situation in a 'routine' and 'automatic' manner.

Our assessment had been of Pat's responses to our intervention rather than of the intervention itself:

... a concentration on outcome alone can render certain intricacies of the social work process immune from analysis.

... adverse responses to social work intervention are all too easily written off as denial or resistance, rather than a failure on the worker's part to achieve a satisfactory 'fit' between their analyses and the meanings ascribed by the family or individual themselves. (White, 1997, p.740 and p.749)

The only opportunity Pat was given, or was able to take up, to challenge or change the premises upon which our intervention methods were based was through her behaviour - with her children, her partners, her friends and the professionals involved in her life. However, it seemed that we accrued the details of this behaviour as 'evidence' of the justification for our actions rather than reading it with the purpose of understanding the 'story' she was offering us about her life. (White, 1997)

That moment at the traffic lights which caused me to change direction came about as a result of a sudden 'immersion in the lived experience of the service user', an empathetic interpretivist understanding seemingly contradictory to a positivist, objective, `professional` notion of social work. (White, 1997, p.741)

Perhaps it had been an unarticulated and unrecognised sense of dissatisfaction with the limitations of this professional objectivity that had led me towards an exploration of concepts of love whilst on my MA course? Whatever my motivation at the time, my reading, thinking and writing upon the subject had equipped me to recognise the significance of both the presence of love (her children) and the lack of love (parents / partner) in Pat's day-to-day life, her 'lived experience'.

Conclusion

This account of part of a journey through a case has highlighted some aspects of the relationship between theory and practice in social work.

I began the journey equipped with a 'map' drawn during my training, I abandoned the route being taken as a result of a 'collision' between my own experience as a young woman and that of Pat, my client. This collision caused me to abandon briefly my professional worker persona and to seek an explanation for my personal response to her and her situation. Once I had identified the route that I now felt should be taken, I was able to draw upon a different theoretical position in order to give professional credibility to my request for resources.

Reflection on this piece of work has affected my teaching of social work in a number of ways:

- I am aware of the dangers of working uncritically from within an espoused theoretical position or a 'preferred professional formulation' (White, 1997, p.746), 'like the carpenter, who, possessing a hammer, tends to see every problem as a nail'. (Blaug, 1995)
- I am clear that articulated theory can be effective in securing resources on the basis of need rather than availability.
- I encourage workers to become aware of the political and organisational contexts in which they are operating.
- I include an emphasis on self-knowledge, personal understandings, values and experience and on how these aspects of the self impact upon the relationship between worker and client.
- I stress the importance of, and the links between, reflective practice and evaluation:

... social workers need to learn how to use theories in an explicit, systematic way and to conceptualise their practice so that they can explain clearly the reasoning behind their decisions and actions if they were to work in an explicit manner, it would be more feasible to evaluate their practice and discover whether or not it was effective. (Munro, 1998, p.103)

Note

1. I use 'client', the terminology in use at the time, rather than 'user', the term currently used in the UK.

References

Bailey R. and Brake M. (eds) (1975) *Radical Social Work*, Edward Arnold, London

Blaug R. (1995) 'Distortion of the face to face: Communicative reason and social work practice', *British Journal of Social Work*, 25, 4, 423-39

Cohen S. (ed) (1971) *Images of Deviance*, Penguin, Harmondsworth

Milner J. and O'Byrne P. (1998) *Assessment in Social Work*, MacMillan, Basingstoke

Munro E. (1998) 'Improving social workers' knowledge base in child protection work', *British Journal of Social Work* 28, 89-105

Pearson G. (1975) *The Deviant Imagination*, Macmillan, London

Rees S. (1975) 'How misunderstanding occurs', in R. Bailey and M. Brake (eds) *Radical Social Work*, Edward Arnold, London

White S. (1997) 'Beyond hermeneutics, reflexivity and social work practice', *British Journal of Social Work*, 27, 5, 739-53

12
You can't teach somebody something that they don't already know: Developing a practice theory of community crime prevention

Chris Shipway

Introduction

I'm going to begin my story with a Zen story that I have always enjoyed and never entirely understood.

> Nan-in, a Japanese master during the Meiji era (1868-1912), received a university professor who came to inquire about Zen. Nan-in served tea. He poured his visitor's cup full, and then kept on pouring.
> The professor watched the overflow until he no longer could restrain himself. 'It is overfull. No more will go in.'
> 'Like this cup,' Nan-in said, 'you are full of your own opinions and speculations. How can I show you Zen unless you first empty your cup?' (Reps, 1980, p.17)

I have reflected on this story at various times for nearly 20 years now but it has only been in the past five that it has begun to have some resonance with my work with communities. Over the past five years I have been employed as Senior Project Officer in the New South Wales Government's Crime Prevention Division with responsibilities for promoting community based crime prevention and supporting the establishment of local crime prevention plans throughout the state.

Perhaps it is not surprising that notions such as 'emptying your cup' should be relevant to community work. One of the fundamental premises of working with communities is that of assisting communities, and the individuals and groups that constitute a 'community', to identify, analyse and respond to the issues that are of greatest concern. You approach the community with 'an empty cup'. You seek to ensure that your own assumptions do not influence the identification and analysis of community concerns. Such an 'empowerment' approach is often contrasted with the 'expert' approach whereby the 'professional' or 'expert' provides the identification, analysis and preferred responses to a particular issue.

Paulo Freire articulates this 'empowerment' approach as an act of dialogue. 'Because dialogue is an encounter among men who name the world, it must not be a situation where some men name on behalf of others' (Freire, 1977, p.26).

Such an approach sounds great in theory. But how do you apply such approaches when working with communities to prevent and reduce crime? Crime is a hot issue in Australia in the 1990s. On a daily basis crime is portrayed by much of the media as a problem which is out of control. Most community members would have a view as to the best means of tackling and reducing crime and these views are diverse and often opposed to one another.

Furthermore, most people have some personal experience of crime and do not approach the issue as something that is removed from them. Individuals, families and groups are concerned that they are not burgled, robbed, assaulted, raped, defrauded or otherwise violated. Crime is personal. People, understandably, respond to it with emotion.

Unfortunately, I know that many of the responses generated by deep community concerns about crime will not work. The United States National Institute of Justice has analysed decades of crime prevention research to identify those crime prevention initiatives that work (and under what conditions) and those initiatives that do not work (Sherman et al, 1998).

The dilemma with which I am always faced is how can an empowerment approach to working with communities be reconciled with an 'expert' understanding of which initiatives may assist a community and which will not. That dilemma has been represented by opposing statements that are often put to me when I first start working with a community.

On the one hand people will often say: 'You're the expert, tell us what to do'. There can be great frustration on their part when I say: 'I don't know what to do because I don't know enough about your community'.

On the other hand when I propose a general framework of crime prevention I am often told: 'That will never work around here, you don't understand what we are facing'.

In the first instance I am being criticised because I am not 'expert' enough to solve problems immediately. In the second instance I am not acknowledging my 'outsider' status adequately and am seen as being presumptuous. The reconciliation of the 'expert' and the 'naive outsider' has been one of the key lessons I have learned over the last five years. Getting the balance right between these two elements has been one of the key factors in getting successful crime prevention outcomes. The balance is not a static balance. Knowing when to shift the balance from 'expert' to 'outsider' and vice versa has also been an important lesson.

When I first began working to promote crime prevention planning I also confronted an additional and more fundamental problem. How do you develop and support effective community based crime prevention initiatives?

These two problems were encapsulated at a 'law and order' meeting I was invited to attend in one of the larger regional cities in New South Wales during 1996. Representatives from many communities within a 400 kilometre radius travelled to attend the meeting and more than 300 people were packed into the local civic centre. It was a hot summer's night a few weeks before Christmas and the mood that evening was anything but charitable. I was overwhelmed by the depth of anger, and in some cases hatred, that was generated during the meeting.

Although crime rates were increasing in New South Wales at that time, the rate of increase could not be characterised as a 'crime wave'. Nonetheless many of the participants were available to identify different groups in the community that they felt were to blame for the incidents of crime that they were experiencing. These groups included: the 'politically correct'; indigenous people; young people; civil libertarians; the current government; the police; the gay community in Sydney; and politicians in general. Despite the ready identification of scapegoats, the Law and Order Meeting was not able to generate specific initiatives that would begin to address the causes of local crime.

I was only an observer at this meeting. At the time, I felt that if I had been invited to speak I would not have known what to say to adequately address the sentiments and concerns expressed that evening. But I was confronted with a series of challenging, indeed threatening, questions. What kind of authority or expertise was required to constructively contain and direct such anger and fear? How could a community be assisted to develop the necessary knowledge and skills to effectively prevent crime? What would be the source of such knowledge and skills? Should we lead such a process or should we follow the community's lead?

This is my story of how I have begun to learn to reconcile and integrate a consultative empowerment approach to crime prevention with an 'expert' understanding of initiatives that may assist a community and those that will not. In so doing I have been exhilarated by the simplicity of what I have learnt. Conversely I am challenged by the complex implications and potential of this approach to community based crime prevention. Furthermore I have been excited to discover that this approach to community based crime prevention actually works and evolves.

In this chapter I will discuss three key themes that have contributed to the development of practice theory of community crime prevention:

- The development of an effective community education approach ('The Pitch');

- The use of 'story telling' as a critical tool in producing a crime prevention plan; *and*
- A process of 'diagnosis' that enables communities to identify crime prevention strategies that are likely to be effective.

The Pitch

In 1995 the New South Wales Government established the Crime Prevention Division in the NSW Attorney General's Department. The Division's role was to promote an integrated 'whole of government' approach to preventing crime and to encourage community based crime prevention initiatives throughout the state.

By then, less than half a dozen community based crime prevention projects had been implemented in the state of New South Wales. Moreover, these projects had achieved little reduction of crime.

In 1996 the Crime Prevention Division undertook a series of five Juvenile Crime Prevention Seminars for local government throughout rural New South Wales. Those seminars promoted a theory of crime prevention that emphasised a collaborative problem-solving analysis and inclusive community building. This approach, while received politely, was also greeted with notable scepticism by many of the participants. Many of those participants viewed such an approach as being of minimal significance to their situations. Rather they favoured a reliance on increased police numbers and powers and the provision of tougher laws, sentencing regimes and punishment. The kinds of issues raised during our seminars included:

- Declining moral values;
- Young people's lack of respect for adults and the community;
- The imposition of city values on rural communities;
- The failure of rural communities to adapt to changing community values;
- Community disintegration, accompanied by a longing for the 'good old days' when everyone 'knew each other' and could leave their homes unlocked;
- Australia's international treaty obligations being in conflict with local community interests;
- The secularisation of society;
- The loss of family values;
- The failure of the education system to instil respect and teach kids to read and write;
- The failure of the political system to invest enough authority in the police to quell crime; *and*

- The decline of local services.

One of my key lessons from the seminars in country New South Wales was an increasing awareness that I was promoting community based crime prevention as a 'theory'. I understood the fundamental principles of crime prevention and could articulate those principles. However when local community representatives would say 'OK we accept what you are saying, so what should we do locally to prevent crime?' I could only respond vaguely and in generalities. I understood the theory but I could not translate it so that communities could use it. I had to learn how the required crime prevention knowledge, attitudes and skills could be effectively transferred to communities so that they could practically engage such competencies.

Prior to my employment with the Crime Prevention Division I had spent six years working as an adult educator. One of the key things I had discovered then was that one of the best ways to learn about a subject was to teach that subject. The fear of public failure can be a great motivator to examine the application of theory from a diversity of different critical perspectives. You anticipate the range of issues that will be presented in the context of a training situation and determine different ways of exploring and resolving such issues. It is not so much a matter of coming up with the 'correct answers'. Rather it is the identification of different ways that those issues can be examined and satisfactorily resolved for all the participants in the learning process.

In 1997 I began developing short presentations (1-2 hours in length) and one day training workshops to facilitate the development of specific crime prevention skills and knowledge in local communities. I experimented with different formats for the short presentations and it was during one such presentation in country New South Wales that I first discovered an approach which assisted communities to put theory into practice. There were several key elements to that presentation:

- An identification of the causes of crime (determined by criminological research);
- Two rules for effective community crime prevention (the recognition that more than one strategy is required for success and the development of effective local partnerships);
- The provision of NSW examples of effective community crime prevention which illustrated the above two points; *and*
- The provision of simple steps for the development of effective local initiatives.

I was astounded by the response to this presentation. In particular the presentation of the causes of crime produced a strong and positive response from the audience. The list of factors that contribute to crime was derived from a report produced by the NSW Bureau of Crime Statistics and Research (Salmelainen, 1995). But it was also a 'common sense' list describing a range of issues that were frequently raised at law and order meetings: family background; drugs and alcohol; peer relations. There were a number of benefits to discussing these causal factors:

- The factors seemed credible and thus provided an opportunity to realistically examine how such factors do, and don't, impact on crime. For the first time I had discovered a means of introducing expert research to local discussions of crime.
- The list provided that community with a number of tangible issues that communities could act upon. It could provide a basis for practical crime prevention initiatives and action, if communities could identify with precision how these various factors interact to produce specific local crime profiles. I emphasised that we would not find such local crime profiles in textbooks. Rather we would have to go into our communities and talk to the different individuals and groups that had a direct knowledge of crime. Those stakeholders would include: the police, residents, local government, local business, government services, non-government agencies, and victims of crime.
- The two 'rules for effective crime prevention' and the 'steps for the development of crime prevention initiatives' provided some principles to inform local crime prevention planning.
- I had also discovered that the use of real life examples of success stories in New South Wales illustrated these factors and principles in a practical manner that engaged many of the participants in the seminar.

For the first time I had an audience that was enthused by the presentation and could see a way forward. They engaged in animated discussion for the rest of the day about what they could do locally. I had discovered some of the elements for communicating the benefits of crime prevention credibly and practically. However, although I had found a 'language' that could enable more effective dialogue about crime prevention I still lacked confidence in the application of the theory. I felt like an imposter who had discovered how to 'talk the talk'. But I was not at all sure that I could 'walk the walk'.

Another event answered this problem of confidence several months later. The Crime Prevention Division had engaged Jon Bright (Field Director of Crime Concern in Britain) as a consultant for a one month period. Jon had over a decade's experience in community based crime prevention and was assisting us in the development of frameworks for community based crime prevention. In particular he was guiding us to recognise opportunities for the establishment of local crime prevention projects.

I found Jon's presence a great inspiration and source of encouragement. He participated in several workshops that I facilitated and also gave presentations on the merits of crime prevention during his one-month stay. I was able to observe both the merits of his arguments and the confident manner of his presentation. As if by osmosis I was able to absorb much of his confidence and his rationales. It was one of those experiences where 'the penny dropped'. Everything that I knew about crime prevention, and its application to New South Wales, just 'clicked into place'. Suddenly I was able to apprehend and articulate that knowledge in the confidence that it could work. In no small measure that confidence was derived from working with someone who had put similar initiatives into place and seen those initiatives effect change in communities.

It was not as if I had not understood the merits of community based crime prevention for much of the preceding two years. However I do not think 'the penny would have dropped' unless I had previously put myself in circumstances where I was unsure of what to say or do. I had to be faced with circumstances where I struggled to develop the concepts and language that meaningfully communicated crime prevention. Only by first understanding the need for an effective 'answer' to many of the concerns and fears raised by communities would I be able to recognise the 'answer' or 'message' when I chanced upon it.

Throughout the remainder of 1997 I undertook a number of trips throughout NSW where I promoted the 'message' again and again. By exposing myself to community after community I was able to test and hone that message so that it had real resonance and meaning in a variety of community contexts throughout the state. By the end of 1997 I had a number of tried and true presentations that could engage communities and enable them to begin a viable process of crime prevention.

It was also at this time that I began to refer to these presentations as a sales pitch or 'the Pitch'. I was surprised that I referred to it in such a way and wasn't sure at the time as to why I had selected such a phrase. It was only later that I began to understand why.

Story telling

Another issue continued to haunt me. It was all well and good to have an effective framework and mechanism for the dissemination of crime prevention knowledge and skills. However I had seen how destabilising local debates about crime (its causes and its prevention) could be.

One of the key foundations of viable crime prevention plans is the development of a 'Crime Profile Report'. The principal purpose of a Crime Profile Report is to employ demographic data, recorded crime statistics, incidents of disorder or incivility that are not captured by official statistics, and, most importantly, crime information from a range of non-police sources. This data - quantitative and qualitative - is then analysed and compiled to form a profile that details and describes:

- where the priority crime occurs;
- the victims of the crime;
- the perpetrators of the crime;
- the circumstances and environments which encourage the occurrence of that crime;
- the times of day when that crime occurs;
- the incentives and opportunities for the commission of that crime; *and*
- the consequences of that crime.

However in my experience communities readily polarised into a number of warring factions none of whom seemed able to communicate effectively with each other. Blame was often apportioned to a range of stakeholders. Considerable anger and hatred often marked local discourse. I wanted to believe that there was a way of overcoming this but I found the ferocity of the debate could be intimidating.

I also knew that much of the emotion underlying such debates was grounded in people's lived experience. I had observed on many occasions that local quantitative crime data were disputed as people would simply recount stories they had encountered about other people's experience of crime. For example a comparatively low rate of assault would be discounted on a basis of ' my neighbour was assaulted last week and I know that this happens regularly around here'.

Many people were frustrated and angry for legitimate reasons. The anger could not be simply rationalised or argued away. If this issue could not be resolved I knew that many initiatives would be doomed to failure. But how could such emotion and concern be engaged and harnessed positively and productively? How could local debates be transformed so that communities were not divided but rather strengthened?

I found the seeds of my answers in a Victoria Health Seminar I had attended in Melbourne in 1996. The 'Power, Participation and Partnerships for Health Promotion Seminar' promoted the value of story telling as a basis for developing community consensus and establishing effective foundations for community action. Elizabeth Reid opened the seminar by describing one means of promoting social capital as:

> ... *the creation, with others, of spaces and occasions in which the involved, diverse social actors can pass through individual introspection and collective reflection, to the strengthening of understanding. This is a process of drawing on what one's self has learned and of collective reflection to create a 'thick' description and out of that*

thick and complex description draw out those key elements which will provide entry points for change of the bases for strategies for action. A 'thick' description as formulated by Denzin (1989) does more than record what is happening.

'A thick description goes beyond mere fact and surface appearances. It presents detail, context, emotion, and the webs of social relationships that join persons to one another. Thick description evokes emotionality and self-feelings. It inserts history into experience. It establishes the significance of an experience or the sequence of events for the person or persons in question. In thick descriptions, the feelings, voices, actions and meaning of interacting individuals are heard.' (Labonte, 1997, p.9)

The two-day seminar provided 'hands-on' tuition in the use of story telling as a means of building partnerships as the basis for action on range of community concerns. As I participated in the process it began to occur to me that most people's experience and understanding of crime was provided by the telling of stories:

- local crime stories that were told over back fences and in shopping malls;
- 'official' stories that were related at meetings such as Neighbourhood Watch and Police Community Consultative meetings; *and*
- the ubiquitous lurid crime reports that seemed to be the staple fare of many newspapers and current affairs shows.

Ron Labonte argued that:

Stories are about people and what they do. They touch listeners in ways that theoretical arguments and statistical data do not and cannot. They hit us at a feeling level, as well as a thinking level. What's powerful about stories is the personal connection. (Labonte, 1997, p.27)

I wondered what would happen if people's stories of crime were encouraged and employed as the basis for Crime Profile Reports. I speculated that valuing such lived experiences could provide the foundation of qualitative data gathering about crime that occurs in communities. It also occurred to me that the opportunity for people to voice their stories, and have those stories heard by other community members, would provide alternative interpretations and appraisals of such stories. Finally I had a strong intuition that this might be a means of transforming divisive and angry local debate to an enriching and enabling dialogue.

In 1998 I had the opportunity to put this intuition to the test. At the close of 1997 the New South Wales Parliament assented to the Children (Protection and Parental Responsibility) Act 1997. This legislation is best known in New South Wales for the section that provides opportunities to authorise police to remove young people from public places and return those young people to their parents when the young people are 'at risk'. Another less publicised section of the Act enabled the Attorney General to endorse local crime prevention plans submitted by local government and financially support the implementation of the endorsed plans.

Suddenly the onus was on the Crime Prevention Division to adequately support and facilitate the establishment of local crime prevention plans. Several local councils were enthusiastically requesting our assistance. The communities of Moree (in the north west of New South Wales) and Ballina (on the far north coast) invited the Division to direct and support the development of their local crime prevention plans. Without having previously observed or undertaken the practice of community crime prevention planning I was about to take the theory I had been espousing and put that theory into practice. It felt like a huge step into the unknown. Although I now had confidence in the theory, I was still apprehensive that either the theory would not work or that I would not have the personal capacities to make the theory work.

The process that I followed was as follows:

* Identify the range of crime issues of concern to the local community;
* Identify priority crime issues;
* Develop Crime Profile Reports (detailed or thick descriptions) for each of the priority issues;
* Identify a number of critical components of a Crime Profile report which combine to cause the occurrence of a particular crime in the community;
* Identify specific strategies that can impact on the critical components of a crime profile report.

In following that process I hoped to employ a story-telling approach to develop the crime profile reports. We engaged key stakeholder groups (such as local business, local government, key government service organisations, indigenous community leaders, resident groups and the police) and asked them to tell us their stories about their experience or understanding of particular crimes. We conducted discrete consultations with each of these groups to provide them with an attentive audience that would not seek to contradict their experience.

As we developed the reports we provided feedback about the stories that other groups had provided and invited comment. Additionally we discovered that we began to develop a number of hypotheses about the specific contributing causes of crime in a particular setting and invited comment on those hypotheses. Employing such an approach produced a number of startling outcomes. I refer to them as:

- Dispelling the 'common wisdom';
- Uncovering the 'hidden knowledge'; and
- Putting the jigsaw puzzle together.

We found that once a priority issue had been identified it was commonly assumed that the factors that contributed to that problem were widely known and understood. For example, in one community it was assumed by all members of the local crime prevention committee (including young people) that malicious damage in a particular area was caused by teenagers. Teenagers were seen walking through the affected area at night. In the morning damage had been done to property. Therefore teenagers were seen to be the perpetrators.

However as we developed the local crime profile the teenagers who frequented the area at night, could only provide information about damage that their parents' homes had suffered. It later became apparent that the perpetrators were actually intoxicated (adult) patrons returning from local hotels and clubs (a reality supported by local licensees). If that local crime prevention plan had developed strategies based on the 'common wisdom' they would have selected the wrong strategies and the plan would have failed.

Although this seems an obvious point, the Crime Prevention Division has found in every situation where we have assisted in the development of a crime prevention plan that there is a 'common wisdom' about an identified crime that is either inaccurate or distorted. As a consequence, the development of a crime profile report has to ensure that an accurate description of the crime phenomena is developed so that strategies can be selected with the confidence that they are likely to be effective.

In seeking such accurate descriptions we also discovered that there is usually a 'hidden knowledge' in communities. This is information that many people possess but the data is so obvious that it is not consciously acknowledged. Rather it is a 'given' that simply exists in the background.

For example in the development of a local crime profile of 'violence against women' in one community key stakeholders were unable to identify particular locations where such violence was more likely to occur. However several hours later when discussing the need to reduce isolation through community transport, a particular street was identified as greatly in need of such a service because of the consistent violence experienced by families there. Everyone present was aware of this given social fact, but it was only with reflection and exploration of the local profile that it was unearthed as a critical piece of information.

Similarly in another rural town every informant group with which we consulted stated that street violence involving young people was perpetrated throughout the town. But as we listened to the stories of street violence, the same local landmarks and street names kept recurring. I requested a map of the community and drew a boundary that included all of the landmarks and streets that had been named throughout the consultation. Approximately 25 per cent of the town was enclosed by the boundary. The members of the crime prevention committee looked at the map and agreed that there was where the violent behaviour occurred. They all possessed that 'hidden knowledge' derived from their lived experience. But the 'common wisdom' was that violent behaviour must co-exist with theft offences. Since theft offences did occur throughout the town it was commonly understood that street violence must be co-located.

I have learnt through subsequent planning processes that when we have dispensed with the 'common wisdom' and uncovered the 'hidden knowledge' we are usually very close to a finalised crime profile report. Additionally the identification of the hidden knowledge' is often a key indicator of the critical strategies that will impact on crime.

In pursuing this process we have discovered that developing a Crime Profile Report can be likened to putting a jigsaw puzzle together. All of the pieces of the picture are available in a community but they are held by a range of diverse stakeholders. To develop an accurate Report those various stakeholders have to be engaged and encouraged to describe and consider what they know and understand of a particular crime.

Inevitably in our experience there are conflicts and contradictions in the development of such profiles. But we have also discovered that it these very conflicts and contradictions that regularly offer up the most valuable information about the manifestation of crime in a given community. The point when you get a piece of the puzzle that won't fit into your pattern is often the moment when you realise that a number of hypotheses are not accurate. It is that point when you are often on the brink of uncovering the 'hidden knowledge'. The example of malicious damage, cited earlier, demonstrates how a seeming contradiction in the local qualitative data actually led to a more accurate and enriched analysis of the local problem.

By the end of 1998 I had finally experienced the theory at work. Furthermore it succeeded in unexpected ways and revealed itself to be richer, more adaptable and empowering than I had ever imagined. I had facilitated two local planning processes that had:

- clearly identified and articulated a number of local issues that underpinned particular crimes;.
- developed a shared language and understanding in regard to local crime problems that could be assented to by previously opposed groups in the community;
- generated many strategies (up to thirty) that would be progressively implemented over the following three years; *and*
- finalised draft plans that were flexible enough to adapt to the changing needs of the community.

I gained great confidence and enthusiasm from these successful planning experiences. In 1999 I facilitated a further five crime prevention planning processes. I had now understood and experienced how local crime prevention planning could be successfully applied in practice. As a consequence I was better equipped to indirectly provide tailored advice and support to other local committees engaged in the crime prevention planning process. My experience could also be applied in a range of other settings such as the training of crime prevention officers funded by our Department or planning processes that developed regional plans to reduce violence against women.

Finally, now that I had experienced the theory at work as a process, I was better equipped to support the effective transfer of this knowledge and skills to a number of colleagues in the Crime Prevention Division. As a consequence a further five local plans were facilitated by other members of the Division in 1999.

Diagnosis

In 1999 I became a member of a national reference group that was convened to provide practitioner guidance in the identification of the core knowledge and skills required by the successful crime prevention practitioner. The reference group was asked to comment on a draft list of crime prevention practitioner competencies. As we considered the draft competencies we were all struck by the fact that the competencies were those that one would expect to find in generic community based work. Indeed if the words 'crime prevention' had been removed from the document there did not appear to be any specific competencies that would distinguish crime prevention from other community related work.

None of us were surprised by the competencies that had been identified. However some of us had a strong sense that something critical was missing from the document. We struggled to identify which community crime prevention competencies were absent from the draft competencies.

As I reflected on my experience of the past four years, it occurred to me that the employment of a process which relied upon the identification of specific local manifestations of crime (crime symptoms perhaps?) and 'expert knowledge' was somewhat akin to a medical diagnosis. The process of consultation for the development of a Crime Profile Report was not a random process. There were particular factors that we expected to feature and actively explored such as: family background; schooling; drug and alcohol use. As those factors emerged in varying combinations we sought to develop further detail about the manifestation of those factors.

We could not make an accurate diagnosis without the active and informed participation of the community (the metaphorical patient). A critical element was the active collaboration of different community stakeholders without whom we could not develop an accurate picture of the local crime problem (the metaphorical symptoms). Simultaneously 'expert knowledge' (the metaphorical doctor) was required to guide the development of the Crime Profile Report and the identification of strategies (the metaphorical cure).

The diagnostic element of community based crime prevention seemed to be the quality that distinguished it from other forms of community based work. This element relied upon criminological knowledge but it was more than this 'expert' knowledge. It was the application of such knowledge to identify and analyse crime problems in specific community settings. In short the diagnostic element was the capacity to determine how particular contributing factors occurred in a community leading to specific manifestations of crime. Without a 'diagnostic' Crime Profile Report a community could not determine the appropriate initiatives that had a high probability of reducing crime. In metaphorical terms 'no cure could be effected' until we had identified all of the symptoms and determined what syndrome or disease was the likely cause of the medical problem being experienced.

However the employment of this diagnostic process was not simply a matter of dispensing 'expert wisdom'. Rather it required the establishment of a partnership between the different stakeholders (local agencies, community members and crime prevention practitioners) whereby the various stakeholders could guide and influence the process when their specific knowledge and expertise was required. I discovered that this involved me in adopting different practice approaches according to the particular stage of the process.

In my experience, the critical elements of a successful community crime prevention planning process have been:

* 'Getting the pitch right' - the promotion and establishment of a framework that will guide the planning process;
* Using people's stories - the employment of story-telling approaches in the development of crime profile reports; and
* Diagnosis - the application of expert knowledge to identify and analyse crime problems in specific community settings.
* The effective employment of these elements relies upon a number of considerations as to when one element or another is employed and to what effect.

One such consideration concerns an appreciation of the purposes of engaging and working with communities. The importance of engaging communities is regularly emphasised in the literature concerning local crime prevention. Phrases such as 'promoting community leadership', 'community-led initiatives' or 'working with communities' are phrases that are invoked as if there is a clear and shared understanding of: who (or what) the 'community' is; and why crime prevention practitioners would seek to engage a 'community'.

In my experience such understandings are neither clear nor shared. As a consequence many of the best-intentioned initiatives face difficulties from the start. In many cases the term 'community' is understood to mean the residents of a certain geographically defined place. The term may also be extended to imply that such residents have a unity of interests. The reality is usually quite different. Many people's experience of participation in a community is not simply, or primarily, that of membership in a local geographical community. Rather their primary experience of community is often associated with: workplace or vocation; friendships or sociocultural interests; ethnicity; age; or sexuality.

When working with communities I have discovered that I am working with multiple communities who may have some common interests but will also have a diversity of attitudes and interests, cultural values, histories and allegiances. My understanding of 'community' seeks to recognise that individual and collective experiences of community are complex, fluid and evolving.

In a crime prevention framework, it has been important to recognise that there are a number of differing rationales and goals that explain why we need to engage communities. It is not simply to maintain inclusive practices like involving more people on a planning committee. The Crime Prevention Division has identified a number of key reasons that underlie and inform our commitment to working with communities to:

- Identify the issues of priority concern to communities;
- Access the diverse sources of information, analysis and 'insider knowledge' to develop detailed descriptions of particular crimes as they occur in a given community;
- Identify and mobilise community leaders for action against crime;
- Gain community agreement on problems to be tackled and the solutions to be employed;
- Ensure that the benefits of crime prevention planning are equitably shared by different communities that exist within a locality; *and*
- Maximise opportunities for crime prevention initiatives to strengthen communities by enhancing the capacity of communities to address or respond to problems themselves.

Each of these rationales involves distinctly different tasks and outcomes. It is clear that without flexible and adaptable concepts of community, and acceptance of its inherently diverse nature, it is difficult to undertake the required tasks to achieve our required objectives.

Appreciating the reasons that underlie and inform my work with communities has assisted in balancing and effectively employing a tension that is implicit in much of this story. On the one hand I have adopted an approach which has an 'expert' orientation. This promotes a particular framework and diagnosis to support successful planning. On the other hand my approach has been that of the 'naive outsider' relying upon the knowledge and values of the community (or communities) to guide and inform the planing process. Learning when to adopt a particular approach has been a critical skill to develop. Understanding when and how to balance the two approaches has relied upon an appreciation of the different rationales that inform community engagement.

For example, identifying and mobilising community leaders for action against crime primarily relies upon an 'expert' approach. In undertaking this task I have found that is important to provide a clear framework for action which can motivate community leaders for action.

On the other hand, when accessing the diverse sources of information and 'insider knowledge' to develop detailed descriptions of particular crimes, I have employed a 'naive' approach to elicit diverse forms of information within the community. However, as such detailed descriptions evolve through story-telling, I increasingly combine an 'expert' orientation to focus on those particular factors which are associated by criminological literature with crime.

Another implicit tension in my experience of community crime prevention has been the balancing of active-listening techniques and the use of personal biography ('use of self'). There are times when it is necessary to employ an 'active listening' approach to encourage different community stakeholders to really speak their mind. One task, which requires such an approach, is the identification of issues of priority concern to a community. At this point it is important to elicit the range of issues which are of concern. On the other hand, when establishing community agreement on problems to be tackled and the solutions to be employed, I have found that the use of personal biography (my own values and experiences) can be a critical element in the process. This is because I am likely to be making a number of recommendations about the best ways of proceeding. However, if communities are to make an informed choice about my advice, they need to appreciate the values and experiences that instruct my advice.

Conclusion: How do I know when I've got there?

Exploring the different modes of working with communities and appreciating the rich and diverse implications of these different modalities has been one of the most exciting experiences of my professional life. In particular, it has been deeply satisfying to engage in this practice of community crime prevention in the knowledge that communities are being strengthened to address or respond to problems themselves.

How do I know that a community's capacity to reduce and prevent crime has been increased? One strong indicator is the moment when the range of diverse stakeholders are able to agree on the detailed description of the problem that will be addressed (the Crime Profile Report). We encourage communities not to proceed to the identification of initiatives for implementation until agreement is reached on this report. Time and time again I have had experiences of convening a stakeholder workshop to discuss a draft report. There is a particular point that these workshops reach when the diverse interests represented are able to state:

This report represents the particular concerns that we have been raising and the issues that we want to tackle.

I usually know when we have reached that point because the various interest groups have ceased to debate the issues and want to talk about solutions. In my experience, when communities have reached that stage a new language or discourse is in place. A language which will enable enhanced dialogue between potentially opposing interests and groupings has been established. At that moment, the community as a whole has moved beyond the 'common wisdom' and identified the 'hidden' knowledge that many people in the community have possessed but had not fully appreciated. For me it is a magic moment when I can sense that something has changed. It is a moment when a community has developed an enhanced capacity to address its problems, on its own terms, in a manner that is likely to succeed. It is a moment when a community in all of its complexity has uncovered and rediscovered what they already knew from their lived experience. It is a moment when a community's collective knowledge and wisdom can be employed so that real change can be effected. When that stage is reached I recall and increasingly appreciate a Sufi saying recounted by Ron Labonte in his seminar on story-telling: 'You can't teach somebody something that they don't already know' (1997, p.27).

I am now comfortable with a role that could be described as 'crime prevention expert' because I appreciate that this role is necessary to assist communities to uncover collective knowledge and skill. If communities already knew how to prevent crime then they would be doing so. But the reality is that many communities are paralysed and unsure how to proceed. The community's 'cup is empty' and requires an expert to come and fill it. However I have seen that one can only make a positive contribution as an 'expert' under particular circumstances.

At other points in the process I must 'empty my cup' and acknowledge that I know nothing of the community values, expectations, social realities and dynamics that profoundly influence crime and the solutions that will be required to address such crime. I have learnt that an effective crime prevention planning process requires an acknowledgment of expertise - the expertise of community members, the expertise of other stakeholders, and the expertise of crime prevention practitioners. When that expertise is recognised, and employed in partnership at appropriate points in the process, community stakeholders gain in knowledge and skills. Greater capacity to prevent crime can be established.

I raised a key dilemma at the start of this story. How can an empowerment approach to working with communities be reconciled with an 'expert' understanding of initiatives which may assist a community and those that will not?

In one sense the answer to the dilemma is quite straightforward. You need to know when you are an 'expert' in a particular situation and when you are not. You need to know when the community has expertise and when it does not. You need to know that, at various stages in the planning processes, the expertise is shared between the crime prevention practitioner and various community stakeholders. In negotiating partnerships between the different stakeholders, the shifting concepts of 'expert' and 'non-expert' must be constantly articulated and examined to ensure that genuine partnerships and agreed goals are being established.

However it is one thing for me to write an answer, such as the one above, to the dilemma raised. It is quite another matter to experience that answer so that you truly understand it. The reality is that I haven't learnt my personal practice theory from a text book. I had to go out and do it - recognising at all times, even now, that I am still learning. My community work theory and practice are constantly evolving and in my experience there is only one way to develop an effective practice theory: you go out and do it; you face your challenges; and you learn from those challenges.

References

Denzin, N (1989) *Interpretative Interactionism*, Sage, Thousand Oaks, CA

Freire, P. (1977) *Pedagogy of the Oppressed*, Penguin, Harmondsworth

Labonte, R. (1997) *Participation and Partnerships for Health Promotion*, VicHealth

Reps, P. (1980) *Zen Flesh, Zen Bones*, Penguin, Harmondsworth

Sherman, L., Gottfredson, D., MacKenzie, D., Eck, J., Reuter, P. and Bushway, S. (1998) *Preventing Crime: What Works, What Doesn't, What's Promising*, US Department of Justice- National Institute of Justice,

Salmelainen, P., (1995) 'The correlates of offending frequency: A study of theft offenders in detention', *NSW Bureau of Crime Statistics and Research*, 1-3

13
Life and death matters

Lindsey Napier

'You are a social worker. Why do you want to know about policy?' I was asked. I was sitting in a light, airy, ordered room in a hospice of world renown. I was really caught off guard. The answer seemed so obvious. I offered what I thought were reasonable answers to the question. I wanted to understand to whom the gates of the hospice were open - and closed - and why. I wanted to understand whether and how changes in the function of acute care hospitals (lower average length of bed stays, for instance) affected the pressures for admission to hospices. I wondered about the effects of community care policy on hospice and palliative care. I wanted to be clearer about the distinctiveness of hospice care, palliative care and palliative medicine. While I had found some general answers to my questions in the literature, I am always interested in how the history of institutions shapes their responses to directions in policy. I wanted to understand how the network of services - general practice, community care, home, hospital and hospice - worked, or did not work, together. 'Who pays for what' is always important to understand.

My questions were greeted with disinterest. I quickly realised that these issues - issues, which I called policy issues - were not what fired people up. I was missing the point. The 'real' work, the work which absorbed and satisfied, was the work of caring for individual patients and their families. All else was someone else's business, reluctantly conducted by medical directors on behalf of Boards of Directors. I continued to avoid the question about social work. I 'covered' myself by explaining that I had worked in health policy as a public servant and that now I teach and research in the area of health policy and social work. I had indeed been 'one of them'. Some jokes followed about 'bureaucrats' who 'haven't a clue' about what it's really like for staff, far less for patients.

I began to assert myself. I explained that the understanding that came from front line experience was invaluable in broader policy work. Such understanding was often in short supply. I bit the bullet and said, 'In any case, you are all involved in policy here - the fact that you are here at all is about policy. The fact that social workers aren't employed much in palliative care or hospice is an expression of policy, isn't it?'

I had stumbled upon this fact simply through introducing myself as a social worker. It wasn't a single instance. 'We don't employ social workers. We all talk to the patients and their families here', I had been informed in the course of a visit to another hospice. In response to my request to speak with a social worker in a palliative care service, I was told 'We used to employ a social worker but we don't any more. We hired a psychologist to do grief and bereavement counselling; that's what is needed'. I have heard such statements many times before and have been known to launch into expositions of the differences between counselling and social work. On this occasion I thought 'I'll show you'.

Then I found I was also somewhat panicked. 'Maybe social work, in a setting like this which espouses 'holistic care' is redundant', I thought. 'And perhaps I am as capable of being as self interested as the next.' I argued with myself, reminding myself of the substantial efforts of colleagues to make a convincing case for the inclusion of social work in palliative care and hospice work (see, for instance, Monroe, 1993; Oliviere, Hargreaves and Monroe, 1998). 'This is not rational', I thought. 'It's all written down'. To quell my doubts, and sideline my quandary, I scribbled down a checklist of knowledge I would expect a social worker to offer as a particular contribution to the work.

On each occasion I backed off. I tucked it away and focused the discussion on policy, on discussing the familiar imperative of doing more with less, on the pressures on hospices to accept patients, in active treatment, for in patient hospice care. I presented myself as a 'policy person' and failed to tackle the two issues: why as a social worker it is 'natural' for me to be interested in questions of health and social policy, and whether in the current environment of health services, there is a place for social work in palliative and hospice care. I tried to convince myself that the timing was not right to 'speak up for social work', that I needed to understand more about the local history and politics to be sure of my ground.

Social work has always had to argue for being a necessity, not a luxury, in health services. It has done this successfully in different ways at different times. On this occasion, I was left uneasy, unsure what to think about the perceived redundancy of social work and dissatisfied about my own behaviour. I did not have at my fingertips, or rather, at the tip of my tongue, a convincing reply about social work that was politically astute and policy informed. I needed to convince myself.

Social work

Over the weeks that followed, two explanations jostled for attention. Social work is not needed, I thought, because the battle has been won. An alternative and more persistent thought, was 'Social work has fled the battleground: we only have ourselves to blame'.

'It's all fine, we've done ourselves out of a job'

I didn't want to believe that social work had become redundant but I didn't feel one hundred percent confident that it might not be true. I pulled back and thought about the fact that the hospice and palliative care movement has been a revolutionary movement, modelling for modern, 'mainstream' health services why and how attention must be paid to the 'whole person'. I reminded myself of the assertions of the movement's pioneers: that people for whom curative and life prolonging medicine has no more to offer are people who are alive and living. They still have important living to do. In palliative care, medicine sets out to relieve pain, discomfort and distress associated with illness to the fullest extent possible. The purpose of hospice and palliative care, including that of medicine, is primarily to attend to quality of life, to the social, psychological, emotional and spiritual needs of patients and of those who are significant to that person, as expressed by them and as perceived by staff. Saunders herself called it 'control of distress' (Saunders, quoted in Kellehear, 1999, p.4). Though a person's physical strength may be ebbing away, calling for time and skill to be deployed attending to bodily comfort, there is more to life. The multidisciplinary team became a hallmark of hospice and palliative care, a recognition that spiritual, emotional and social needs cannot be an 'add-on', secondary to bodywork. More recently it has been pointed out that the principles and practices of palliative care pertain as much in the earlier stages of illness as in the later and final stages (Kellehear, 1999). I agree with this.

So it is possible, I argued with myself, that at least as far as work with people who are close to death is concerned, everyone has become responsive to the social situations in which they, their families and friends find themselves and the social resources that may be needed. Perhaps when you are dying or facing the death of your child or best friend, you don't get labelled 'difficult', 'uncooperative', 'demanding', 'objectionable' or 'manipulative' - all common reasons for referral to social work in the large treatment hospitals familiar to me.

I doubted that. In any case, social casework, a term I think that is still appropriate, is only one part of social work. The trouble is, I tell myself, perhaps I 'agree' to this partial definition of social work. Or perhaps I am belatedly catching on to the idea that health promotion and health education activities, which encourage us to bring death in from the cold and stop sealing it off from life, are now part of everyone's job. Perhaps there is a lot of skilled work going on encouraging the activities of patients, friends, partners and families, to comment on the effectiveness and adequacy of policies like mainstreaming, home hospice and respite care. In the main, self-help groups, as we know, welcome the assistance of professionals, particularly in their formative stages.

There are other possibilities.

We have only ourselves to blame

I find it very easy to come to such a conclusion and have no trouble finding supporting arguments. In general I am better at advocating for clients and causes than I am at advocating for social work and myself as a social worker: I am not alone in this. I have a 'built-in' resistance to advancing professional interests, on the basis that there is a danger of their being advanced at the expense of the interests of the people we are there to serve. I prefer to demonstrate social work in action and to negotiate for authority every step of the way rather than assuming a right to be there. (Nothing like making it hard for yourself!)

But I had other, more substantial, grounds for concern. In my head, I return to the original incidents, to try and make sense of what might have been said if I'd had the courage to hear it. I assume that social work is included in what is labelled the 'psychosocial' domain. This seems to mean everything other than medical and body care. It seems to mean talking to patients and offering support, the nature of which isn't specified, so all the team members can do it. It seems to be about loss and grief, which some people 'do' normally (and therefore don't need professional help) while other people don't. For those who don't, counselling is needed; and psychologists are specialists at counselling about loss and grief. I gather steam thinking about this question of the 'psychosocial'.

It seems to me that 'the psychosocial' has come to mean the narrow world of emotions and of communication. Death as 'the final stage of growth' is the language 'everyone' has discovered. Psychosocial work has come to mean providing opportunities (setting expectations?) for people who are dying or bereaved to express their emotions. The language is one of coping, of adaptation by people to their terminal illness, to changes of lifestyle and to the knowledge of imminent death. It is about risk factors and people at risk - at risk of abnormal grief, for instance. There is less talk about the need for the world around dying people, their families, partners and friends to adapt and change, for a questioning of this separation of the normal and the abnormal. (How broad is the definition of next of kin, for example?) Counselling is 'everyone's' business with health professionals gathering information, assessing stages of adjustment and assisting dying people to adjust to loss and death, assisting families to continue functioning and the bereaved to do grief work. There is sloppy talk of providing 'support' (as if everyone agrees about the meanings of support) and who is best placed to provide these different kinds of support.

There is less discussion of how to bring death in from the cold; how to challenge the stigma some people who are dying experience (as untouchables, for instance); how to pursue Saunders' mission of making institutions more sensitive to the special needs of dying people; how the professional power accrued by the much vaunted interdisciplinary team will guarantee the empowerment of the person at the centre of events and not their exhaustion or exclusion from 'the team'.

If I am 'reading' the situation accurately, how have we only ourselves to blame? I acknowledge that social work has placed reliance on psychological, psychoanalytic and systems frameworks for practice; and just as health promotion has omitted dying and death from its purview (Kellehear, 1999) in social work I think we have tended to concentrate on emphasising 'clinical' roles. Perhaps this has placed us in a precarious position, particularly if we think about the processes of dying and grieving as potentially touching off underlying pathology. If that is so, then we do place ourselves in direct competition with all the other 'counsellors'. For myself, I want to relinquish this tendency to identify myself as 'therapist', and concentrate on finding ways for social institutions to become more inclusive of people who are dying and bereaved. It's taken a while for me to reach this point.

As I think and write, my anger rises and gives me the cue to consider a third explanation. Perhaps profound changes are taking place in hospice and palliative care, much more important than the concerns of any one profession.

The exclusion is deliberate

This is not a conclusion I reach easily. I am wary of universal explanations. I remind myself of the explanation now advanced (see, for instance, Rumbold, 1999). It runs as follows. The ruling paradigm for work with people who are dying is being reclaimed by biomedicine. This means that biomedical services, particularly sophisticated symptom control measures, are now privileged. Those who execute them must naturally occupy positions of overriding authority. Palliative medicine is now a medical specialty, albeit struggling to boost its numbers and to be fully accepted. It is now distinguished from palliative care. Successful outcomes must be gauged in terms of rates of cure and remission of symptoms. Other services are just that - 'other', and therefore subordinate, limited or excluded (Willis, 1989). This is a significant concern for nursing, which has established a leadership position in community based palliative care services (Street, 1998).

Parallel with this trend is one, which espouses the original goals of the pioneers of the doctors and nurses of hospice - of enabling more people to die at home. Dying 'in the community' is now writ large in policy. 'Home' is now defined to include residential care facilities like nursing homes. Community based palliative care comprises both direct 'generalist' care at home, supported by specialist consultation and admission for respite and short stay hospice management. At the heart of this new policy is efficiency: dying must be 'mainstreamed'. The principles of palliative care are reiterated, but staffing of programs comprise only nursing and medical staff. Anything more is presumably regarded as a luxury or the work able to be subsumed by these two occupations.

I turn to the recent Strategic Plan of an area health service to examine the evidence for this portrayal of current policy trends (WSAHS, 1998). At the outset the plan defines those who can benefit from palliative care as

> ... *all residents of WSAHS who have an incurable disease that is at an advanced stage and is progressing, and is causing them* physical, psychological, social *or* spiritual problems, *whether they are close to dying or not.* (p.15) [my emphasis]

It proceeds to include the following in the stated principles of palliative care:

- *'the patient/client and their family or support group are the focus of care,*
- *the needs of the patient/client as a whole person is* [sic] *the basis of care,*
- *a multidisciplinary team approach will provide coordinated medical, nursing and allied service to patients/clients and families or support group,' (p.16).*

The key providers are named as general practitioners, community nurses and the family/carer (in that order!), complemented by specialist palliative care doctors and nurses, allied health workers, volunteers and other support services.

As the plan unfolds, the words 'psychosocial support' and 'social support' appear, but without definition and without any clear logic for their inclusion and exclusion. The adoption of the Australian Hospice and Palliative Care Association's description of patient needs at different phases of terminal illness adds further confusion. According to this assessment, it is only when the patient is in stage 3 - 'deteriorating' - that social and practical difficulties are named. Emotional and spiritual issues are attached to the terminal stage alone, when 'Death is likely in a matter of days' (p.19). Care is then focused for the family on emotional and spiritual issues 'as a prelude to bereavement' (p.19). Planned support programs and counselling are proposed as the solution to such difficulties in care 'management'. In-patient palliative care units, functioning to support 'the community', should employ 'allied staff' (social workers, physiotherapists, occupational therapists and counselling) in addition to medical and nursing staff.

I am struck as much by the absence of discussion about how the plan intends to address spiritual needs as I am by the confusion over meanings of the words psychosocial and social. I search and find that while the 'strategic vision' identifies only medicine and nursing as core service providers, pastoral care personnel and volunteers do at least rate a mention after specialist palliative care physicians, allied health professionals, surgeons and physicians in acute care facilities. The emphasis on 'management' seems a far cry from the idea that the person who is dying actively participates in what is after all their life. The idea of sharing a uniquely lonely journey is a foreign language.

The conclusion is inescapable: with the planned shift in emphasis for 'management' of 'increasingly complex cases' to take place in the community, comes a medical / nursing model of dying, with psychosocial and spiritual needs (however defined) secondary, to be dealt with by as yet undefined counselling of individuals and families. Like most plans, this one provides a clear statement of the policy direction: away from the policy principles espoused by the founders of the hospice movement. Is it not still true that dying is not simply the final and inevitable page in a record of supervised medical treatment?

Where to?

Where did all my disquiet lead me? to create, out of my years of practice and academic experience as a social worker, some simple, working concepts, which might arm me as a social worker to respond to the current policy context. The following simply emerged, as I reflected on the learning I have previously taken for granted. I imagine that for many social workers, indeed many workers, in hospice and palliative care, they will seem obvious, or worse still, oversimplified. However, I hope that for others, my articulation of what may seem obvious can help build a new way of seeing. For me at least, the process of reflection leads to a renewed clarity and reaffirmation of the importance of the holistic, social work perspective in palliative care.

Dying is not a disease

Dying is not a disease, any more than living with a life threatening illness is a disease. This seems so obvious as to make elaboration redundant. Of course, dying may take longer these days, when mortality is called to heel.

Death can be held at bay when body parts can be replaced and when modern treatments can extend life and hope.

But regardless of the body's frailty or strength, human beings are more than their disease; and their experience is more than their experience of illness. However much disease may cause just that - dis-ease, pain, sickness, the loss of bodily control, and in turn fear, resilience, embarrassment or despair, there is always more to attend to than the body. There are many differing ways of bringing relief to the body. This is explicit in the aspirations of hospice and palliative care work, without for a moment underestimating the life changing effects of (chemical) pain alleviation, for instance, or even the knowledge that pain and distress will not be the overwhelming factor in the last days or hours of life. People are more than systems of biomedicine. People are complex and very private amalgams of regrets, fears, hopes and dreams; of acceptance and anger; of compliance and rebellion; of inner strength and weakness.

Just as dying is not a disease, neither is the experience of anticipating the death of another or the struggle of getting on with living after they have died. This does not mean that listening, understanding and sharing are irrelevant. Rather that attention can be paid to the process of 'letting go'. But grieving is not, of itself, a sickness. It is a natural part of the pattern of coming to terms with a bewildering reality that can only partly be shared.

Thinking back to the series of 'critical incidents', with some trepidation, I will not object too strongly to leaving the competition over 'counselling' to others. Social casework is a different matter. One obvious aspect of this is providing information, and helping make sense of it, a service valued by patients and carers (Australian Community Health Association, 1997).

Diversity

Social workers concentrate primarily on people's personal and social situation; and we are expected to be committed to reducing inequality. Dying is not the same for everyone. While death may be the great leveller, it is socially distributed. Genes aren't everything. A person's risk of contracting life threatening illness is associated with occupation, education and social and economic position. When dying, the resources, which people can command – resources like health insurance, networks of influence, avenues to knowledge, car rides to the day hospice, willing and able friends, airline tickets, employment flexibility, money to hire round-the-clock personal care – vary. Personal resources, like the confidence to ask questions, aren't equally distributed either. Social work practice is inevitably political, because it is required to respond to such inequalities, by advocacy, negotiation, resource provision, lobbying, involvement in policy processes.

In postmodernity, dying is accomplished in many different ways. It may be shaped by the factors influencing the person's life course - income, culture, sexuality, gender, age, for instance and the meanings made of those. People when approaching death authorise particular persons to help them accomplish their dying. The medical complex is the most obvious to be accorded such authority, but the cleric or priest, the trusted confessor or the old friend, may be equally or more significant for some. Some people, in approaching death, may take their own authority to produce, direct and enact the drama. For others it may be the first time ever that they take the authority to exclude persons from their presence - a violent partner, an unforgiving parent, for instance; or the authority to bring back an important figure into their life - a lost child, brother or sister, for instance. Potentially, social work becomes part of the project assisting people to construct and re-order their own life narratives and 'sense of self', a project somewhat different from 'coming to terms' with dying and death through a lens of fixed identity (Mellor and Shilling, 1993; Napier, 2000).

People anticipate death in many differing ways - with relief, with dread, with pragmatism, in anger, ignorance or disbelief, or with calmness. 'To die will be an awfully big adventure,' said J.M. Barrie's Peter Pan. There is no one policy prescribed pathway to dying. 'Care begins when difference is recognised' suggests Frank. One of the policy issues then is about inclusion: how inclusive is it? How capable is it of individualising care?

So in answer to this question about policy, I will say that there are challenges for hospice and palliative care in relation to redressing inequality and responding to diversity at the end of people's lives. A biomedical focus reduces interest in difference. When there are explicit imperatives to provide holistic care, to attend to quality of life, and to enable an 'acceptable' and 'unembarrassing' death - one definition of a 'good death' (George, 1999) - they must surely include the provision of the necessary social resources to make that possible. Knowing how to find out about resources, assisting people to negotiate resource systems, finding ways through 'roadblocks' to access resources, lobbying for more adequate or appropriate resources, might be considered quite proper and equally important tasks in pursuit of 'quality of life'.

Talk and talking

We all talk to patients.

It is important not to be naive about talking, listening, comprehending and the consequences conversations carry. Different occupations hold different disciplines of knowledge; their members are able to hold different and quite particular conversations. These carry differing kinds of authority and different consequences. Some things have to be talked about. Some things are better left unsaid. Talking and silence involve politics too. A holistic approach in social work and in hospice and palliative care is alert and responsive to this dimension of power.

It is emphasised in hospice and palliative care work that the dying person is entitled to 'make the running', to decide what is important and what needs attention. Ideally this includes deciding when to talk and when to stay silent; what it is safe to talk about and with whom. It is also emphasised that it is the patient and the people centrally involved with them in their lives that constitute 'the client'. They may not wish to talk to each other. They may have become 'lost' to each other. They may not know what to say to each other; they may not know how to say what they want to say; they may have different ideas about what needs to be talked about. They may have secrets from each other (with dying, games are often played), secrets to be kept or unwillingly revealed. There may always have been someone in the family who does the talking, and therefore claims to know what is best for everyone, what has to happen. This time may provide the opportunity or demand that other voices are heard.

Sometimes things are unspeakable. For the patient, protection from demands to talk and 'unburden' themselves may be required. Skilled judgment is required whether, when and how to open up opportunities for the central actor, the dying person, to listen to and talk with the people who are involved with them in this part of their life. Rightly or wrongly, I think it is a good idea if someone on the team concentrates primarily on all these questions about 'talk' and 'silence', not as an add-on to their job, maybe even a social worker.

On the other hand, making the decision to divulge information to any professional is a risk. For instance, in describing the management of his treatment and care in a cancer centre, Frank (1991) writes, 'The first time we went to day care, a young nurse interviewed Cathie and me to assess our 'psychosocial' needs ... she began asking some reasonable questions ... The problem was where they were being asked. ... Our response was to lie ... Nothing she did convinced us that what she could offer was equal to what we would risk by telling her the truth'. (p.68) The decision about with whom it is possible to share worries, hopes and fears, may be linked to whether the person can do anything about it, or whether the person on a first encounter can be deemed to be trusted with confidences. This is one of the perceived dangers of speaking to an interdisciplinary team.

Being able to talk with people who are going through similar experiences may be preferable to talking with professionals, though it may be policy to forbid such encounters. 'Those who best affirmed my experience were often people who had been through critical illness themselves or with someone close ... these friends seemed able to look at me clearly and to accept what they saw'. (Frank op cit, p. 104)

Social workers have a duty of care to offer opportunity for talk about particular things, all of which are social: they are discussed in all the literature about social work in palliative care, They include talk about practical things like wills and funerals; talk about planning ways to leave something of oneself behind for children as they grow up; talk about relationships and resources in families; talk about the possible helpfulness of self help groups. They include talk about whether and how to deal with rejection and loneliness; talk about how to support or create social rituals for honouring and mourning. Much of social work talk is with people other than the patient - employers, schools, childcare agencies, friends and families, advocacy groups, for instance.

Such talk is purposeful and theoretically informed: it focuses on improving the environment around the dying person. How inclusive is it? For instance, in early social work/ general practice collaboration research, clients were able to distinguish different kinds of talking. Huntington's research (1981) revealed that the outcome of talk with social workers was that 'patients' felt they were put back in touch with the potential that was within themselves, potential which they had been unable to grasp and utilise' (p.81). It was 'no ordinary talking and listening' (p, 79); theory and technique were consciously employed.

Perhaps most important of all, talking is but one medium of communication, and one part of the work for everyone. Dying is, by definition, lonely; at least it has to be accomplished alone. Spending time with patients may be more important than talking, if the original meaning of hospice care still resonates. Policy has to be clear about the purposes of talk, whose purpose talk is there to serve and who can best help fulfil those purposes.

Time and timing

All this is important because time for many people, who know they are dying, is of the essence: the sands are visibly running out. How much time is left is unknown: some may not want to know how long they've got. For others a sense of time or an informed prognosis is crucial and a matter of consuming interest. How to live each day is decided against that uncertain certainty.

Daily living may be an experience of a battle against time, a battle to complete a cherished project, say, or to be 'spared' for long enough to see a daughter married or a grandchild born into the world. The rigours of illness, with its attendant inactivity, may mean that time suddenly hangs heavily on a person's hands; from being a diary driven or compulsively active person, there is suddenly too much time. It is a burden. For others, each day is experienced as a gift, and each moment is precious. It becomes urgent to spend time wisely and well, putting affairs in order, for instance. For the person dying, there may be regrets about time misspent, about the likelihood that there is little time to make amends, to right the balance. Spending more time with partners, parents, children and particular friends and less time concerned with work are familiar examples.

Setting new priorities, trying to achieve some long cherished dreams, or to fulfil one last wish may become paramount, or such prospects may get lost along the way in the more urgent struggle simply to exist. There may be competition for the dying person's time. Good hospice and palliative care is clear on this. As much as illness allows, command over the way time is spent is in the hands of the person who is living with terminal illness or who is dying. Making time available to patients to do with it what they will is highly valued. Flexibility and responsiveness are talked of as professional duties: discretion is exercised about use of time to fit in with patients' needs and wishes. Enabling a person to eat when hungry instead of at routine times is one small and important example. Planning with a patient to delay a treatment of chemotherapy in order to be 'well' to celebrate a birthday is part of 'juggling time' and therefore puts illness in a bigger picture of lifetime priorities. Understanding what this time means for a person dying and for their family and responding is one essential part of holistic care.

It is of course more common to read about how precious is the time of the 'professionals'. General practitioners have been known to say that time alone prevents them undertaking 'the pastoral role of caring and advice and understanding for problems 'social" rather than purely 'medical"' (Huntington, p.58)'. An unhurried approach has been valued by people in touch with social workers. Time is a limited resource for everyone, but in hospice and palliative care, professionals have traditionally named time as an explicit resource and an important part of care.

Policy therefore has to address how to cost and cost in time. The availability of time is one measure of the adequacy and appropriateness of policy. But the meanings of time are contested in policy circles. At what stage in life threatening illness palliative care should helpfully be introduced is disputed. To me it makes sense to offer holistic, palliative care early on in illness. When it is offered late, it may be rejected, because it signifies 'the end', for which someone may not be ready. In an Australian study (Lord and Pockett, 1998) patients have reported that they would value social work involvement early on in illness, particularly when the doctor breaks 'bad news' But while policy may espouse the strategy of early intervention, resistance from other 'treatment' professionals may make that impossible.

Time also bears a cost tag. 'Time is money' is the immediate thought in these days of economic stringency. Health insurance companies may decide what length of time they will cover for a patient's last months of life, before they are expected to die. 'Is the money going to last?' is a frequent anxiety. The question of who is in control of the time and manner of death is a complex policy question. Many people, in particular many old people, who do not die of 'something', wish to die in their own time.

The time required for mourning by people who outlive the dying may be governed by custom and ritual, by their own choosing or, again, by the kind of people they are, or indeed by their state of exhaustion from months or years of caring. The amount of time provided is often at odds with the time needed, by professionals, by employers, by family members and friends, who may regard time needed for mourning as time lost - from jobs, duties and obligations. (I do not disregard the 'protections' these may offer). Providing a holistic service must, for social work, mean documenting and reporting the match or mismatch between personal needs and social provision.

In retrospect, I am glad I held my silence at the time when asked the questions about policy and social work. I needed time to think. Before I am ready to speak, there is one more concept, the concept of a fair death.

A fair death

There has been much discussion of what constitutes 'a good death', but the pressing policy question now is as much about fairness as about goodness. Is a fair death the one people can personally afford to pay? If capacity to pay does not designate equality, what price tag is to be put on the care of people who are dying? What are we all prepared to pay for everyone? With increasing privatisation of responsibility for caring, in many countries greater control by health insurance companies over length of stay in hospital, the rapid transition of the hospital to be a place of acute, surgical procedures and intensive diagnostic and medical management and the home as the expected place of convalescence and ongoing care, it is hard to imagine that many will be able to afford the ultimate postmodern dying experience described by Small (1997). How are these rationing decisions to be made? If the principle of holistic care is followed through, then, in fairness, are not people whose dying and death may come sooner, and people, who have cared for a person dying, entitled to participate in the finding of answers to these questions? Empowerment, in social work and holistic hospice and palliative care, does not stop at providing individual care.

Policy practice

Writing this chapter has helped me confront what lay behind my silence. I wanted to see more clearly what has to be argued for and over, and to integrate the 'policy person' with the 'policy informed' practitioner in me. I do this by writing the political dimension into my view of social work practice in this field. The argument is for hospice and palliative care to return to their roots, wherever they are offered - in hospitals, homes, nursing homes or hospices. This will cost money. Attention to social and spiritual matters is being lost, and patient management favoured over holistic care. The person at the centre of it all is made passive, a passive recipient. The argument is bigger than social work's competence or diffidence, though advocacy skills are part of it. In arguing for holistic care, we also argue for ourselves.

Richardson (1998) has suggested that 'Writing is also a way of "knowing" - a method of discovery and analysis. By writing in different ways, we discover new aspects of our topic and our relationship to it.' (p.345). Like her, I have tended to write only when I know what I want to say, when there is something 'complete'. Here, it has felt less like a breakthrough and more like a concentrated gaze. Out of it have come some working concepts, a checklist to call on the next time round. The list is incomplete, as is their potential meaning. In the process, my 'positioning' in social work in what is known as the field of dying and death has changed.

These words speak to the situation now. My hope is that, being armed with the working concepts I have reclaimed, I will be more able, as a social worker, to contribute to changing current policy directions. Living and dying, after all, are more than breathing and heartbeats. Life and death, policy and practice, go together. Together they matter.

References

Australian Community Health Association (1997) *Health Outcomes: the case of palliative care*, Australian Community Health Association, Bondi Junction, NSW 2022

Frank, A. W. (1991) *At the Will of the Body*, Houghton Mifflin, Boston/ New York

George, J. (2000) 'The allied health professions and death', in A. Kellehear (ed) (1999) *Death and Dying in Australia: Interdisciplinary perspectives*, Oxford University Press, Melbourne.

Huntington, J (1981) *Social Work and General Medical Practice. Collaboration or conflict*, George Allen and Unwin, London

Kellehear, A. (1999) *Health Promoting Palliative Care*, Oxford University Press Australia, Melbourne

Lord, B. and Pockett, R. (1998) 'Perceptions of social work intervention with bereaved clients: Some implications for hospital social work practice', *Social Work in Health Care*, 27, 1, 51-66

Mellor, P. and Shilling, C. (1993) 'Modernity, self-identity and the sequestration of death', *Sociology* 27, 3, 411-431

Monroe, B. (1993) 'Social work in palliative care', in Doyle, D. et al *Oxford Textbook of Palliative Medicine*, Oxford University Press, Oxford

Napier, L. (2000) 'For ever beyond' in Fawcett, B., Featherstone, B., Fook, J. and Rossiter, A. (eds.) *Practice and Research in Social Work. Postmodern Feminist Perspectives*, Routledge, London and New York

Oliviere, D., Hargreaves, R. and Monroe, B. (1998) *Good Practices in Palliative Care*, Ashgate, Aldershot

Parker, J. and Aranda, S. (eds.) (1998) *Palliative Care. Explorations and challenges*, MacLennan and Petty, Sydney

Richardson, (1998) 'Writing. A method of inquiry', in Denzin, N. Y. and Lincoln, Y. (eds.) *Collecting and Interpreting Qualitative Materials*, Sage, California

Rumbold, B. (1999) 'Traditional hospice ideals and health promoting palliative care: What's new, what's not?', in Box, M. and Kellehear, A. (eds.) *Sink or Swim: Palliative care in the mainstream?* Palliative Care Victoria and Palliative Care Unit, La Trobe University, Melbourne

Small, N. (1997) 'Death and difference', in Field,D., Hockey, J. and.Small, N. (eds.) *Death, Gender and Ethnicity*, Routledge, London

Street, A. (1998) 'Competing discourses with/in palliative care', in Parker, J. and Aranda, S. (eds.) *Palliative Care. Explorations and challenges*, MacLennan and Petty, Sydney

Western Sydney Area Health Service (WSAHS) (1998) *Palliative Care Services. Strategic Plan. 1998-2001*, WSAHS, October

Willis, E. (1989) *Medical Dominance*, Allen & Unwin, Sydney

14
The lone crusader: Constructing enemies and allies in the workplace

Jan Fook

Once upon a time, I was teaching in a skills subject in a social work course with a team of several other staff. I had concerns about the cross cultural relevance of some of the skills training, particularly the training for interviewing skills, which was assessed by role plays. I have been a long term critic of the type of laboratory training model that was used, and I had previously published several articles which were critical of this approach (Fook, 1988, 1989). However I was not in charge of this subject, which had in fact been developed some years earlier by someone else who had since left that university. I was also concerned about one of the other staff, who I shall call Annette (not her real name), who I felt held quite discriminatory attitudes, albeit unwittingly, towards students of non-English speaking backgrounds. Annette, although junior to me, was also the current subject coordinator.

On one particular day, during the examination period, many of these issues came to a head for me. Some of the teaching staff in this subject had viewed a role played interview from behind a one-way screen, and were meeting to discuss the assessment of the student's performance. The people present were: myself, Annette, and a sessional staff member, whom I shall call Maria (not her real name). Maria was closer to me as a colleague than she was to Annette. She was an experienced field educator who had worked with Asian people over a long period, and who shared many of my views about cross-cultural work.

The interview in question was conducted by an Asian male student about whom Maria already had concerns. She had taught this student in a small tutorial group. In my opinion the interview was not too bad, especially if allowances were made for cross-cultural differences, such as grammatical expression. Annette was quite critical, and pointed out some 'faults' which I believed could be considered as cultural differences, such as the student not picking up on the exact feelings being expressed, and being too task focused in the interview (as opposed to following up on feelings). I could feel myself becoming more and more angry, as the discussion progressed, and Annette kept pointing out more of these instances, particularly as she would not consider other viewpoints which I thought I was raising in a reasonable manner. I remember thinking at the time that she was probably incapable of doing so, since I assumed that she had not read any of the literature which was critical of the culture bound nature of micro-skills training, as acknowledged in many of the mainstream text books on counselling and social work practice (such as Nelson-Jones, 1992; Davis & Proctor, 1989). I finally became so angry that I raised my voice, and criticised the whole laboratory model of skills training as epitomised in the writings of Ivey (1988) and Egan (1990). This seemed to take Annette by surprise. This took the debate to another level, and I do not now remember exactly what the team decided to do with regard to the specific role play being assessed. I think we did decide not to fail the student outright, but to allow him to resubmit his work. This aspect is particularly blurred in my memory because of my anger towards Annette. I was also puzzled by the behaviour of Maria, as I expected some support from her, but she remained almost silent throughout the whole incident, which lasted about half an hour. Afterwards some of us went for lunch (without Annette), but with some other staff whom we had previously arranged to meet to plan an allied subject. Annette had been invited but couldn't make it. During lunch Maria still only expressed noncommittal remarks to me about the incident, so I still didn't really know where she stood.

The critical incident as a reflective tool

What I have just described above is a true story, an example of a critical incident from my practice, an incident which was significant to me for many reasons. I hope, that by reflecting upon this experience, I will learn some new way of seeing, some way of 'breaking through' the web of preconceptions and experiences which seem to have conspired to construct the situation in ways which rendered my practices ineffective and my memory of it unsatisfying. In this chapter I want to reflect upon this incident, following a process and approach I have developed for reflective learning (Fook, 1996; Fook, 1999). In this process, which is loosely based upon the early work of Argyris & Schon (1976), participants begin by choosing a concrete incident from their experience, which is for them significant in some way, and then reflect on their own description of this incident, deconstructing the implicit conceptions which contribute to their way of seeing the situation. This opens people up to the possibility of many different perspectives and interpretations, which in turn allows them to reconstruct the situation in ways which may enable them to create different types of practice. This parallels a type of theory building process, in which theoretical assumptions are re-examined, and rebuilt in ways which are consciously more congruent with desired ways of thinking and acting. It is also a process which is valuable in enabling critical practice, since it facilitates awareness of implicit power structures and relationships, and ways of challenging and changing these (Fook, 2000).

You will notice that I have also written the incident as a fairy tale, a happening which, although it did occur (in broad terms) as I have written it, could recur, in many different guises, in many times and places. My account and memory of the incident in a sense is like a fairy tale, a story whose features and interpretations may change over time, but which will always have significance. The critical reflective analysis which I undertake in this chapter, in this sense, shares commonalities with narrative analysis and therapy (White & Epston, 1989), which recognises that people construct ways of understanding their experience (stories) which may simply be reflections of other imperatives, perhaps social, personal, structural or historical. It is in the deconstruction and reconstruction, or reframing of these stories, that they might find liberation from disempowering ways of thinking.

Why the incident was critical for me

I actually chose to present this incident and my reflections to a group of human service workers who were engaged in critical reflection with me in a relatively recent workshop. As part of my teaching practice, I normally deliberately model whatever process I ask students to participate in, so my presentation of this incident formed part of my introductions to the workshop series. I chose this incident initially because I was surprised at the amount of anger the memory of it still engendered for me, so many years down the track. On further reflection however, it seemed to encapsulate, in that half hour, so many of the dissatisfactions I had felt about that particular workplace, and my own undervalued position in it. It also raised issues for me about how to work effectively with people who I regard as politically and ideologically different, and how to bring about change in them, and the workplace, along lines which I consider to be socially more just. These are issues with which I still struggle, and which have been pertinent in all of the many workplaces in which I have found myself. Although it was an experience which happened some years ago, its significance spanned twenty years of experience for me in multiple workplaces. It pushed so many buttons, personal, professional and political, that it begged for more in-depth reflection. The reflection on my critical incident, my 'fairy tale' will therefore need to be 'self-searching in the fullest sense of the word, since it touches upon and brings together so many aspects of myself.

Embedded assumptions and main themes

It is really interesting to reread and rewrite descriptions of this incident so many years after it occurred. Each time I rewrite it, I make conscious decisions about what I will put in, how I position the points in relation to each other, and what descriptors I will use in relation to each of the elements. In writing the account this time, I was conscious of trying to write it as freshly as possible from my original memory, rather than from the number of subsequent reflections I have engaged in.

On analysing the account this most recent time, the first theme which strikes me is my assumptions about loyalty and support. I am surprised at Maria's lack of support, almost an implied disloyalty. It is as if I take for granted that her 'closeness' to me, through a shared set of beliefs around cross-cultural work, means that she should agree with me in this instance, perhaps every instance, despite her own more specialised knowledge. I seem to disregard the fact that Maria already had concerns about this student, presumably from other experiences in teaching him. I seem to construct the whole situation as one of a 'war' with Annette, in which people must take sides on the basis of loyalty. Annette is definitely the enemy, and colleagues must show allegiance by allying with me against her.

Bound up with this theme are concerns about authority and status. Several times I mention the issue of who is in charge of the course, and the relative status of Annette, myself and Maria. I am also miffed that my own authority, built up through an established reputation of writing in the area, seems to be completely disregarded. Status is clearly important to me, in both informal and formal manifestations. This comes as some surprise to me, as I pride myself on democratic ways of relating, especially in the workplace. There are several distinct ways in which I unwittingly reaffirm status differentials. I assume:

- that the person who has an established academic experience in the area should be the one in charge of the subject;
- that the person who is in charge does have the authority to take some lead (I am reluctant to question the position of Annette I think, partly because she is subject coordinator);
- that the authority of an established academic track record should carry its own legitimacy

It is interesting then, in the light of these assumptions, that I expected that Maria, the sessional staff person, should feel able to 'take sides' in a situation which would mean alienating at least one of the two people who were senior to her. I expect her to disregard her own relatively powerless position, and ultimately risk her own position in doing so. It is easy for me to 'risk' mine, since I do not have anything to lose, but to expect this of a person who has much to lose is another matter.

Another striking feature is the fact that I seem to disregard Maria's voice. Maria is an experienced worker, particularly in work with Asian communities. She has already noted concerns with the student, and would be in the best position to make this assessment, having taught the student in a small group for a whole semester. It would be fair to say that her assessments would be unlikely to be based on any discriminatory attitudes, or at least that she would be aware if her behaviour could be disciminatory. However I seem to be at particular pains to support this student whom I do not know (simply because he is Asian), and I do not seem particularly interested in taking Maria's views into account, except for expecting her to agree with me, and being surprised that she does not. I clearly have another agenda operating, the 'cause' of Asian students in social work education. I am on a mission, and for this I need an enemy (just one will do) and some allies (the more the better).

Another omission that is telling, by its very omission, is the fact that I am myself of Asian descent. Although I do not identify as totally Asian, my background as an Australian-born Chinese person means that I do feel a special responsibility towards Asian students in social work. I am also aware that I have an Asian appearance, and for many people who know me superficially, my Asianness would be a paramount aspect of my identity. When I factor these issues back into the incident, I can imagine that Maria might have had great trouble disagreeing with me (if that is indeed what she might have wanted to do) simply because she might have seen me as an Asian person taking up the 'cause', and did not want to undermine this. Also, she may not have wished to offend the Asian part of me. It was I who constructed the situation in these terms, effectively not giving Maria another way to respond or put her point of view across. Far from being disloyal, Maria might simply have been 'gagged' in several complex ways.

Interestingly, it also says something about Annette's sensibilities, that she was not deterred from arguing about an Asian student's capabilities with an Asian staff member. While I and Maria might have recognised the authority and relative privilege of speaking from the marginalised position, it seems that Annette did not. This racial 'blind spot' is perhaps an example of the type of attitudes which had annoyed me, but also goaded me into trying to assert my authority in a number of ways, to the point of feeling utterly frustrated. I felt that my authority as an academic was ignored, as was my personal authority derived from my marginal position.

I am forced to reflect further on the meaning of authority for me, and how it can be used effectively and appropriately in the workplace. I also detect an ambivalence about authority, as if on the one hand I am proud of it, yet uncomfortable in exercising it. I want to have my cake, and to eat it too. This incident also sends me back to questioning what types of situations I create and whether they are enabling for other people to speak and have their views recognised. I have always been a little impatient with people who do not seem to have their own strong views on matters, and who will not take the opportunity to speak up and voice these. I now reflect on how and whether I may contribute to creating situations which make it difficult for people to voice opinions in the first place. Other people may not want to be forced into fighting my wars in my ways. For others, the more diplomatic route may be more comfortable, and not necessarily less effective.

The 'lone crusader'

I am tempted to term this tendency of mine as wanting to be the 'lone crusader', and I feel this stance comes across strongly in the account of this incident. I clearly see myself as someone 'on a mission'. I take this aspect of my professional life very seriously. I have missions about all sorts of things, ranging from creating a more inclusive workplace, to flying the flag for social work against other professions, and to reaffirming women's ways of doing things. The trouble is that I seem to assume that no one else is on these missions (except for perhaps a few very close professional colleagues and friends, who I see as being as beleaguered as I am, so that they are to some extent simply an extension of my own identity and position). I have to do it all by myself. It is all up to me. Not only this, but I want to do it all as well. In the lone crusader mentality, this means that all injustices have to be righted, that everyone else has to come around to my way of thinking and acting. Of course I am speaking in somewhat hyperbolic terms here, because I am articulating unexamined assumptions, the stuff of fairy tales. But nonetheless, it is the 'fantastic' (as in fantasy) type of thinking which subtly guides our thinking, in the same ways in which the lessons of childhood fairy tales stay with us at our darkest and happiest moments.

Constructing the enemy

It is quite humbling to see that my own fairy tale doesn't include room for anyone else, except the enemy. It is strangely comfortable to have 'Annettes' in my professional life. Not only do they serve as scapegoats, but they give me a target, a defining point against which to test my commitment, my ideology, my personal longings and professional failings. This type of 'othering' process in which the category or label of 'the enemy' is created, performs many functions for lone crusaders. In the language of postmodernism, by creating binary opposites ('us vs them') (Berlin, 1990), we are better able to see and reaffirm privileged categories. By labelling others as 'different', we create the space and excuse to treat them in ways different from ourselves. (The problem of difference is well-documented in the literature—see for example, Minow, 1985; Williams, 1996; Crinall, 1999). By creating Annette as a problematic person, I am able to reaffirm my identity as a socially aware, right-minded educator. I create a privileged category for myself. I am not commenting here on the issue of whether or not Annette's behaviour and attitudes were really problematic or not (I still happen to believe they were and are, and I still experience a great deal of anger when I reflect upon her behaviour). What I am reflecting on is the fact that I also participate in constructing her in this way – I have a need, socially and personally, to see her in this way, because I have a need, socially and personally, to see myself as different from her.

Interestingly, if I construct my enemies in this way, I also give myself a way out. It is a comfortable position in some ways, because it implicitly absolves me of responsibility. 'Oh, I couldn't really do anything about it you know, because you know what they're like - they're all so conservative.' 'She's got a vested interest in things being like that so what can I do?' It is easy to shift blame and responsibility to 'enemies', those vehicles who carry the can for all the things we couldn't do, or the things we don't like.

Of course, we then have a vested interest ourselves, in ensuring either that we have no allies (because they are likely to want to change things) or our allies become like us, disempowered and alienated as well. There is a certain comfort in not changing, or not being able to change, a situation. There is therefore, a certain comfort in creating enemies, and a lack of allies, so that we feel we can't change things.

Laragy (1996) notes a similar phenomenon, in that caseworkers often identify with their clients, feeling powerless, in the same way that they see their clients as powerless. Workers tend to construct themselves as advocates of the client and enemies of employers or managers. This attitude is often coupled with an ambivalence towards power and authority. (Laragy, 1997). Whatever the genesis of these phenomena, the upshot is a situation in which the social worker is unable to change what they regard as an unacceptable situation for the client.

Oppositional thinking can therefore function as disempowering, if the self, the social work identity, is constructed as the powerless element of the binary opposite. This is an example of 'complicity with oppression' , in which relatively disadvantaged groups take on 'victim' identities which automatically confer a powerless status (see Fook & Pease, 1999, p. 225).

Such binary thinking is coupled with a modernist way of thinking about power, in which power is seen as a commodity, which can only be transferred from powerful to powerless people.

The only change is total change

This type of alienated thinking is also inherent in the way the idea of change is constructed. In my account, it is implicit that I feel that the only worthwhile outcome of my argument with Annette is that she change her views and behaviour. She should think like me, no less; and, furthermore, other people, like Maria, should not only think like me, they should voice the same opinions as well. The notion of the only meaningful change as being total change, is another fantasy which I suspect is harboured by lone crusaders. It is their mission to change the whole world alone.

I wonder where this idea of change comes from? I have found, in participating in many reflective group discussions, that many social workers share this view of change. Any changes they have brought about are somehow never enough. They really wish to have changed the whole organisation, to have gotten rid of that bad manager, to have elicited a confession out of that dodgy claimant, to have stopped that colleague from discriminating against Asian students and admit the error of her ways. Notions of these scales of changes are I think implicit in many of our social work practice texts. We must change that counsellee's views, we must eschew personal change and seek to change the social structure, we must take a systemic view of families and change the way they operate.

Why do we put such pressure on ourselves, and construct change in such seemingly unattainable ways? Is there also a degree of comfort in this? We define the goal as unattainable, and therefore feel excused when it is not reached? Or do we have a need to sell ourselves short, to see ourselves as people who are always trying, perhaps little succeeding? Is there a fear of agency and responsibility? Or are we perhaps simply too idealistic, and in cultivating pride in this idealism, we 'shoot ourselves in the foot'?

Retheorising 'the enemy': Constructing allies

How do I participate in creating situations which need an 'enemy' and which freeze out potential allies and their voices? How do I limit colleagues from fighting their wars (which might also be my wars) in their ways? How do I perhaps even stop the enemy from fighting beside me, in my wars, because of my need to fight against them? How did I know Annette was being deliberately discriminatory against an Asian student? How did I know that if she was aware of this, in her terms, she might not have been as appalled as I? How could I have created spaces so that Maria might have spoken up, in her own way, and found a 'solution' to the situation which did not mean that one of us had to lose, or feel betrayed or unsupported? In short, how could I have reframed the situation, acted differently, so that I might have constructed allies out of Annette and Maria?

Part of the process might lie in creating opportunities for other people to express differing opinions in ways which are not threatening or intimidating. I have become aware of what I have always known (but often not remembered in specific situations) that the person who speaks first, or speaks the strongest, or speaks from the highest position of authority, is often the opinion maker, the person who sets the scene. If this is me, then it may be unlikely that I will hear other views. I can open up situations for differing viewpoints by sometimes voicing differing viewpoints, creating a climate where it is acceptable to air difference. I can counter one strong view with two or three (not just one) others. I can delay expressing my viewpoint, until differing perspectives have been heard. I could have reframed the situation with Annette and Maria by simply posing a hypothetical cultural explanation for the Asian student's poor performance, and asking Maria and Annette what suggestions we could all make, if we accept such an idea. This would be positioning myself as an ally of theirs, all of us equally concerned about the student's performance, and all of us equally committed to exploring several explanations in order to most effectively assist the student.

'Unfinished change'

If we wish to retheorise our notions of change, away from 'all or nothing' conceptions, then Mathieson's idea of 'the unfinished' (as quoted in Cohen, 1975, pp. 92-97) is helpful. Perhaps we need to redefine radical possibilities as simply incremental change, aiming towards more macro level changes. All change is 'unfinished' in this sense, but nonetheless valuable.

Interesting in my account is how I seemed to frame the only acceptable change as a change of viewpoint, and, therefore, a change of attitude and behaviour on Annette's part. Did I really think this was possible, and what egocentric right had I to think this? I am sure I would not extend Annette the same courtesy in relation to my own thinking and behaviour. What gives me the right to assume this superior and privileged position? Would it not have been enough for me, in this specific instance, to secure an outcome which did not discriminate unduly against the Asian student? And had this not in fact been done? If I remember correctly, it was decided not to fail the student, but to give him benefit of the doubt and allow him to redo his work, after having been given some assistance in this. Upon reflection, this was not a bad outcome. The student would have to do more work, but he might also have benefited from the extra assistance and learning. Under the circumstances, this might have been the best possible outcome, and accompanied by an analysis about the culture-bound nature of many of the taught micro-skills, a beginning might have been made towards changing how the course was run. In fact, an apparently small 'practical' change of this nature, might have contributed to broader theoretical and ideological shifts further down the track. In many ways a change of practice policy, for instance, so that all students from non-English speaking backgrounds whose performance is in doubt were automatically granted a chance to redo their role plays, might contribute to more immediate ways of lessening discrimination, than a more amorphous change of ideology (since ideology does not necessarily translate into practice).

Dissenting voices

What has been the breakthrough for me, through my reflections on this critical experience? Do I really think it is possible to retheorise my enemies, to reconstruct them as allies? Is any change enough change? Whither ideals and passionate (if unrealistic) goals? Can I, simply through reflection, change my way of relating to my enemies enough to get them on side, and even, in effect, to change them?

I still feel and believe strongly that Annette was in the wrong, that her behaviour and attitudes, whilst perhaps not deliberately racist, were inexcusable, particularly in a social work educational setting. The strength of my 'lone crusader' mission is not assuaged by my protracted reflections on the incident. On the other hand, what might the situation have been if our positions were reversed, if it was I who believed the Asian student's capabilities were not satisfactory, and it was Annette who argued his case on cultural grounds? This is the question of how I fight for the cause, develop more sophisticated permutations of anti-oppressive practice, introduce a potentially more complex view, which undermines a unified approach. To some extent Maria was in this position. Although a committed and accepted worker amongst Asian communities, she was placed in the position of having to make a negative assessment of an Asian student, perhaps on culture-bound criteria. Politically such a decision loses ground against a more mainstream anglo-centric view, whether or not the student in question needs to improve his skills. How do we concede the battle but win the war? Lee FitzRoy discusses the politics of this dilemma in regard to her study of offending mothers, and its potential to undermine the feminist cause (1999). How can difference be incorporated so that it strengthens rather than weakens the collective struggle? (Fook & Pease, 1999, p. 226).

For me these questions are still caught up in notions of power, structure and positionality. It is difficult for me to change some aspects of my positionality - I am a woman, of Australian-born Chinese descent, originating from a lower middle class background. It is a perhaps a quirk of my genetics, my family upbringing, my cultural background, that I am not comfortable with open confrontation. I am also an established social work academic, someone respected within professional circles. It is interesting that some aspects of my position seemed to come into play for me more than others in this situation, that I perhaps felt my marginal status more keenly than my more senior formal status. Do I have less options available to me because of my socially marginal status? Would a white middle class man have handled the situation differently, and been seen differently by colleagues? How much can reflection, and hence more creative manoeuvring, compensate for a lesser social position, and in fact why did my more senior academic status not compensate for this? Was it purely discrimination against me on the part of my colleagues, or did I also perhaps participate in this? Perhaps the option of lone crusader was really the only one available to me. As I write this I reflect on Narda Razack's chapter in this book, and also Amy Rossiter's lucid and honest account of her own position as a white middle class woman attempting to transform the social work curriculum with respect to race and ethnicity (Rossiter, 1995). Would the struggles have been different for either of them?

These questions are intimately bound up with notions of difference, and how 'the other' is created and maintained. On one level it is tempting to retreat to the idea that someone from a socially marginal background like myself must always be the lone crusader, a maverick It is in itself, a privileged position. On the other hand, I must inevitably contribute to this view of myself, in the way I position myself in relation to others. It is this positioning, and the functions it serves or does not, which a critical reflective approach can shed light on. Just how much does it originate from preconceived ideas which do require challenge, or from structures which cannot be changed? In so far as my positioning is born of ideas which can be challenged, there is a window of opportunity for change, yet the opportunities may not be the same for every situation. The extent to which my positioning is a given and can be changed in varying situations, will depend on the ideas I and other players bring to each situation. Perhaps as a relatively marginal person, my position will normally be one of having to work hard to gain respect and authority, that which might normally be given more easily to those of mainstream background and status. However, what critical reflection allows me to do is to maximise my ability to influence each situation. I cannot guarantee an outcome, or how different players will react to my changed strategies and ways of relating. However it is likely that in the changes which do result, new ways will be found to rewrite the story. Maybe it is not a question of winning or losing battles or wars, but reconstructing the struggle as an ongoing one. Maybe it is enough to ensure that it continues, is unfinished, that it never disappears off the agenda.

How will the fairy tale look, now that I have generated these new insights?

Rewriting the story and reconstructing the ongoing struggle

Annette, Maria and I are about to view an Asian student's role-played interview and discuss the assessment. I am open to the idea that the student might not perform satisfactorily, but I also want to ensure that cultural factors and differences are taken into account. Before the viewing begins, I don't assume that I know what either Maria's or Annette's assumptions are, so I ask both of them how they see cultural factors influencing interviewing skills criteria, and how they see these as an issue with this particular student. I recognise that the accepted discourse can determine the views that dominate, so in this way I try to seize this position by setting the agenda, in a relatively non-threatening way, of discussing cultural dimensions *collegiately*. But I also acknowledge and use a position of formal and informal authority. It is informal in that it introduces a discussion of relevant ideas in a collegiate three way discussion. It is formal in that it gives me a potential forum to use some authority to introduce material about which I have written, in a way which is relevant to us all. In this way, rather than denying my position, I acknowledge and try to use it beneficially. I find, for instance, that Annette is not aware that traditional forms of counselling and pyschotherapy are not congruent with Chinese cultures, which prefer more directive approaches (Martin, 1998). And so I use my personal (and professional) authority to assure her that this is the case. Maria agrees with this, but argues that she believes the student in question is also not very capable of appreciating the full complexity of his interviewee's situation. Together we discuss and develop some criteria for establishing some reasonable interview assessment criteria for the student in this case.

By introducing this initial discussion (which may only be brief), I also gain the advantage of learning more about how Annette and Maria think, so that I can enlist their skills and attitudes in improving the course. It gives me information about how to frame our common goals, rather than assuming that our goals are different. I am thus not assuming that Annette, Maria and I are necessarily the same or necessarily different in our commitment to the subject and its teaching approach. I am instead assuming that, whatever position we come from, we can negotiate a position which will be shared to some extent. What I have been able to identify up to this point is that Annette, Maria and I are all working and teaching to a notion of what we regard as the 'good' interview, but that our expectations and standards of what is 'good' vary in certain aspects. For Maria the issue hinges on where we draw the line regarding what interviewing skills are acceptable across all cultures. Annette shrugs and says that she is really only interested in proper standards, and she does not want the university to earn a bad reputation with social workers in the field because it will jeopardise field placements. I am most concerned that students from different cultural backgrounds are able to graduate as social workers, and that we make sure our education thus uses and acknowledges the skills that they bring, rather than turning them into clones of a Western style of interviewer. This leads us into revisiting what our 'bottom line' is in regard to interview standards. We decide that we'll have lunch next week to re-examine these criteria in the light of what is already written in the subject guide. I offer to chase up some literature and research on the topic and to circulate it to other staff.

We are all, in common, daunted by the idea that some work and energy might be involved in rewriting the subject to take into account cultural differences, so we light upon the idea of using resources amongst the student group. We decide to include, as one of the teaching sessions, a 'focus group' of students which brainstorms these issues from each student's own cultural and social position.

We don't know what criteria we are going to redevelop, but what we have started is a process of change, in which common goals might be met, or, at the very least, rearranged. Although the outcome is uncertain, staff and students are at least united in the process of discovering new ways of seeing, of recreating new criteria, and in changing the course. In the process we will argue and disagree, yet we are allies in a broader concern. It is not a war between parties to see whose view can dominate, but a struggle to improve a course in which all positions can be sustained. My position has become more that of initial catalyst than of lone crusader. I am happy to have allies, albeit argumentative ones. And if their ideas of change are different from mine, then I will have to take the responsibility to discuss, accommodate and negotiate. If they refuse to budge, I may still end up the lone crusader, but throughout this process their relationship with me, and mine with them, will have changed. I may still dislike Annette and disagree with many of her views, but it is unlikely that she or I will remain unchanged through the joint process we have undertaken. And in the seeds of changes which have been planted, other changes may eventuate further down the track. An uncertain process will have begun in which power relations may become slightly unseated which will ensure the struggle continues.

Postlogue and breakthrough

The original fairy story occurred many years ago, and so it is not possible for me to rewrite the story in action, since that particular situation no longer exists. However, it is interesting to note that a few years after that incident occurred, I did challenge my alienated thinking, in assuming that the conservatising environment would not allow for any change. I simply proposed a rewrite of the course. It was accepted, and I did it.

Acknowledgements

I am indebted to Helen Jessup and Steve Rogerson, who first introduced me to the idea of 'constructing enemies'

References

Argyris, C. and Schon, D. (1976) *Theory in Action: Increasing professional effectiveness*, Jossey Bass, San Francisco.

Cohen, S. (1975) 'It's allright for you to talk', in Bailey, R. and Brake, M. (eds) *Radical Social Work*, Edward Arnold, London, 76-95.

Berlin, S. (1990) 'Dichotomous and complex thinking', *Social Service Review*, March, 46-59.

Crinall, K. (1999) 'Challenging victimisation in practice with young women', in Pease, B. and Fook, J. (eds) *Transforming Social Work Practice: Postmodern critical perspectives*. Routledge, London, 70-83.

Davis, L.E. and Proctor, E.K. (1989) *Race, Gender and Class: Guidelines for Practice with Individuals, Families and Groups*. Prentice Hall, New Jersey

Egan, G. (1990) *The Skilled Helper*. Brooks Cole, Califormia.

FitzRoy, L. (1999) 'Offending mothers: Theorising in a feminist minefield', in Pease, B. and Fook, J. (eds) *Transforming Social Work Practice: Postmodern Critical Perspectives*. Routledge, London, 84-96.

Fook, J. (1988) 'Teaching Casework: Incorporating radical and feminist perspectives into the current curriculum', *Advances in Social Welfare Education*, UNSW, Kensington, 43-53.

Fook, J. (1989) 'Teaching Casework: Incorporating radical and feminist perspectives into the current curriculum: Part 2', *Advances in Social Welfare Education*, UNSW, Kensington, 93-105.

Fook, J. (ed) (1996) *The Reflective Researcher: Social workers' theories of practice research*, Allen and Unwin, Sydney.

Fook, J. (1999) 'Critical reflectivity in education and practice' in Pease, B. and

Fook, J. (eds) *Transforming Social Work Practice: Postmodern critical perspectives*, Routledge, London, 195-208.

Fook, J. (2000) 'Critical perspectives on social work practice', in O'Connor, I., Smyth, P. and Warburton, J. (eds) *Contemporary Perspectives on Social Work and the Human Services*, Longman, Australia, 128-138.

Fook, J. and Pease, B. (1999) 'Emancipatory social work for a postmodern age', in Pease, B. and Fook, J. (eds) *Transformimg Social Work Practice: Postmodern critical perspectives*, Routledge, London, 224 - 229.

Ivey, A.E. (1988) *Intentional Interviewing and Counselling*, Brooks Cole, California.

Laragy, C. (1996) *Professionals in the Changing Workplace*,. Thesis presented for the degree of PhD, La Trobe University, Melbourne, Australia.

Laragy, C. (1997) 'Social and welfare workers in the Year 2000', *Advances in Social Work and Welfare Education*, 2 (1) , Australian Association for Social Work and Welfare Educators, La Trobe University, Melbourne, 104-113.

Martin, J. (1998) 'Chinese culture and social work', *Australian Social Work*, 51(2), 3-8.

Minow, M. (1985) 'Learning to live with the dilemma of difference', *Law and Contemporary Problems*, 18(2), 157-211.

Nelson-Jones, R. (1992) *Lifeskills Helping*, Holt, Rinehart and Winston, Sydney.

Rossiter, A. (1995) 'Entering the intersection of identity, form and knowledge: Reflections on curriculum transformation', *Canadian Journal of Community Mental Health*, 14 (1), 5-14.

White, M. and Epston, D. (1989) *Literate Means to Therapeutic Ends*, Dulwich Centre, Adelaide.

Williams, F. (1996) 'Postmodernism, feminism and the question of difference', in Parton, N. (ed) *Social Theory, Social Change and Social Work*, Routledge, London, 61-76.

15
Some notes on the government of death

John Drayton

There are a couple of reasons why I don't have many notes on the case I want to write about. It was a few years ago, firstly; before we had a computer in the counselling office. In those days we used to keep everything on files which, due to lack of space, we cleared out annually, leaving only those cases that were receiving on-going attention. And this case didn't get much of that. Second, there seemed so little to write. I suppose I could have made do with a few sentences like 'Parents arrived at mortuary with body. Did not want to release body to mortuary. Finally agreed.', or 'Ambulance transported body and parents. Booked into mortuary after some discussion in ambulance.', or 'Parents uncooperative re release of body to morgue staff. Agreed reluctantly after some time.' As it happened, though, I made do with recording a viewing of the body later the same day. So I don't have notes to work from.

I wondered for a while if this would pose a problem. It means, after all, that I can't vouch for accuracy in what I'm going to relate, or be sure that my memory has not somehow fiddled around with timing and tone. In fact, it probably has. I don't intend to grossly misrepresent what happened, but won't try to avoid the standard 'case study' mix of post-hoc analysis, fiction in the name of 'confidentiality' and back-watching. What I don't want is sentimentality, which has little to do with grief, or to depict myself as some consistent figure 'learning from experience'. What I intend is to relate this set of situations: a particular story which seems to me to sum up the job that I do. The hard part lies in deciding whose story it is.

It isn't mine. My story changes too often; or, to put it differently, my perception of the role I played shifts. Actually, that's not right either: I played a few roles that day, not all of them consistent, not all of them edifying, but all of them directly involved. And it is that involvement - that sense of both crisis and novelty within a situation of flux - that undermines any sense of ownership. I'll give you a version of what I did, what I felt, a sanitised version of what I thought, but I won't pretend that that's the story.

It isn't the parents' story either. All I know of that is what I saw and heard; what they let me see and hear. It would be presumptuous to claim that I could speak for them.

And it isn't the story of the dead boy, although he was there. His story has been broken down into a series of documents and reports - pathologist's findings, witness statements, police summaries, birth and death certificates, coronial correspondence, photographs, funeral company invoices - memories, empty rooms, guilt, quiet and resentments. The conflict in the story went on literally over his head. He was involved in every event: cause, motive and object; present throughout, never moving but imperceptibly changing as the conversations went on. In contrast to his olive-skinned parents, he was as pale as children are who have rarely been able to walk outside unassisted. He was never a symbol, never a literary device, but he had the shifting meanings of a metaphor to everyone involved. Not empty enough to be a corpse, not oblique enough to be sublime, the dead boy had, by the time I joined his parents in the cramped back of the ambulance, begun to decompose to the extent that I was aware of his smell and the first marks of lividity on the side of his head. This isn't his story either.

A shifty, unreliable narrator, characters unreadable but through the language and gestures of shocked desperation, a dead child blurring the edges of object and context. Maybe it's nobody's story. Maybe it's the story, rather, of the conflicts inherent in the unreliability, the obscurity, the blurring. Maybe there are so many perspectives that it's not possible to assemble anything coherent. And maybe that's not a problem. There is, after all, a bit of a cult around 'coherence' these days, a romantic faith that it is possible, through individual effort and insight, to construct order out of the essential riot of events. Social workers straining like someone in a comic book as they squeeze meaning from the primordial muck of other people's lives. Of course, it's nonsense, but it's got that purple prose feel that suggests Sincerity and Engagement.

I think it's nonsense because I don't believe in the essential chaos. Instead, I think, events always make some sense to everyone involved. It's just that the sense is not always the same and that sometimes the sense a thing makes is 'a mystery'. This only looks like a riot if I stand too far back. It only looks like it needs order if I want everyone's story to be the same as mine. It's only as dark as the Europeans thought Africa if I feel like setting up a colony.

When I write here about the dead boy, however, I'm telling a story. I've made things up, I've distorted and I've conflated. It's a theft, really: the appropriation of someone else's tragedy for dissection, analysis and interpretation in much the same way that the boy's body was treated in the investigation of his death. And on the same basis. I steal this story for you, by virtue of a set of qualifications and involvements I use to make money. It is nobody's story, but I'm doing the writing.

What has this got to do with the project this book of essays addresses? In a sense, the way I've put these notes together is as good an answer to that question as I can manage. If I look in practice for theory (or vice versa) I'm looking nowhere. Theory tells us what practice is, but can't exist without material to theorise. It tells us not only where to look, but how to look, why to look and even what looking looks like. Then it tells us how, why and where to describe what we've seen. Theory, rather than the imposition of meaning on the meaningless slime, is - in this sense - no more than a recognition that nothing comes naturally. Nothing can be seen in the wild because we can never have those kind of eyes; and anyway, nothing is ever purely itself: not a 'Case Record', a 'Case Study', a 'Social Work Intervention', not the 'Sudden Death of a 9 Year Old Boy' and not the 'Delivery of a Body for Forensic Examination'.

I don't intend to bore you by going over the legislative context in which I work. It's important, but not what interests me here. Some basic facts, though, are unavoidable. I'm going to put them here in point form, because I want them to appear as the landscape of my work. Each point represents a series of assumptions based on ideologies of bourgeois family and social structures, empiricism, patriarchy and surveillance. I'm putting them here in point form because they should read like they work: bare statements that indicate bare facts, features designed for the comfort of Somebody Else. They are not unchanging, they are not 'common sense', they are not objective. They are the political circumstances in which some grief is done: important, disturbing, but not what I want to talk about.

- In New South Wales, every 'sudden and unexpected' death is reported to the Coroner. This includes any death a medical practitioner is unable, for medical or legal reasons, to explain such as suicide, accidents such as drownings, homicide, motor vehicle accidents, overdoses, deaths in custody and deaths under an anaesthetic.
- The coronial investigation into these cases generally involves the conducting of a post mortem examination by a Forensic Pathologist.
- I work at the mortuary at Westmead, in the western suburbs of Sydney: an unfashionable area treated with a sort of nervous distaste by legislators and funding bodies. Stigmatised and patronised by the broadsheet media, rabble-roused by the tabloids, the region is stereotyped by the liberal urban middle class of Sydney in much the same way that same class in England stereotypes Australia.
- From the time a body is received at the mortuary to the time it is released to a funeral company, it is the property of the Coroner. Relatives need to make an appointment to see the body, and are subject to restrictions in obtaining physical contact.
- The investigation comprises the autopsy report, witness statements as provided to police and any other documentation considered relevant

to the four basic areas of coronial interest: the identity of the deceased, the date and place of the death, the cause of the death and the manner of death.

*

The mortuary where I work as a grief counsellor is designed to make a profusion of corpses acceptable to those of us working here. That probably wasn't the conscious intention, of course, but that is how things have worked out. Not that the staff are never affected by a particular 'case', but that, in the midst of being affected is the refuge of having a job to do. In other words, the place is industrial. Clean without being surgical, light green concrete floors which are hosed down regularly, dull silver refrigerator doors arranged in columns of three in the central area adjoining a 'loading bay' of metal grill, orange sidings and what, in the summer, feels like a tin roof. It has the security of being unsentimental: the advantages of uniforms and production lines: the safety of knowing that these appalling things are here to be processed, labelled and investigated. That no matter the look or circumstances of the death, the body is here, in a workplace. Everyday sees an average of six to eight dead bodies (in all states) being brought to the bay by government contracted funeral companies and ambulances. From there the bodies are weighed, measured and 'tagged'. Their property is recorded and they are assigned a refrigerator. The post mortem is usually conducted on the morning of the next weekday.

When I walk from my office to the staff lunchroom or another office, I expect to see a dead body. It is not the case that I stumble upon some traumatised cadaver in a shadowy nook: rather that here is where the labour pursuant to sudden death is conducted. I say 'labour' intentionally: we are selling particular knowledges, skills and behaviours to our employer the state government. In my case I am selling labour in the form of a series of interactions with bereaved and traumatised individuals. Intrinsic to this sale is the presence of corpses.

Still laden with meaning and a variety of taboos and fascinations, the bodies are, as it were, where they should be, when within the mortuary. Almost anywhere else the sentiments and superstitions surrounding them would be so stark as to be distressing. Within the confines of our workplace, however, tasks and procedures contain those other factors. A further meaning emerges as a consequence: the body as the vehicle of labour. Within a political and economic context of the private ownership of capital, it is hardly surprising that this industrial sense - in conjunction with the functional design of the workplace - proves, for those of us involved in sudden death as employees, to be compelling.

What I don't expect to see in this part of the mortuary is a bereaved person. There is a sense of security in knowing that we can walk around the offices and the post mortem room without at any time being faced with that most disturbing of sights, a stunned or weeping relative. So where do I place them? I am, after all, employed as a counsellor, not a technician or a pathologist.

There is a small suite dedicated to use by families at the western extremity of the building. It is here – amidst carpet, plush couches, tasteful lamps, and tissues – that we sit with our clients and work through the process of 'viewing the body'. We tend to refer to this suite collectively as 'the viewing room': a term which serves the dual function of indicating both the place where the bereaved are prepared for seeing the body and the place where we are prepared to see the bereaved.

I'm not concerned here with going through the viewing process with you. What interests me is the dedication of space for that process - a dedication which, as you will have guessed, protects us as workers as much as it provides a more 'domestic', as opposed to industrial, environment for clients. We know, of course, that it's as domestic as any waiting room so for us the industrial meaning remains. So do the families. But they recognise at the same time the symbolic nature of the gesture. It's as if the state is saying: 'Reference is made to your current situation and the processes consequently imposed. We are making this room look Nice. Your pain is hereby acknowledged.' Every flower in every hospital ward says the same thing, as woodenly. None of which means it shouldn't be said.

I'm aware of writing 'the body': it's a term we quickly learn to avoid. It sounds clinical to our clients - the relatives and friends of the deceased person: detached, maybe a little brutal, as if the person is somehow more and less than dead.

When the coroner is formally notified of a death, we are given contact details for the next of kin and a brief description of the circumstances. This usually happens on the morning of the autopsy. We then attempt to make contact: to answer procedural questions, to determine whether a viewing is required, to make an early assessment of trauma and to provide assistance in addressing any immediate practical issues which have arisen.

They're hard to make, these calls. We know in advance that we are entering a situation in which, potentially, the worst thing that can have happened, happened yesterday and now the shock is wearing off so that it hurts like crazy. But the pain isn't crazy. It's not chaotic, either. It's ordered in the same way as what we wear or what we see as clean or dirty or beautiful is ordered - and by the same mix of (themselves) ordered interests and re-negotiated habits and beliefs about normal and allowable.

So we make the calls and we get abused, thanked, blessed, threatened, sometimes in the same conversation. We ask how they are - knowing it's a dumb question but knowing too that the dumb questions are the ones they most need to answer. We give information

slowly,

calmly,

repeating,

emphasising and
leaving space for expressions of hurt.

We don't pretend we can fix things, but we come on with authority. We sound in control. We tell people the post mortem is happening to someone they loved (they are being surgically eviscerated, their skulls sawn open, their organs removed and examined and weighed, then replaced in the chest and abdominal cavities in a large plastic garbage bag to minimise leakage through the coarse stitching) and they thank us.

No, we don't go into that detail, but it is what 'post mortem' means where I work. When we use the words, that's what we refer to. It goes on like a bass line throughout the conversation: the person is more and less than dead. The people we speak with rarely choose to be conscious of this undercurrent. In rare cases they insist on it, in others they react aggressively against it, hearing any awkward phrase or hesitation as sounding a disjuncture in the system, which our call represents, like it or not, as an affirmation of its existence. So we ask our dumb questions and give information. We telephone 'clients' and discuss procedures. We 'normalise' and 'empathise' and suggest that they aren't really as alone as they feel, even though they know as well as we do that they are. It makes a difference. Then we hang up, make some joke the way people rub their hands after coming in from a frost, get a coffee and ring the next one, just as we're employed to do.

What does this have to do with theory?
Counselling for fun and profit

WCY and I were discussing ways to adapt our service so as to be both more productive and more efficient. We had been agreeing for some time that we should work smarter and finally took the plunge by contacting an acquaintance of ours (trained as a social worker but long since employed as a consultant in personnel and marketing with a multinational firm in the city) and discussing our vision. Pleased to help, she spent a few non-billable hours with us, story-boarding, brainstorming and butchering-paper. We then went off, fine-tuned, costed and prepared to roll-out.

Prior to the big day, we invited guests from the middle echelons of the bureaucracy and providers of religious and fee for service counselling to attend the premiere of our newly structured experiment. Cost minimisation being, along with customer satisfaction and the prevention of media difficulties for the Minister of Health, our natural focus, we decided to meet our guests in the re-named 'Viewing Centre' rather than hire an expensive venue.

WCY began proceedings by introducing our 'Vision Statement for a

Customer's Charter'. This document neatly sets out our new aims and objectives. We work to ensure that:

- customers leave each session happy;
- customers view themselves as 'Surviving Victims';
- customers are not so overwhelmed by their emotions that they cease paid work and become a burden to the tax payer;
- customers recognise that 'they have gone to a better place';
- customers view us as caring experts; and
- customers enjoy and utilise the right to grieve like middle class white men, regardless of age, gender, sexual orientation or ethnic background.

Our vision being roundly applauded by all present, we went on to unveil the new look Centre. The foyer was decorated by a mural drawn ourselves. Against a background of rolling green hills, at the end of what looks like a crisp autumn day, a golden sun is setting. Challenged, happily, by a limited budget, we had to make do with sheets of cardboard for our canvas, stuck together with masking tape. Ingeniously, we devised a system of strings and pulleys so that, as customers enter the room, the sheet showing the sun begins a gradual descent, finishing behind the furthest of the hills. Neither of us being skilled in art, it lacked a certain realism: in fact, in our darker moments, we both felt the drawing looked really cheap and childish, despite the hours we had spent with our texta colours, tongues poking out of the sides of our mouths so we stayed inside the lines. Talking about this, however, we realised that our picture was no less realistic than those glossy photos of natural scenes environmentalists buy: an apposite consideration given the strong links between Green ideology and the middle class liberalism towards which we now aspire. Down-sized, we agreed, is beautiful.

Consoled both by this realisation and the reaction of our guests, we led them into the waiting room of the Centre. Totally re-engineered to provide all the benefits of a counsellor without the need for one to be present, each corner of the room boasted life-size cut-outs of ourselves smiling kindly into oblivion. By these cut-outs we had buttons placed, each of which activates a pre-recorded tape. In the northern corner was the 'Symptoms' button: a list of feelings and actions the self-help manuals identify as normal. In the east lay 'Hints': a recording of practical ways to get customers back on track ASAP. To the west is a button marked 'Professionals Only'. When pressed a list of necessary skills for service provision is played. In the south is the 'Condolence' button: a recitation of some of the most helpful expressions we have encountered, including 'They wouldn't want tears', 'You'll meet again on the other side of the rainbow', 'We know how you feel', 'God wanted the best, now He's got the best' and 'You aren't too old to adopt in some parts of South America'.

The premiere went off splendidly. That evening, prepared for patriotic redundancy, we remarked that we were satisfied we had demonstrated a true synthesis of Theory and Practice: a caring, apolitical service using modern techniques for the benefit of customers and tax payers. Best of all, we had achieved this without once mentioning 'death', 'bodies', 'grief' or 'pain'. Final roll-out will occur as soon as we have raised funds to laminate our cut-outs. Pending this, we have placed the buttons and tapes in storage. We have, however, left the sunset where we put it.

The End

*

The dead boy had drowned in the bath seven hours ago. Nine years old, he had buck teeth and mousy-brown hair. From his mouth came a clear plastic tube. His parents sat in the back of the ambulance, on either side of the stretcher where he had been put. One of his eyes was open and his mother alternated between trying to make it stay shut and opening the other. Neither parent looked up as I entered.

I'd been called earlier that day by a hospital worker because the parents steadfastly refused to leave the child's body for transportation to Westmead. Rather than force the issue, the staff had arranged for them to be transported by ambulance to the mortuary together. Less safe by their presence, I met the family in the ambulance in the Loading Bay.

I'd not been in an ambulance before and remember it as being cramped with a confusing array of lights, switches, buttons and tubes. Crouched to the left, the father was watching as his wife stroked the boy's breast. There were, by this time, early signs of decomposition: blood had begun pooling at the back of the boy's neck, tinting his ears purple. The skin around his nipples was too clear, the veins light green and blue, starting to marble. Through everything was a smell of metal, plastic, disinfectant and the almost sweet odour recently dead bodies can exude. The woman, apparently oblivious to every change, continued stroking the body, speaking quietly to him in defiant intimacy, every now and then adjusting his eyelids.

She said he was cold to her husband and he nodded.

'My name's John. I work here as one of the counsellors.'
'You're not taking him.'
'I know that. I'm not here to take him. I've come out to see if there's anything I can do to help.'
'What could you fucking do to help?'
'Maybe you've got some questions ...'
'No.'
'He's not dead.'
'Yes. He is dead.', letting my voice down gently into the space between us.
'It's not fair.'
'No. It's not fair. It's never fair when this happens.'

Silent until now, the father mentioned a younger child at home with his parents.

'I don't care about her.'

He went to speak, then stopped.

'She doesn't fucking need me.'

'She does.' and he started to cry.

'You're not fucking taking him.'

'No. But soon someone will.'

'Yeah. And cut him up like meat.'

'Not like meat, but they will cut him.'

'It's not fair.'

'No. None of it's fair.'

'You don't even fucking know him.'

'No. I didn't know him.'

The father told me his wife was really upset.

'That's OK. I guess you are too.'

'He just shouldn't have died.'

'No. I guess it's not making any sense.'

'None mate. Not a fucking scrap.'

'Does it even seem real?'

The mother answered, not looking up.

'It's not real. Never. Everyone's always been telling me what to do with him, like I didn't know he was sick, like he wasn't mine.'

'And here I come and I guess you feel like I want to do the same thing.'

They both nodded then, like I'd said something true.

'What if you see him inside?'

'Why? We can see him here.'

'Not for much longer: they have to take the ambulance.'

'I know that. They'll just have to wait.'

'They won't for much longer.'

'I'm not fucking stupid.'

'I know. I can't imagine what this is like for either of you.'

'No. 'cause you didn't fucking leave him in the bath did you? Stupid, stupid.' And she muttered apologies into his chest.

'He's mine and you just want to take him. You reckon you can be all nice like you give a shit and then we'll do what you want.'

'Yes. I want you to do it. We both know it's going to happen and I'd prefer you to go out to them so they don't come in here.'

'They won't.'

'Yes. They will.'

Her voice was firm still, but had a tone suggesting somehow that the whole thing had gone on too long. Her nose was running. The dead boy's fringe was twirled about the index and middle fingers of her right hand.

I'm not going to tell you what happened. This isn't that sort of story.

There is no real story

That's why I've been jumping around a bit. Not to pretend to give you alternative versions, but to stretch in some way the words I write in; as if writing like I talk belies definitive consolations and condolences. I could have done all of this in a steady tone (like in this sentence), but that would be no more than a sham: at best the 'Real Story of Me Writing About an Incident at Work for a Chapter in this Book you are Holding'. And maybe that would have been enough. More than enough, even. But that would suggest to you the existence of a template, a standard (in both the senses of quality and quantity). Of course, useful templates exist, some are even consoling, but they aren't the point.

I can't leave it at that, can I? I don't want you to think I'm making some case for relativism, as if 'Everyone has their own Truth, each as valid as every other' because I don't believe that. Some beliefs aren't valid: free-marketeers, privateers (from schools to enterprise), bourgeois liberals, racists. These aren't valid: they're just ascendant.

So by a 'multitude of stories' I mean that process of ascent and descent: the class struggle. The way things like 'grief' are defined as 'normal' or 'pathological'; the way a body is defined as 'dead' or 'alive' or 'mine'; the way 'counselling' is defined. All these things change over time and place. But we take it for granted that we'll know a dead boy when we see one. And of course, we will. We just can't take it for granted he'd have been as dead twenty years ago.

So the stories involve the conflicts which are always going on: winners and losers tussling over what things mean and how they should look. These conflicts go on in places, at times. But these locations aren't the real story either: to focus on them is to miss the way they themselves have been put together. Or how the winners tell us that this is the World and that it's Natural. If we take something as natural as death and look for the cheap bit in the scenery - the masking tape joins in the cardboard - then maybe we can get hints about why it's put together the way it is: some glimmer of capitalism and patriarchy making the rules of dying. None of which means that people don't need support. In fact, it is in the need for support, the pain and its consequences, that those rules are clearest. Which itself doesn't mean that it doesn't 'really' hurt like crazy. It just means that support - the job we do here, as well - is itself located within relations of capital and ownership and experts.

Tussles, loss and every awful thing;; each power struggle, each piece of information; acts of compassion and oppression, attempts at empathy, analysis, intervention; every technique, strategy, symptom; lies, compromises, orders; silences. The world is roofed. Each place as cramped with meanings and negotiations and betrayals and loyalties as the back of an ambulance. We are, all of us, surrounded by switches we don't understand, weird lights and tubes which go from nowhere to nowhere before our eyes, all surrounded by industrial steel and a floor that can be hosed down when necessary. Each natural consolation is cheap and badly painted, with us looking out, a vague, welcoming smile on our faces. All of us, I mean. Not trapped: there really is nowhere else.

If such a bleak vision is true, do the acts of consideration (for which some of us are paid) mean any less? Does the contingency of things make tragedy less tragic, consolation less consoling? I hope not. I guess the story I tell myself involves the usefulness of these things - cheap and inefficient as they are - among a collection of rusty pulleys, strings and masking tape. The only problem I can see is the shaky way the sun - bright yellow until the texta started to run out two-thirds of the way down - sets as I walk off into it, a jaunty but moved spring in my step, like I've made a difference and look forward to doing more good tomorrow.

Acknowledgments

Cathie Peut provided invaluable support and suggestions in the composition of this chapter. It is a better piece of work for her input, yet she should not be held responsible for any errors of fact, judgement or taste which it contains.

I owe a particular debt also to WCY, whose work has been both an inspiration and a support over many years.

The following people have, over a number of years, provided the information and support which give the lie to notions of individual insight: John Merrick, Gina Paleologo, Jane Mowll, the Westmead medical staff and the Technical staff, and the staff of the Coroner's Court at Westmead.

Much of the writing was done to the accompaniment of Frank Zappa's You Can't Do That On Stage Anymore series. The discussion of reification and 'cheapness' owe clear debts to this oeuvre and to Ben Watson's entertaining analysis, *Frank Zappa: The Negative Dialectics of Poodle Play*, Quartet, London (1994).

16
From dilemma to breakthrough: Retheorising social work

Jan Fook and Lindsey Napier

We began this book with the claim that we were show-casing different ways in which practising social workers demonstrate their ability to improvise, to be intuitive, creative and responsive in context. The critical reflective process enables practitioners to create theory from practice experience, to devise breakthroughs in thinking from dilemmas in professional life. Our main concern in this book has been to demonstrate this practice of reflective practice.

In some ways the book invites readers to engage in a type of peer review process, in that we as contributors have opened our practice, in all of its uncertainty, spontaneity and honesty, to public scrutiny. This has not been an easy process. Whilst reflection might be entered into somewhat glibly with intentions to confine it to intellectual levels, the process is often disturbing, involving a courage to name and ask the hard questions, to change long standing and comforting conclusions and convictions. For these reasons, all of us, whilst not perhaps converts to a reflective approach, are certainly colleagues who share a view of social work as complex, situated, and necessarily open to interpretation and the use of discretion. We all share a commitment to improving our practice, and to scrutinising it thoroughly in order to do so.

In this last chapter we want to interrogate the different contributions, to reflect upon and analyse what they bring to us about professional social work practice, and indeed about the critical reflective process itself. It has been claimed that reflective practice does not exist and that there is no adequate theory of reflection (Ixer, 1999). What response to that claim do the contributions of this book make? What is critical reflection in practice? Does it make a difference, and what difference can it make? Given that critical reflection may be practised in a variety of ways, and that theories of it are still being developed, we hope to develop theorising around critical reflection by illuminating the contributions made in this book.

Differences in the critical reflection process

Let us begin with a word about differences. Although we all worked with the same guidelines in preparing our chapters, each of us has chosen a process which was meaningful for her or him. Each of us has engaged with the reflective process in markedly divergent ways. Some, like John Drayton, have spoken of specific instances in their practice which have illuminated the entire job. Others, like Sheila Sim and Andrew Lowth and Michael Bramwell, have relived entire cases with people, which have been watersheds in their development. Authors like Chris Shipway and Mark Baldwin have taken a different point of entry, that of reworking a particular theoretical stance through a case study of a program. Yet another type of reflective process is modelled by Narda Razack, who has reflected on her professional development, through the prism of different incidents which marked major breakthroughs for her.

The reflective process also differs markedly in the ways in which we integrate our theorising with experience. Some, such as Rachel Balen and Jan Fook, are initially most struck by how a long ago happening has stayed with them, sometimes because of the degree of emotion the incident engendered. The theorising is not immediately evident, but happens as they revisit the earlier experience. Others, like Cathie Peut and Lindsey Napier, are aware their experience is already reflective of particular theorising, which in part represents the dilemma for them. Their reflection involves another level of theorising which assists them to see it in new ways. For still others, like Narda Razack, the theories with which they are currently familiar, allows them to make some more coherent meaning of numerous experiences. Some authors, like Nigel Hinks, use the reflective process to re-examine and develop a chosen theoretical practice framework. The reflective process then reaffirms the use of theory in many different ways, as catalyst and template, in restricting and liberating ways. The process of creating theory also involves the process of relinquishing theory.

Each contribution differs in other major substantive ways. We vary widely in terms of experience, and stage of career. Some authors are relative new-comers to the profession. Others are longer stayers, who are nonetheless reflecting on very early professional experiences. Some are experienced professionals for whom basic issues still have credence in current experience. We come from a variety of practice settings (medical, statutory, educational, community) and cultural contexts (Canada, the United Kingdom, Hong Kong, Australia). We work in a variety of roles (direct practice, program development, research, education). The range of formal theories drawn upon reflects place and time of education. The issues range from queries about the adequacy of practice theory to the pull of personal involvement, the rage of social injustice to the grief of personal inadequacy. For some readers, some dilemmas presented will seem trivial or obvious. For others, the illumination will be surprising and moving. Still others may find breakthroughs for themselves, not in the content of authors' experiences, but in the reflection on their own practice which is stimulated by these practitioners' stories.

The reflective process clearly takes different forms, for different people, at different times. It is this diversity, this multiplicity, this inclusiveness, which is one of the very valuable features of critical reflection. Its flexibility allows meanings, new and changing, to be developed, throughout the vicissitudes of a professional career and a personal life. We are never too experienced to learn from the newest graduate or the most 'down and out' service user. We are never too inexperienced to create insights into the most enduring professional dilemmas. We are never too practised to revisit our successes or failures, our certainties or uncertainties, to recreate new theories for new situations. Professional social work practice must be critically reflective to stay alive.

Let us revisit the reflective processes of the contributions by reflecting on the content of what they have raised.

The dilemmas

Control, power and change

How much control should we have, and do we have, as social work practitioners? What is the nature of power, and who exercises it? How much change should we be able to bring about, and how responsible are we for the different scales of possible change?

Many of us expressed different degrees of *Angst* about these questions. While for most contributors, assumptions about change and power run like an undertone through their accounts, for some they constitute the most burning questions. In some cases, the questions are tied up with the social justice mission of social work. Silvia Alberti was reacting to a misuse of power in a prison, about which she felt she could do little about. Sheila Sim felt very strongly that she should have been able to do more to protect the rights of the young mother Sandra, when her new born child was removed. Jan Fook, like Narda Razack, was highly concerned about issues of anti-racist practice, and the extent to which racist practices can be changed amongst colleagues. Jan, whilst wanting to preserve the rights of an Asian student, also wonders about the extent to which the attitudes and behaviour of a colleague (and indeed the curriculum) can be changed to be more inclusive of different cultures. Narda explores these issues through her own experience of becoming a social work practitioner and academic, describing the dilemmas and breakthroughs involved for her in manoeuvring between her own, and more mainstream, cultures.

Mark Baldwin is concerned, like Nigel Hinks, with how research can change organisational practice, and practice within organisations. For Mark the dilemma is one of how research can be conducted so as to be owned by – and incorporated into the practice of – workers whose practice is being researched. For Nigel the issue is more one of how organisational practice can change to incorporate ongoing processes of reflective practice learning, a question which has remained with him throughout twenty years of professional experience.

Rules, and breaking them

The theme of professional rules, and their restrictive nature, as an even more common dilemma. For some contributors the rules take the form of particular theories or concepts which seem too stilted to guide practice. This leads Rachel Balen to question the relationship between theory and practice through a case which has haunted her for many years. For May Wong, the concept of self-determination doesn't account for the complexities, ethical ambiguities, and contextual considerations which affect professional practice with a young woman involved in the sex industry.

For Molly and John Harvey, the rules involve professional labels and boundaries. The dilemma for them is that when the professional labels are removed, relating to everyone becomes much easier and more authentic. Yet on the other hand, there are costs involved in the resultant partnership.

Andrew Lowth and Michael Bramwell also question the rules surrounding personal involvement, and the sorts of barriers which are set up through labelling. In what was for both of them a landmark experience, they speak of Susan, and how they were aware of changing traditional professional ways of relating to this remarkable woman.

Problematic conceptualisations

Yet for others, the dilemmas lie in problematic, oppositional ways of conceptualising aspects of social work. Lindsey Napier speaks of her discomfort with the apparent split between 'policy' and 'practice', and the unacceptable assumptions about social work which this entails. Cathie Peut raises the familiar dilemma of the 'care vs control' debate, and the over-simplifications which are sometimes made about practices like 'referral'. Chris Shipway discusses the dilemma of 'empowerment vs expert', how community groups can be empowered at the same time as relevant expertise from professionals is recognised.

Finding meaning and understanding

A different kind of theme is a broader type of dilemma. It is more about the finding of meaning, an ongoing quest to affirm the work, and the worker, in broader professional context. John Drayton wonders what is the 'real' story of his work in a mortuary, and whose it is, given the interplay of economic pressures, organisational contexts, the loss and grief of families, and his own imperatives to 'do good'. Narda Razack struggles to construct her professional identity between what seem to be the opposing worlds of the 'mainstream' and the 'marginal' in social work practice and academia. Nigel Hinks' goal is to develop a way of linking theory and practice, of introducing action research and reflective practice in a participative way into an organisation, and at the same time to resolve his own concerns about enhancing meaning and understanding in respectful work with colleagues and service users. Molly and John Harvey seek a reaffirmation of their approach to partnership.

Theorising the Dilemmas

What concerns underlie these differing dilemmas? What are the more embedded ways of thinking in social work, which point us towards the more unspoken culture of the profession?

The dilemmas arise as such for the contributors, because they encapsulate particular ways of thinking, constructions which pose sticking points for practitioners. They constitute stumbling blocks to creative, meaningful, assertive and effective practice. Whilst this sounds obvious, it is important to note that, since each of these stumbling blocks arises out of a particular way of thinking or theorising in social work, then the identification of that particular way of theorising may point to new ways of theorising which are more enabling.

What are these particular problematic ways of theorising identified by the contributors in this volume?

A clear theme in all the chapters is how simple dichotomies, oppositional ways of thinking, have produced unhelpful ways of characterising social work. Dichotomous thinking has been identified by postmodern and poststructural theorists (for example, Berlin, 1990; Sands & Nuccio, 1992) as a feature of the way in which language constructs power relations. Binary opposites are sets of categories which involve two elements, always characterised as the opposite of each other, and in which one element of the pair is privileged or valued over the other. Often it is a male characteristic valued over a female-associated one (as in the binary opposite 'male-female'). When ideas are deconstructed, these binary opposites are often at the foundation of accepted ways of characterising thinking. They have become unquestioned assumptions, which are often embedded in culturally acceptable ways of thinking and relating. Such binary characterisations may often be unhelpful in social work, in that they may construct social work and its practices in ways which actually work against the intended aims and philosophies of the profession.

A number of these binary opposites, or splits between two opposing categories, are evident in the work of all of us.

The 'professional/personal' split underlies Andrew Lowth's and Michael Bramwell's doubt about the way they relate to Susan, and is at the heart of their reconstruction of their practice. These are also issues for the Harvey's, who illustrate the changed nature of practice without professional labels. To some extent, the split between 'professional/client' is also related to this dichotomy, the assumption that keeping this clear boundary is a proper way to practice. For May Wong, this split also underlay her concern about suspending her personal judgement in order to best assist her young client.

The 'theory/practice' dichotomy is of course one of the most recognised, but yet the one that still probably concerns us most. Much has been written about, and criticised, regarding this dichotomy (Hindmarsh, 1992), yet it still manages to underpin much of our teaching of social work (Solas, 1994). It is a long remembered problem for Rachel Balen, who questions the adequacy of some early radical theory in helping her understand and practice with a child protection case. Nigel Hinks voices similar concerns in a different way, in his need to discover how we can continually learn from practice, to foster practice learning within an organisation. For May Wong, the theory of self-determination seems far removed from the practice of it, especially in relation to the case of a young woman choosing to be employed in the sex industry.

There are other less obvious, but perhaps not less-widely held, dichotomies. Lindsey Napier speaks pertinently about the 'policy/practice' split, the assumption that the two are mutually exclusive, and that policy is superior to practice (in some circles), or is not the concern of practitioners (in others). Cathie Peut points up many commonly encountered dichotomies. First, the 'care/control' opposition has been well-noted in much social work literature (Howe, 1996). This split is associated with 'radical' thinking, which tends to oppose 'statutory' against 'community' and obviously 'radical' against 'conservative'. Control functions are irrevocably associated with statutory bodies, and, obviously, care with voluntary, community-based organisations. Interestingly, other oppositions also arise from these. One is the dichotomising of 'casework' functions against 'counselling', a more highly valued activity. Casework activities, like referral, are seen as basic and simple, whereas counselling is seen as more complex and advanced. She uses Rojek's term, the 'gladiatorial paradigm' (1986) to refer to the almost warlike relationship between these two camps, and to the respective workers' so constructing one another (where is the place for service users?).

Jan Fook picks up on this imagery, by posing her dichotomy as 'enemies/ allies', particularly in the struggle to develop anti-oppressive practices in the education of social workers. The tendency is to divide colleagues up into two mutually exclusive and opposing camps, and to construct the struggle as a war. There is an element of this type of dichotomising in Silvia Alberti's account, in which she had constructed the prison authorities as 'the system' about which nothing could be done. Her dichotomy became one of 'the system vs the worker', one which alienated her from the ability to change the situation.

To some extent, this type of construction comes across in Narda Razack's account, where she seems to construct two main cultures, the 'mainstream' and the 'marginal', with her dilemma being one of constantly negotiating her positions between these two camps.

Chris Shipway has also constructed two camps, the 'to be empowered' and the 'expert', assuming that in order to empower one group, the expertise of the other may be denied. His chapter tells the story of how he resolves this oppositional dilemma. This dichotomous thinking about power and authority is evident in other accounts. Sometimes the power is invested in the statutory authority (as in Cathie Peut's conceptualisation), but this sometimes means to the detriment of the non-statutory worker. This is the case in Sheila Sim's account, where she seems to assume that she does not have power because she is only the hospital worker, not the child protection worker. This assumes a dichotomy of 'powerful/powerless', equating with a dichotomy of 'statutory worker/non-statutory worker'.

Another theme around power and authority is the discomfort with it. Jan Fook illustrates this in a type of ambivalence around the exercising of authority and power. The dichotomy in operation here is that of 'authority and power vs collegiality', assuming that only one can be practised to the detriment of the other. Lindsey Napier echoes this ambivalence in relation to the profession of social work, as if somehow speaking up for social work will somehow work against service user interests. This is a re-run of the 'professional/client' dichotomy, but in an entirely different guise. In this case Lindsey is wary of supporting the profession against the needs of service users, but it still assumes the mutual exclusivity of both sets of interests.

Breaking through into theory building

The dilemmas contributors have identified have helped us create theories about how we have constructed social work and its practice in unhelpful ways. How do we as contributors retheorise, help reconstruct our notions of social work, which allow us to break through these limitations of thinking?

Notions of professionalism

We tend to reject the idea that professional practice is somehow opposed to personal involvement. Instead we recreate a notion of professional practice which incorporates, and values, the ability to relate to service users as holistic human beings, with as much, if not more, to offer workers, as workers can offer them. For Andrew Lowth and Michael Bramwell, Susan taught them to remake professional boundaries, to have confidence in relating as whole people, to service users who are also whole people like them. They affirm their capacity to be congruent and confident with how they use themselves, and develop a closeness for therapeutic ends. Like Molly and John Harvey they no longer feel bound by professional labels, and find deep satisfaction in work in which they participate as people, rather than solely professionals. In a sense, rather than splitting the personal and professional, their remade practice can be characterised as involved and connected, as 'label-free' practice, in which the person's story is valued for its own sake, without professional preconception.

In this type of practice, workers are able to acknowledge, value and use their own experiences, personal, emotional and social, in relating to, understanding, and working negotiatively with service users. This type of practice is modelled in both Cathie Peut's and John Drayton's accounts, in which they try to set up a situation which allows for mutual dialogue. It is interesting that in this type of model, Cathie and John do not use the language of power in speaking about themselves, but only in reference to other workers. It is as if they do not seek power for themselves, and do not see it as being important for themselves.

Professionalism is also not necessarily 'anti-client'. What Lindsey Napier discovered was that in resolving the 'policy-practice' split in social work, she was also freed to speak up for social work. In recreating practice theory around social work in palliative care to embrace policy dimensions, she realised that the social work professional orientation does speak for the client. Sometimes professionalism may involve boosting the status of the profession so that the needs of service users are better met. Professionalism can also therefore promote client interests.

Contextuality

Whilst the notion of context has long been regarded as integral to social work's definition of itself, the contributors go some way towards reworking the notion of contextuality. Whilst traditionally we have recognised that context plays an important part in social work practice, indeed that we practise with people in context, contributors extend this understanding to develop how we actually work *with* context, rather than simply *in* context. Narda Razack illustrates how taking into account her positionality, she constructed a number of different identities (positions) which allowed her to make meaning of social work. By understanding how she related (reflexively) to her changing contexts, she was able to create identities for herself which helped her to practise meaningfully. Contextuality in this sense involves a reflexive understanding of positionality.

This reflexive understanding also allows for practice to be reconstructed in negotiative terms, and in different contexts. Once the practitioner appreciates his or her own position and influence, it is possible to use this understanding to set up relations of negotiation, rather than inevitable conflict. Since the practitioner is able to recognise that her or his own position, rather than being necessarily privileged, is 'implicated' (like John Drayton) or 'situated' as much as any other, then the focus becomes one of negotiating between different positions, rather than trying to enforce the domination of one position over another. The practitioner is able to reflexively reframe the situation, to write themselves back in as being at least partly responsible for constructions which may frame the situation in unworkable ways. Cathie Peut therefore tries to reframe the 'care/control' dichotomy, and in this way tries to set herself up as ally with Mary and Diana, the youth worker. Jan Fook attempts to reframe the 'enemy/ally' dichotomy in efforts to create a more collaborative team to establish culturally inclusive curriculum policies. Using an understanding of how they themselves, their ideological and theoretical preconceptions, their status and roles, and personal characteristics contribute to the specifics of the situation, they build a vision of practice which uses these features to advantage in specific contexts, rather than as limiting factors.

Shifting positions and making meaning

As Narda Razack so clearly illustrates, the process of reflection is a dual one of constantly making meaning out of new situations, which involves a shift in position, a continual change in identities. This change of social positioning, as ourselves as subjects are made and remade, is also a process which applies to other players with whom we interact. Cathie Peut is aware of how her client is made a social subject in different ways by different referring agencies.

There is a sense in which this identity change also incorporates personal change. Lindsey Napier's identity is able to change, so that she no longer needs to incorporate the counselling role as part of the social work identity. Jan Fook's sense of herself has to change in order to incorporate herself as authoritative academic and person of Asian descent, so that she can practise effectively. This is a process which has some parallels with Chris Shipway's journey, in that he needed to find a way to incorporate both the participative and authoritative aspects of himself. Sheila Sim needs to reframe herself as a more powerful person. May Wong, in redeveloping her notion of self-determination, also redevelops a notion of who she is in relation to her client - their needs are allied, rather than opposing.

Theory

Notions of theory are remade in many different ways. The dilemmas contributors raised tended to assume fairly rigid notions of theory, whether formalised sets of theories such as 'empowerment' theory, or specific concepts like 'self-determination'. Dilemmas arose because these sets of ideas did not sit with practice experience.

Some authors now see their relationship to theory quite differently. Rachel Balen speaks of the need for constant evaluation, taking into account both complexities and personal reactions. Nigel Hinks discovers the benefits of an iterative cycle of evaluation and learning, and the ongoing struggles which will always be involved in maintaining an environment where this process of theory creation can be fostered.

The practice theory around supposedly simple concepts like 'self-determination' and 'referral' are redeveloped in more complex ways by May Wong and Cathie Peut respectively. May reworks her notion of self-determination to include more room for the client's views, as well as social and organisational context. Cathie shows how the practice of referral is irrevocably constructed by a host of other constructions operating in a particular context. For her, theoretical constructions both mould the ways she sees, and also allow her to see the way other players see, and therefore interact, with her. Theory is always relative to other constructions.

Theory is also understood in broader ways. For some contributors, there is a sense in which a reaffirmation of broader values, which are not always easily identifiable with particular theoretical formulations, provides the meaning and understanding which is crucial in 'breaking through' their dilemma. For Nigel Hinks, his discovery of the action research and reflective learning approaches, put him back in touch with longstanding values of respect for colleagues and service users. For John Drayton, the meaning is ultimately in 'doing good' - despite all the different theoretical constructions, different perspectives and interpretations, the uncertainties and contingencies of practice, there is value in what we do. His story is ultimately one which both reaffirms the basic values of social work, and at the same time is reaffirmed by them.

Empowerment and power

Questions of how to empower, of how to gain equality for disadvantaged groups and a voice for the marginal, tend to become reworked as notions of inclusivity. Rather than assuming that less powerful groups can only be empowered at the expense of the more powerful, contributors develop the ways in which both more and less powerful can work together, and how different voices and groups can join in a collaborative endeavour so that respective talents are valued and utilised. Chris Shipway models this in his chapter, in which he redevelops his theory of community crime prevention so that it incorporates shifting roles for the 'expert' and 'non-expert', as they continually renegotiate where the expertise lies in each instance. He learns to value his own expertise as facilitator, as well as his expertise in identifying the expertise of others.

In a slightly different way, Jan Fook's ambivalence about power and authority is turned into potentially empowering strategies for all. By recognising her own power, authority (both personal and professional) and status, she is empowered to use this in creating a more enabling environment for colleagues to voice their views, and to negotiate a shared position.

Mark Baldwin begins from this type of position, in that he has already learnt the pitfalls of conducting research which is not 'owned' by participants. By establishing an environment, through the model of cooperative inquiry, in which practitioners reflectively and collaboratively create their own practice theory, they are able to empower themselves to both improve practices based on their own imperatives, rather than those of managers.

Coming from an entirely different angle, Sheila Sim discovers her own power and agency. By deconstructing her own position in her own story, she redevelops her notions of power by writing herself back into the story, and discovering the many points at which she did, and could have, acted. Silvia Alberti learns that by reconstructing her notion of 'system' as more fragmented, she is able to find ways to break through her impasse with prison authorities, and to devise a program for drug offenders which is both more empowering for them, and more attractive to authorities.

Conflict

It is interesting to note that the issue of conflict is present in most accounts, although it is generally not raised explicitly as the presenting dilemma. Andrew Lowth and Michael Bramwell regard themselves as in conflict with the professional norms of emotional closeness to clients. Sheila Sim and Silvia Alberti are at the same time awed and alienated by 'the system'. Lindsey Napier is struck by major disagreements about the role of social work in palliative care. Cathie Peut was placed in a conflictual situation by a non-statutory worker, and John Drayton spent time with grieving, and hostile parents. For Jan Fook and Narda Razack the conflict is also tied up with issues of marginality. Narda's chapter is replete with instances, where she is either in disagreement with, or feels oppressed by, authority figures who represent a mainstream social work culture. Jan tries to deal with the dual position of being both marginal and powerful, to argue for anti-racist practices.

How do we deal with conflict if it is not perceived as a dilemma by us? There are very few accounts of 'head on' confrontations, of overtly aggressive encounters, but rather the theme is one of trying to find a way through or around conflictual positions. Lindsey Napier both seeks a stronger case and a better timing, in order to win her ground. Silvia Alberti invents a programme which meets the needs of opposing groups. Jan Fook reframes the debate. A major theme, as in Cathie Peut's chapter, and as we have noted earlier, is the construction of dialogue with allies, of establishing relationships for joint negotiation, rather than assumed conflict.

Does critical reflection make a difference?

For most of us, the experience of critical reflection was empowering and liberating, for ourselves, and sometimes for others involved in our stories. The breakthroughs allow new ways of seeing, new possibilities for action. In providing different constructions, we are freed from old ones, and in the process are able to reaffirm the values which make the practice of social work meaningful.

What claims do we make for critical reflection?

We are not claiming that critical reflection answers, or should be able to answer, all the current ills of the workplace, and the social ills, contexts and structures we are called upon to work with. What it does do, is create opportunities where before they might not have been evident. It maximises the practitioner's ability to see possibilities for change, and thus maximises (but does not guarantee) their ability to influence change. Change is comprised of many factors, many unpredictable and unknown. Critical reflection simply maximises one aspect - the practitioner's agency and role. By retheorising change and its possibilities, so that the social worker actor is located directly within the possibilities, critical reflection can be an enabling and empowering tool. And we cannot foreclose on saying whether, when these new possibilities are enacted, that they might bring about structural changes. Certainly for some people, the changes and breakthroughs which were wrought in situations which had previously seemed stalemated, may have felt like structural change. Given that the significance of change will vary from situation to situation, the process of critical reflection even throws into question the need to define to define structural change.

Critical reflection is at the same time enhanced, and limited, by the theories, the ways of seeing, which are available. In this sense, it is only as good as the theories available. For instance, Hess (1995, p.81) notes how particular concepts, such as 'use of self', can be used to structure the reflective process. In principle, the value of the reflective exercise is maximised by the input and feedback from other people, since this potentially maximises the numbers of theories and concepts which can be used to understand and reframe the experience.

However, it is also important to note that critical reflection can also create the possibilities of being open to other theories, by creating the propensity to be open, and therefore the propensity to create anew. In this sense it might not matter what theories are available, since the critical reflection process might actually develop the ability to create new theory. However, this variability, this difficulty in 'pinning down' a uniform view of critical reflection and its value is unfortunately characterised as a weakness of critical reflection. It may, however, be its very advantage. It is the open-ended nature, the way in which critical reflectors are at once affirmed in their work whilst constantly humbled; the way in which experts are able to work with confidence yet remain receptive to uncertainty; these are perhaps the contributions of a critical reflective process.

Interestingly, Schon (1995) notes the findings of a study in which eight successful projects were reflectively analysed. The practice of leaders of more successful programs differed markedly from traditional clinical models of practice. They did not see themselves as experts, but prided themselves in meeting clients on a person to person basis.

They saw themselves as client-focused and were prepared to begin with the client's view of what needed to be done, even if that task would have seemed unprofessional according to established professional norms. ..... As a consequence ... practitioners could not claim to know ahead of time just what needed to be done nor could they keep their transactions with clients under unilateral control. They were continually called on to cope with uncertainty and surprise. (Schon, 1995, p.45)

These findings closely echo the practice features in the accounts in this book. Perhaps reflective practice does share some identifiable common features.

How do these changes in practice, brought about through critical reflection, make a difference, particularly in a work world which seems to increasingly value top-down management, and technical measurements of performance?

In technocratic terms, critical reflection, as the process which creates theory from practice, is invaluable since it allows contextually appropriate responses to new and changing situations. Service users whose stories are valued, relatively free from preconceived labels, will presumably be more satisfied customers.

Ironically, although reflection is often criticised as a 'navel-gazing', introspective, and therefore, by implication, a largely useless internalised process, it can have very real externalised outcomes. The potential for increased accountability is significant, since subjecting the details of practice to rigorous scrutiny is in itself an evaluative, and therefore an accountability, mechanism. This is well-illustrated in Mark Baldwin's chapter.

Workers whose practice is valued, through the organisational enabling of critical reflection, will experience better morale, more enthusiasm for their work, and will create better opportunities for team and collaborative work. If they are not suited to their work, or not committed, a process of critical reflection will clarify their position, and allow them to make better choices about where they fit.

Because it is potentially an inclusive process, it should be adaptable to many situations and types of workers. It should allow a diversity of practitioners to reach their full potential, that is, be relatively unencumbered by constrictive thinking.

Revisiting the beginning

We undertook the project of this book with the express purpose of modelling the reflective process, its potential for meaning making and its contributions to practice theorising. Each of our chapters speaks for itself, and we have also integrated the separate experiences with our own interpretations in this last chapter.

But what else has happened? What has the experience of reading and rereading, understanding and reinterpreting, each chapter given to us, Lindsey and Jan, the editors?

We are both moved and humbled by the accounts. We are moved by the enormous degree of 'self' which is used by each contributor, the range of intellectual and emotional resources which come into play in practising professionally. We are also humbled by the personal and professional generosity, a type of selflessness, which is involved in engaging with difficult, unpleasant and challenging situations. This tremendous integrity, in which each person displays an ability and commitment to see through, to persevere in changing situations, sometimes at great personal cost, bespeaks the ethical and value mission which for us is the 'calling' of social work. Social work is, first and foremost, a valued-led practice.

We are surprised at the multiple identities each contributor has exposed: surprised that they exist; surprised that we are not normally aware of these in professional practice; surprised at the personal courage in revealing, perhaps less than flattering self-portraits, to colleagues. In this process we have gained considerable respect for each other, and for our social work colleagues in general.

The existence of multiple identities, of the many facets of personal, professional and social selves, reminds us that we relate to each other in a myriad of ways, and that fixed ways of seeing each other are at best oversimplified, stultifying our choices of action. Our colleagues are as diverse and changing as ourselves - the only appropriate way to relate is therefore assuming uncertainty, with a constant preparedness for dialogue.

But what does all this say about the political project of social work? If one of the few certainties we have is that all is changing, how do we engage with, and change, what are presumably fixed political structures? For us, a window is foreshadowed in the reflective experiences of our colleagues in this book. A critical reflective process has enabled each of us to integrate an understanding of our personal position as structural. Positionality in this sense is structural, personal, cultural and historical, affected by our inherited and learnt psychology, the vagaries of our family life, our bodies and physical appearances, sexuality, and relative job status's. By reflecting on our positionality, each of us has implicitly linked the personal and political through the prism of our own experiences.

Professional practice experiences, therefore, are both individual and collective experiences. They are individually perceived and interpreted, but they take place within a broader social and cultural fabric, many aspects of which are shared. They are collective experiences in that they only make sense when interpreted through the prism of collective structures and socially inherited ideas. Whilst therefore we accept and acknowledge individuality and diversity, critical reflection also allows us to identify the commonalities of our experience. In this sense, perpetuating differences between the 'personal and political', 'policy and practice', different cultural or social groups misses the 'big picture', and distracts us from engaging with the more important struggle. The big picture becomes 'real' through critical reflection on personal experiences of the big picture. The big picture is that all of us, with all our differences, all exist within the same social fabric, which we make, and which makes us. The struggle is in changing the fabric, not each other. Differences are preserved and respected as we unite in a common cause to change what makes us, and how we make ourselves. This is the possibility which critical reflection makes real for us.

References

Berlin, S. (1990) 'Dichotomous and complex thinking', *Social Service Review*, Mar., 46-59.

Hess, P. M. (1995) 'Reflecting in and on practice' in Hess, P.M. & Mullen, E.J. (eds) *Practitioner-Researcher Relationships*, NASW Press, Washington, 56-82.

Hindmarsh, J. (1992) *Social Work Oppositions*, Avebury, Aldershot

Howe, D. (1996) 'Surface and depth in social work practice', in Parton, N. (ed) *Social Theory, Social Change and Social Work*, Routledge, London, 77-97.

Ixer, G. (1999) 'There's no such thing as reflection', *British Journal of Social Work*, 29, 513 - 527.

Rojek, C. (1986) 'The "subject" in social work', *British Journal of Social Work*, 16, 65-77.

Sands, R.G. & Nuccio, K. (1992) 'Postmodern Feminist Theory and Social Work', *Social Work*, 37 (6), 489-94.

Schon, D. (1995) 'Reflective inquiry in social work practice', in Hess, P.M. & Mullen, E.J. (eds) *Practitioner-Researcher Relationships*, NASW Press, Washington, 31-55.

Solas, J. (1994) *(De)Constructing Social Work Education*, Avebury, Aldershot

The contributors

Silvia Alberti
Silvia is a Senior Project Officer at Turning Point Alcohol and Drug Centre. In her previous position, one of Silvia's roles was the development, oversight and management of drug treatment and education services across 11 prisons in Victoria. She also has clinical experience in the area of alcohol & drug treatment and youth & family work.

Mark Baldwin
Mark is a social work academic teaching and researching at the University of Bath in the UK. He is particularly interested in the congruence between research and social work methods that seek to work with co-researchers or users in order that their voice should be heard in knowledge created and lessons learnt.

Rachel Balen
Rachel is a Senior Lecturer in Social Work in the Centre for Applied Childhood Studies at the University of Huddersfield. She teaches on the BSc in Social Work and is pathway leader of the MA in Child Protection. Her background is in local authority social work.

Michael Bramwell
Michael is a social worker who is currently employed as a counsellor with both the Victorian AIDS Palliative Care Consultancy and the Anita Morawetz HIV/AIDS in rural and remote regions. Michael is currently completing a Masters in Public Health focusing on concepts of sexuality in marginalised communities.

John Drayton
John is a social worker working at the Department of Forensic Medicine at Westmead, Sydney.

Jan Fook
Jan is Professor of Social Work at Deakin University, Geelong, Australia. She specialises in teaching practice using critical reflective approaches. She has published widely in the area of critical practice and research.

John and Molly Harvey
John is a Church of Scotland minister, who has been involved in both parish and community ministry - with the Gorbals Group; as Leader of the Iona community and warden of Iona Abbey; now interim minister in Greenock. He and Molly are parents of four children and four grandchildren. Molly was a member of the Gorbals Group, a member of the resident group in Iona Abbey, foster parent with the Barnardos special families project, and is currently Project Coordinator of Glasgow Braendam Link.

Nigel Hinks
Nigel began his social work career in Liverpool in 1972. He worked for Liverpool and Northamptonshire Social Services Departments and was Director of the Corby Juvenile Liaison Bureau in the 1980s. He then joined the voluntary sector, working first for NCH as Regional Manager, and latterly for The Children's Society where he is currently employed with national responsibility for Practice Learning.

Andrew Lowth
Andrew is the social work team leader in HIV and Sexual Health Services at Royal North Shore Hospital, Sydney. His present research interests include the impact the advances in HIV treatments are having on service providers and models of service provision, and gay men's relationships with the public health sector. Andrew previously taught social work at James Cook University, and has been involved in HIV in a range of capacities since graduating from social work in 1986.

Lindsey Napier
Lindsey is Senior Lecturer in the Department of Social Work, Social Policy and Sociology at The University of Sydney. Her current research interests are in the fields of dying and death and of critical reflection in social work.

Cathy Peut
Cathy is a social worker working for Centrelink at Parramatta in Sydney.

Narda Razack
Narda is an Assistant Professor/Field Education Coordinator in the School of Social Work, York University, Toronto, Canada. Her research and publications relate to anti discriminatory practice; inclusive field education; critical pedagogy and transnational collaborations. She is currently critically

examining curricula and professional international exchanges and working on a text examining diversity and differences for field education.

Sheila Sim
Sheila is Social Worker in Charge, Royal Hospital for Women, Sydney

Chris Shipway
Chris is Senior Project Officer with the Crime Prevention Division of the NSW Attorney General's Department. He is a social worker; with experience in alcohol and drug prevention, adult education, community work, mental health and you work.

May Kwan Wong
May Kwan Wong has been practising as a social worker since 1990, after achieving her Bachelor of Social Sciences from the Chinese University of Hong Kong. Her field of interest is work with youth. Having completed her Master of Social Work from La Trobe University, Australia, in 1997, she now works in the Boys's and Girl's Clubs Association of Hong Kong.